MW01575819

إن الذين يبايعونك إنما يبايعون الله

Selections from

The Muhammadan Covenants

Selections from

The Muhammadan Covenants

SINCERITY IN KNOWLEDGE AND ACTION

IMAM ʿABD AL-WAHHĀB AL-SHAʿRĀNĪ

Translated by

TALUT IBN SULAIMAN DAWOOD

SELECTIONS FROM THE MUHAMMADAN COVENANTS:
Sincerity in Knowledge and Action

COPYRIGHT © 2025 BY IMAM GHAZALI PUBLISHING (USA)

All rights reserved. Aside from fair use, meaning a few pages or less for non-profit educational purposes, review, or scholarly citation, no part of this publication may be reproduced, stored in a retrieval system, or transmitted in any form or by any means, electronic, mechanical, photocopying, recording, or otherwise, without the prior permission of the Copyright owner. For permission requests, please write to the publisher at the address below.

IMAM GHAZALI PUBLISHING
INFO@IMAMGHAZALI.CO
WWW.IMAMGHAZALI.CO

Bulk ordering information: Special discounts are available on quantity purchases. For details, please contact the distributors:

SATTAUR PUBLISHING
INFO@SATTAURPUBLISHING.COM
WWW.SATTAURPUBLISHING.COM

PRINTED IN THE USA, MALAYSIA, & THE UNITED KINGDOM.

The views, information, or opinions expressed are solely those of the author(s) and do not necessarily represent those of the publisher.

ISBN: 978-1-966329-75-6 (PAPERBACK)
979-8-2954-5979-5 (INTERNATIONAL)

FIRST EDITION

10 9 8 7 6 5 4 3 2 1

CONTENTS

PUBLISHER'S MESSAGE IX

IMAM AL-SHAʿRĀNĪ XV

SELECTIONS FROM THE MUHAMMADAN COVENANTS:
Sincerity in Knowledge and Action

Encouragement to Act in Accordance with the Muhammadan Sunnah 16
Encouragement to Manifest Good 32
Urging Pursuit and Review of Sacred Knowledge 42
Urging Travel in Search of Sacred Knowledge 52
Encouragement to Rehearse the Hadith Reports 56
Sticking to the Company of the People of Knowledge 62
Honouring the People of Knowledge 66
Transmitting Knowledge Even If We Fail to Act upon It 72
Things to Avoid The Prohibition of Taking Reprehensible Innovations as Part of One's Religious Practice 76
The Prohibition of Answering Questions Pertaining to Sacred Knowledge Unless We Know That We and the Petitioner Are Sincere 96
The Prohibition of Boasting One's Knowledge 120
The Prohibition of Being Careless in the Narration of Hadith 128

The Prohibition of Being Deluded with the Memorization of Knowledge That Is Unaccompanied by Practice 134
The Prohibition of Laying Claim to Knowledge Unless It Is for a Reason Sanctioned in the Sacred Law 140
The Prohibition of Disputing in Matters of Knowledge 150

Publisher's Message

WHEN IMAM ʿABD AL-WAHHĀB AL-SHAʿRĀNĪ sat down to write in sixteenth-century Cairo, he was addressing a problem that feels strangely familiar today. Students memorized entire books. Teachers gave brilliant lectures. People filled mosques for prayers. But something was missing. Knowledge had become divorced from sincerity, and worship had turned into performance.

The Imam saw scholars who could debate the finest points of law yet showed no humility. He watched students chase certificates and jobs while their hearts remained unchanged. This disconnect troubled him deeply. So he compiled a work that would inspire a return: the covenants that Prophet ﷺ made with his community.

This book you hold contains selections from that larger work, *al-ʿUhūd al-Muḥammadiyyah* (The Muhammadan Covenants). The original spans hundreds of pages and covers every aspect of religious life. We've chosen sections that focus specifically on knowledge and action, because these speak most directly to our current moment. Today's readers face the same challenges the Imam addressed. We have access to more Islamic texts than ever before. We can watch thousands of lectures online. Yet many of us feel that our learning doesn't translate into spiritual growth.

Imam al-Shaʿrānī in Context

Born around 1492 in a village near Cairo, ʿAbd al-Wahhāb al-Shaʿrānī lived during the early days of Ottoman rule in Egypt. His early life was marked by loss; his father died when he was young, leaving the family in difficult circumstances. Perhaps this hardship shaped his later emphasis on humility and his criticism of scholars who lived in luxury while common people struggled. He studied at al-Azhar, the great center of Islamic learning, where he mastered the traditional sciences. But what set him apart was his refusal to specialize in just one school of law. While most scholars of his time aligned themselves with a single madhhab, al-Shaʿrānī studied all four Sunni schools deeply. He wanted to understand the full spectrum of Islamic thought, to see where the schools agreed and where they differed. This comprehensive approach would later influence his teaching that there's often more than one valid way to practice Islam.

The Imam lived through interesting times. The Ottomans had recently conquered Egypt, bringing new administrative systems and religious debates. Coffee had just arrived in Cairo, sparking fierce arguments about its permissibility. Sufi orders were growing in influence, sometimes clashing with more traditional scholars. Al-Shaʿrānī navigated these controversies with remarkable balance. He defended Sufism against its critics while also condemning excesses within Sufi practice. He respected traditional scholarship but criticized scholars who had lost touch with spiritual realities.

What really distinguished him was his concern for ordinary Muslims. Many of his works address practical questions that everyday believers faced. Can a poor person who can't afford meat still achieve spiritual excellence? How should someone balance work and worship? His answers consistently emphasized that sincerity matters more than outward forms. A small act done with pure intention outweighs grand gestures performed for show.

The Structure of These Selections

The original Muhammadan Covenants is organized around specific pledges that the Prophet ﷺ asked from his followers. Each covenant begins with the phrase "The Messenger of Allah has taken from us a covenant that..." and then describes a particular commitment. Some are broad, like making all worship purely for Allah. Others are quite specific, like the proper etiquette for transmitting Hadith.

For this edition, we've selected covenants that deal with the pursuit and transmission of religious knowledge. The Imam believed that learning without sincerity becomes a spiritual poison. It inflates the ego rather than purifying the heart. These selections offer practical guidance for anyone engaged in Islamic learning, whether as a student, teacher, or someone simply trying to understand their faith better.

The text moves between different levels of discourse. Sometimes the Imam quotes directly from the Qur'an and Hadith. Other times he shares stories from earlier scholars and saints. Occasionally, he speaks from his own experience, describing the spiritual practices that helped him achieve sincerity. This variety keeps the text engaging while reinforcing his central message from multiple angles.

One thing readers might notice is the Imam's frequent warnings. He cautions against showing off, against arguing over religious matters, against claiming knowledge one doesn't possess. Some might find this emphasis on warnings heavy. But remember, he was writing for people who already considered themselves religious. His audience wasn't those far from faith but those who thought they were close to it. He wanted to shake them out of their complacency.

What Readers Can Gain

First, these covenants offer a framework for examining our own intentions. Why do we seek religious knowledge? Is it to draw closer to Allah, or to win arguments online? Do we share what we learn to benefit others, or to display our learning? The Imam's probing questions force us to look honestly at our motivations.

Second, the text provides practical advice for spiritual development. The Imam doesn't just say "be sincere." He explains the practices that cultivate sincerity. He discusses the importance of finding qualified teachers, keeping good company, and maintaining consistency in worship. These concrete steps give readers something to actually work with.

The book also offers comfort for those who feel overwhelmed by the vastness of Islamic learning. The Imam repeatedly emphasizes that Allah judges us by our sincerity and effort, not by how many books we've memorized. A person who knows little but practices it faithfully ranks higher than someone who knows much but doesn't live by it. This message particularly resonates today when we have access to so much information that we can feel paralyzed by how much we don't know.

Perhaps most valuably, the text reminds us that struggling with our intentions is normal. Even great scholars battled pride and showing off. The Imam shares stories of renowned figures who worried about their sincerity, who took extreme measures to ensure their actions were purely for Allah. If they struggled, we shouldn't be surprised when we do too. The struggle itself is part of the spiritual path.

Why This Book Now?

We live in an age of performance. Social media encourages us to broadcast our good deeds. Religious discussions often become competitions to prove who knows more or practices better. The pressure to project an image of piety can overwhelm the actual pursuit of piety. The Imam's call to sincerity feels urgently relevant.

At the same time, we have unprecedented access to Islamic knowledge. Books, lectures, courses, and scholars are more available than ever. But this blessing brings its own challenges. How do we navigate different opinions and approaches? How do we avoid becoming confused by conflicting information?

How do we ensure our learning leads to spiritual growth rather than intellectual pride? The Imam addresses these questions throughout these selections.

His balanced approach offers something valuable for our polarized times. He respects scholarly tradition without being rigid. He values spiritual experience without dismissing the importance of sound knowledge. He criticizes both dry legalism and ungrounded emotionalism. This middle path provides a model for contemporary Muslims trying to navigate between extremes.

How to Read This Book

These selections reward slow, contemplative reading. The Imam intended his words to be absorbed and acted upon, not just intellectually processed. Readers might consider taking one covenant at a time, reading it carefully, and then spending several days reflecting on how it applies to their lives before moving to the next section.

The text assumes familiarity with basic Islamic concepts and Arabic terms. Readers without this background might want to keep a glossary handy or read alongside someone who can explain unfamiliar references. But don't let occasional confusion discourage you. The Imam's main points come through clearly even if some details require further study.

Above all, approach the text with the sincerity it advocates. Read it seeking benefit, not just information. The Imam would say that someone who reads a single page with genuine intention to improve gains more than someone who finishes the entire book without that intention. Let his words prompt self-examination and inspire positive change.

This is ultimately a book about the heart. Behind all the specific guidance about seeking knowledge, teaching, and transmitting Hadith lies a deeper message. Our relationship with Allah and His Messenger ﷺ is what matters most.

Everything else, including religious learning, should serve that relationship. When it doesn't, when it becomes about our ego or reputation or social standing, we've lost our way. The Imam calls us back to that fundamental priority.

May these selections serve their intended purpose: helping readers align their outward pursuit of knowledge with inner sincerity, bringing together learning and practice, and ultimately drawing closer to Allah and the Beloved ﷺ through both study and action.

Imam al-Shaʿrānī

IMAM AL-SHAʿRĀNĪ (1493–1565 CE), was a prominent Ottoman-Egyptian scholar, prolific writer, and *Ṣūfī* master of the 16th century, renowned for his extensive contribution during the Ottoman era. His spiritual lineage traced back to prominent figures of the Shādhilī order, including Abū Madyan. His early education was shaped by his grandfather Nūr al-Dīn ʿAlī, a pious scholar, while his spiritual development was influenced by Shaykh ʿAlī al-Ḥawwās. Al-Shaʿrānī maintained strong connections with both scholarly circles and the ruling class of Cairo.

He established a significant *zawiya* in Cairo, serving as a hub for both spiritual guidance and social welfare, providing food and shelter for hundreds daily. His works include *Ṭabaqāt al-Kubrā,* a vast collection of biographies, alongside works focused on *adab*, theology, and spirituality. The shaykh held a deep concern for social justice, spiritual integrity, and the spread of normative Islam, especially in rural areas where scholars were scarce.

After his death, his legacy was preserved through his writings and disciples, though his son was unable to maintain his level of influence. His order, however, continued for several generations. Al-Shaʿrānī's balanced approach to Ṣūfism, emphasizing both insight and adherence to Islamic law, solidified his status as a key reviver in the Ottoman spiritual history. His works remain widely read for their clarity, humanistic style, and profound moral guidance.

Selections from

The Muhammadan Covenants

SINCERITY IN KNOWLEDGE AND ACTION

IMAM ʿABD AL-WAHĀB AL-SHAʿRĀNĪ

Translated by

TALUT IBN SULAIMAN DAWOOD

THE MESSENGER OF ALLAH ﷺ HAS TAKEN FROM US A GENERAL COVENANT, [where we are] to hope for its fulfilment – through the grace of our Lord – by purifying our intentions for Him (Exalted is He) and to purify our knowledge, acts, and states of all impurity – even the witnessing of our own sincerity or entitlement of rewards for it. If the thought to seek reward were to occur to us, we should rather witness it through the door of grace and bounty.

If someone desires to act upon this covenant, he needs to travel the path of the Sufis at the hands of a true *shaykh*, who is an expert in the knowledge of the Sacred Law to the point where he can rule by the four schools of law and others, knowing their evidences and differing opinions, and halting at the Mother of the Book from which all opinions branch off.

Thus, if someone desires sincerity in his actions, he should occupy himself with the remembrance of Allah ﷻ until the veils of his humanity are pierced and he enters the presence of excellence (*iḥsān*), where Allah (Exalted is He) is worshipped as if He is being seen. There, he will witness that all actions are creations of Allah ﷻ, in which the slave has no part – except as the place from which such acts emerge, for actions are accidents (*aʿrāḍ*), which only manifest on bodies. At that, all dissimulation, arrogance, and pride, along with all other deficiencies, will leave the slave; they only occur due to his assumption that he is the doer of such acts, which entails his neglect in witnessing the Creator of those acts. It is known that a slave's dissimulation, arrogance, and pride over someone else's act can never be valid – we have never seen anyone who sleeps until morning and then wakes up showing pride and arrogance over the acts performed by someone who stood the entire night. Hence, if someone does not enter into the presence of *iḥsān* – where, through unveiling, he witnesses with certainty, not mere assumption and conjecture, that all his actions are creations

أُخِذَ عَلَيْنَا الْعَهْدُ الْعَامُّ مِنْ رَسُولِ اللهِ ﷺ أَنْ نَرْجُوَ مِنْ فَضْلِ رَبِّنَا الْوَفَاءَ وَأَنْ نُخْلِصَ النِّيَّةَ لِلهِ تَعَالَى فِي عِلْمِنَا وَعَمَلِنَا وَسَائِرِ أَحْوَالِنَا، وَنُخْلِصَ سَائِرَ أَعْمَالِنَا مِنْ سَائِرِ الشَّوَائِبِ، حَتَّى مِنْ شُهُودِ الْإِخْلَاصِ وَمِنْ حُضُورِ اسْتِحْقَاقِنَا ثَوَابًا عَلَى ذَلِكَ، وَإِنْ خَطَرَ لَنَا طَلَبُ ثَوَابٍ شَهِدْنَاهُ مِنْ بَابِ الْمِنَّةِ وَالْفَضْلِ، وَيَحْتَاجُ مَنْ يُرِيدُ الْعَمَلَ بِهَذَا الْعَهْدِ إِلَى سُلُوكِ طَرِيقِ الْقَوْمِ عَلَى يَدِ شَيْخٍ صَادِقٍ مُتَبَحِّرٍ فِي عُلُومِ الشَّرِيعَةِ بِحَيْثُ يُقَرِّرُ مَذَاهِبَ الْأَئِمَّةِ الْأَرْبَعَةِ وَغَيْرِهَا، وَيَعْرِفُ أَدِلَّتَهَا وَمُنَازِعَ أَقْوَالِهَا وَيَقِفُ عَلَى أُمِّ الْكِتَابِ الَّتِي يَتَفَرَّعُ مِنْهَا كُلُّ قَوْلٍ فَيَشْتَغِلُ مَنْ يُرِيدُ الْإِخْلَاصَ فِي أَعْمَالِهِ بِذِكْرِ اللهِ عَزَّ وَجَلَّ، حَتَّى تَرِقَّ حُجُبُ بَشَرِيَّتِهِ وَيَدْخُلَ حَضْرَةَ الْإِحْسَانِ الَّتِي يَعْبُدُ اللهَ تَعَالَى فِيهَا كَأَنَّهُ يَرَاهُ، وَهُنَاكَ يَشْهَدُ الْعَمَلَ كُلَّهُ خَلْقًا لِلهِ تَعَالَى عز وجل لَيْسَ لِلْعَبْدِ فِيهِ مَدْخَلٌ إِلَّا كَوْنُهُ مَحَلًّا لِبُرُوزِ ذَلِكَ الْعَمَلِ لَا غَيْرُ، لِأَنَّ الأَعْمَالَ أَعْرَاضٌ، وَالْأَعْرَاضُ لَا تَظْهَرُ إِلَّا مِنْ جِسْمٍ، وَهُنَاكَ يَذْهَبُ مِنَ الْعَبْدِ الرِّيَاءُ وَالْكِبْرُ وَالْعُجْبُ وَسَائِرُ الْآفَاتِ؛ لِأَنَّ هَذِهِ الآفَاتِ إِنَّمَا تَجِيءُ لِلْعَبْدِ مِنْ شُهُودِ كَوْنِهِ فَاعِلًا لِذَلِكَ الْعَمَلِ مَعَ غَفْلَتِهِ عَنْ شُهُودِ الْخَالِقِ لَهُ، وَمَعْلُومٌ أَنَّهُ لَا يَصِحُّ الرِّيَاءُ وَالتَّكَبُّرُ وَالْعُجْبُ مِنَ الْعَبْدِ بِعَمَلِ غَيْرِهِ أَبَدًا، وَمَا رَأَيْنَا أَحَدًا نَامَ إِلَى الصَّبَاحِ وَأَصْبَحَ يُرَائِي أَوْ يُعْجَبُ أَوْ يَتَكَبَّرُ بِفِعْلِ جَارِهِ الْقَائِمِ طُولَ اللَّيْلِ أَبَدًا، فَعُلِمَ أَنَّ مَنْ لَمْ يَصِلْ إِلَى دُخُولِ حَضْرَةِ الْإِحْسَانِ وَيُشْهِدُ أَعْمَالَهُ كُلَّهَا خَلْقًا لِلهِ تَعَالَى كَشْفًا وَيَقِينًا لَا ظَنًّا وَلَا تَخْمِينًا فَهُوَ مُعَرَّضٌ لِلْوُقُوعِ فِي الرِّيَاءِ وَلَوْ حَفِظَ أَلْفَي كِتَابٍ، فَاطْلُبْ يَا أَخِي شَيْخًا صَادِقًا إِنْ طَلَبْتَ التَّرَقِّي إِلَى مَقَامِ الْإِخْلَاصِ، وَلَا تَسْأَمْ مِنْ طُولِ طَلَبِكَ لَهُ، فَإِنَّهُ أَعَزُّ مِنَ الْكِبْرِيتِ الْأَحْمَرِ، فَإِنَّهُ مِنْ أَقَلِّ شُرُوطِهِ التَّوَرُّعُ عَنْ أَمْوَالِ الْوُلَاةِ، وَأَنْ لَا يَكُونَ لَهُ مَعْلُومٌ فِي بَيْتِ الْمَالِ وَلَا مَسْمُوحٌ

of Allah (Exalted is He) – he will be subject to dissimulation, even if he has memorized two thousand books.

So, O brother, seek a true *shaykh* if you seek elevation to the station of *iḥsān* – and rarer is he than the red sulphur, so do not despair despite your long search for him. Among the most minimum conditions of a *shaykh* is abstainment from the wealth of rulers, for Allah (Exalted is He) provides for him whence unexpected; He selects for him the pure and lawful from the ugly and doubtful. If that is not the case, the *shuyūkh* of the path are all unanimous that sincerity in action is impossible for someone who consumes the unlawful or the doubtful, for he cannot be sincere unless he enters the presence of *iḥsān*. Nor can anyone enter its presence except those purified of all inward and outward impurities, who are Prophets, Angels, or saints. A condition of those groups is protection from consuming the unlawful and the doubtful; hence, a *shaykh* incapable of guarding himself will not cause others to reach such presence, except in the case that Allah (Exalted is He) blesses some of the disciples with rapture without observance of traditional wayfaring. There is no impediment to that.

Thus, the seeker of knowledge who has not reached sincerity is obligated[1] to follow a *shaykh* who will teach him the path to its arrival. He (Exalted is He) has said, "And they were only commanded to worship Allah, making their religion exclusively for Him as pure monotheists, to establish the prayer and give *zakāh*. That is the upright religion."[2] "Establish (*yuqīmu*) the prayer" means to perform it without deficiency, such as inattentiveness to Allah (Exalted is He). And "give *zakāh*" means to do so without expecting reward or punishment, and only

---

(1) It is obligatory from the standpoint of "If an obligation cannot be completed without something, then that thing is also an obligation."
(2) *Al-Bayyinah*, 5.

وَلَا هَدِيَّةٌ مِنْ كَاشِفٍ وَلَا شَيْخِ عَرَبٍ وَلَا شَيْخِ بَلَدٍ بَلْ يَرْزُقُهُ اللهُ تَعَالَى مِنْ حَيْثُ لَا يَحْتَسِبُ، وَيَسْتَخْلِصُ لَهُ الْحَلَالَ الصَّرْفَ مِنْ بَيْنِ فَرْثِ الْحَرَامِ، وَدَمِ الشُّبُهَاتِ، وَإِلَّا فَقَدْ أَجْمَعَ أَشْيَاخُ الطَّرِيقِ كُلُّهُمْ عَلَى أَنَّ مَنْ أَكَلَ الْحَرَامَ وَالشُّبُهَاتِ لَا يَصِحُّ لَهُ إِخْلَاصٌ فِي عَمَلٍ، لِأَنَّهُ لَا يُخْلِصُ إِلَّا إِنْ دَخَلَ حَضْرَةَ الْإِحْسَانِ، وَلَا يَدْخُلُ حَضْرَةَ الْإِحْسَانِ إِلَّا الْمُطَهَّرُ مِنْ سَائِرِ النَّجَاسَاتِ الْبَاطِنَةِ وَالظَّاهِرَةِ، لِأَنَّ مَجْمُوعَ أَهْلِ هَذِهِ الْحَضْرَةِ أَنْبِيَاءُ وَمَلَائِكَةٌ وَأَوْلِيَاءُ، وَهَؤُلَاءِ مِنْ شُرُوطِهِمُ الْعِصْمَةُ وَالْحِفْظُ مِنْ تَنَاوُلِ الْحَرَامِ وَالشُّبُهَاتِ، فَكُلُّ شَيْخٍ لَمْ يَصِحَّ لَهُ الْحِفْظُ فِي نَفْسِهِ فَهُوَ عَاجِزٌ عَنْ تَوْصِيلِ غَيْرِهِ إِلَى تِلْكَ الْحَضْرَةِ، اللَّهُمَّ إِلَّا أَنْ يَمُنَّ اللهُ تَعَالَى عَلَى بَعْضِ الْمُرِيدِينَ بِالْجَذْبِ دُونَ السُّلُوكِ الْمَعْهُودِ فَهَذَا لَا مَانِعَ مِنْهُ، فَعُلِمَ أَنَّهُ يَجِبُ عَلَى كُلِّ طَالِبِ عِلْمٍ لَمْ يَصِلْ إِلَى الْإِخْلَاصِ أَنْ يَتَّخِذَ لَهُ شَيْخًا يُعَلِّمُهُ طَرِيقَ الْوُصُولِ إِلَى دَرَجَةِ الْإِخْلَاصِ، مِنْ بَابِ: مَا لَا يَتِمُّ الْوَاجِبُ إِلَّا بِهِ فَهُوَ وَاجِبٌ، قَالَ تَعَالَى:

﴿وَمَآ أُمِرُوٓاْ إِلَّا لِيَعۡبُدُواْ ٱللَّهَ مُخۡلِصِينَ لَهُ ٱلدِّينَ حُنَفَآءَ وَيُقِيمُواْ ٱلصَّلَوٰةَ وَيُؤۡتُواْ ٱلزَّكَوٰةَۚ وَذَٰلِكَ دِينُ ٱلۡقَيِّمَةِ ۝٥﴾ [البينة: ٥].

أَيْ يُقِيمُوا الصَّلَاةَ مِنَ الْعِوَجِ؛ كَالْغَفْلَةِ عَنِ اللهِ تَعَالَى فِيهَا، وَيُؤْتُوا الزَّكَاةَ يَعْنِي بِلَا عِلَّةِ ثَوَابٍ وَلَا خَوْفِ عِقَابٍ بَلِ امْتِثَالًا لِأَمْرِ اللهِ تَعَالَى؛ كَالْوَكِيلِ فِي مَالِ مُوَكِّلِهِ.

in obedience to the command of Allah (Exalted is He), like an agent who spends the wealth of the one he represents.

I heard Sīdī ʿAlī al-Khawwāṣ ﷺ say:

> Among the lowest levels of sincerity (*ikhlāṣ*) is that a person is, with his actions, as an animal carrying a load. Such an animal becomes tired from the heft of its load, not knowing whether what it carries is of value. It knows not to whom it belongs or to where it is carrying it. It sees no merit for itself over other animals through it nor seeks any reward for carrying it.

I also heard him say, "If a slave boasts his actions or knowledge, all his acts – by proof of the Book and the Sunnah – are destroyed. If all his actions are destroyed, it is as if he has never done anything at all."

I say: Likewise, it is necessary for the faqir isolated in a cave or a *zāwiyah* to inspect his ego in its claims of sincerity and dedication to Allah (Exalted is He). If he sees that it is saddened by the loss of people's love and regard for him, he is thus untruthful in his claim. For the truthful person is happy when people neglect him, forget about him, and omit from him their gifts and greetings. In fact, he would be happy if all his companions were to turn away from him and gather to another guiding *shaykh*, just as we have explained in detail in our book *ʿUhūd al-Mashāyikh* (*The Covenants of the Shuyūkh*). And Allah knows best.

On *ikhlāṣ*, Ibn Mājah and al-Ḥakīm[3] have also narrated a tradition attributed to the Prophet ﷺ: *If someone leaves this world utterly devoted to worshipping Allah without any partner,*

(3) The latter stated that it is authentic according to the conditions of al-Bukhārī and Muslim.

وَسَمِعْتُ سَيِّدِي عَلِيًّا الْخَوَّاصَ رَحِمَهُ اللهُ يَقُولُ: مِنْ أَقَلِّ دَرَجَاتِ الْإِخْلَاصِ أَنْ يَكُونَ فِي أَعْمَالِهِ كَالدَّابَّةِ الْمُحَمَّلَةِ، فَهِيَ تَعْبَانَةٌ مِنْ ثِقَلِ حَمْلِهَا مُنَكَّسَةُ الرَّأْسِ لَا تَعْلَمُ بِنَفَاسَةِ مَا هِيَ حَامِلَتُهُ وَلَا بِخِسَّتِهِ وَلَا تَعْلَمُ هُوَ لِمَنْ، وَلَا إِلَى أَيْنَ يَنْتَهِي حَمْلُهَا؟ وَلَا تَرَى لَهَا بِذَلِكَ فَضْلًا عَنْ غَيْرِهَا مِنَ الدَّوَابِّ، وَلَا تَطْلُبُ عَلَى حَمْلِهَا أَجْرًا ا هـ.

وَسَمِعْتُهُ يَقُولُ: إِذَا رَاءَى الْعَبْدُ بِعِلْمِهِ وَعَمَلِهِ حَبِطَ عَمَلُهُ بِنَصِّ الْكِتَابِ وَالسُّنَّةِ، وَإِذَا حَبِطَ عَمَلُهُ فَكَأَنَّهُ لَمْ يَعْمَلْ شَيْئًا قَطُّ فَكَيْفَ يَرَى نَفْسَهُ بِذَلِكَ عَلَى النَّاسِ مَعَ تَوَعُّدِهِ بَعْدَ الْإِحْبَاطِ بِالْعَذَابِ الْأَلِيمِ، فَلْيَتَنَبَّهْ طَالِبُ الْعِلْمِ لِمِثْلِ ذَلِكَ ا هـ.

قُلْتُ: وَكَذَلِكَ يَنْبَغِي لِلْفَقِيرِ الْمُنْقَطِعِ فِي كَهْفٍ أَوْ زَاوِيَةٍ أَنْ يَتَفَقَّدَ نَفْسَهُ فِي دَعْوَاهَا الْإِخْلَاصَ وَالِانْقِطَاعَ إِلَى اللهِ تَعَالَى، فَإِنْ رَآهَا تَسْتَوْحِشُ مِنْ تَرْكِ تَوَدُّدِ النَّاسِ إِلَيْهَا وَغَفْلَتِهِمْ عَنْهَا فَهُوَ كَاذِبٌ فِي دَعْوَاهُ الِانْقِطَاعَ إِلَى اللهِ تَعَالَى، فَإِنَّ الصَّادِقَ يَفْرَحُ إِذَا غَفَلَ عَنْهُ النَّاسُ وَنَسُوهُ فَلَمْ يَفْتَقِدُوهُ بِهَدِيَّةٍ وَلَا سَلَامٍ، وَيَفْرَحُ إِذَا انْقَلَبَ أَصْحَابُهُ كُلُّهُمْ عَنْهُ وَاجْتَمَعُوا بِشَيْخٍ آخَرَ مُرْشِدٍ، كَمَا بَسَطْنَا الْكَلَامَ عَلَى ذَلِكَ فِي كِتَابِ [عُهُودِ الْمَشَايِخِ] وَاللهُ أَعْلَمُ.

وَمِمَّا رَوَاهُ الْأَئِمَّةُ فِي الْإِخْلَاصِ مَرْفُوعًا قَوْلُهُ ﷺ: «مَنْ فَارَقَ الدُّنْيَا عَلَى الْإِخْلَاصِ لِلهِ وَحْدَهُ لَا شَرِيكَ لَهُ، وَأَقَامَ الصَّلَاةَ، وَآتَى الزَّكَاةَ.. فَارَقَهَا وَاللهُ عَنْهُ رَاضٍ». رَوَاهُ ابْنُ مَاجَهْ وَالْحَاكِمُ وَقَالَ صَحِيحٌ عَلَى شَرْطِ الشَّيْخَيْنِ.

establishing the prayer, and paying the zakāh, he will have left this world in Allah's pleasure.

In a *mursal* tradition, in which the Companion has been omitted, al-Bayhaqī narrated: A man said, "O Messenger of Allah! What is faith?" He replied, "*Ikhlāṣ.*" The man then said, "What is *yaqīn* (certainty)?" He said, "*Truthfulness (ṣidq).*"

Declaring the chain authentic, al-Ḥakīm narrated that Muʿādh ibn Jabal said, "O Messenger of Allah! Counsel me!" He said, "*Purify your intention and a small amount of action will suffice you.*"

Al-Bayhaqī narrated, in a *marfūʿ* tradition attributed to the Prophet ﷺ: "*Glad tidings to the sincere. They are the lamps of guidance; every great tribulation is dispelled by them.*"

He also narrated, in another tradition attributed to the Prophet ﷺ: "*Indeed, Allah (Blessed and Exalted is He) says, 'I am the best partner. If anyone performs an act in which he associates someone else with Me, that act is for the one associated, while I am free of it.' O mankind! Perform your acts solely for Allah, for He does not accept any act except that which is done purely for His sake. And do not say, "This is for Allah and for us", for none of it will be for Allah.*"

Abū Dāwūd and others narrated the following Prophetic Hadith with a good chain: "*Indeed, Allah does not accept any act except that which is purely to seek His Countenance.*"

Al-Ṭabarānī narrated the following Prophetic Hadith: "*The world is cursed. And all in it is cursed except that by which Allah's Countenance is sought.*"

On the authority of ʿUbādah ibn al-Ṣāmit, al-Bayhaqī narrated the following Prophetic Hadith: "*The world will be brought on the Day of Judgement, and to it will be said, 'Separate whatever*

وَرَوَى الْبَيْهَقِيُّ مُرْسَلًا: أَنَّ رَجُلًا قَالَ: يَا رَسُولَ اللهِ؛ مَا الْإِيمَانُ؟ قَالَ: «الْإِخْلَاصُ»، قَالَ: فَمَا الْيَقِينُ؟ قَالَ: «الصِّدْقُ».

وَرَوَى الْحَاكِمُ وَقَالَ صَحِيحُ الْإِسْنَادِ: أَنَّ مَعَاذَ بْنَ جَبَلٍ قَالَ: يَا رَسُولَ اللهِ؛ أَوْصِنِي، قَالَ: «أَخْلِصْ نِيَّتَكَ يَكْفِكَ الْعَمَلُ الْقَلِيلُ».

وَرَوَى الْبَيْهَقِيُّ مَرْفُوعًا: «طُوبَى لِلْمُخْلِصِينَ، أُولَئِكَ مَصَابِيحُ الْهُدَى، تَنْجَلِي عَنْهُمْ كُلُّ فِتْنَةٍ عَظْمَاءَ».

وَرَوَى الْبَيْهَقِيُّ وَالْبَزَّارُ مَرْفُوعًا: «إِنَّ اللهَ تَبَارَكَ وَتَعَالَى يَقُولُ: أَنَا خَيْرُ شَرِيكٍ، فَمَنْ عَمِلَ عَمَلًا أَشْرَكَ فِيهِ غَيْرِي فَهُوَ لِشَرِيكِي وَأَنَا مِنْهُ بَرِيءٌ، يَا أَيُّهَا النَّاسُ؛ أَخْلِصُوا أَعْمَالَكُمْ لِلهِ فَإِنَّ اللهَ لَا يَقْبَلُ مِنَ الْأَعْمَالِ إِلَّا مَا خَلَصَ، وَلَا تَقُولُوا هَذَا لِلهِ وَلِوُجُوهِكُمْ فَإِنَّهَا لِوُجُوهِكُمْ وَلَيْسَ لِلهِ مِنْهَا شَيْءٌ».

وَفِي رِوَايَةٍ لِأَبِي دَاوُدَ وَغَيْرِهِ بِإِسْنَادٍ جَيِّدٍ مَرْفُوعًا: «إِنَّ اللهَ لَا يَقْبَلُ مِنَ الْعَمَلِ إِلَّا مَا كَانَ خَالِصًا وَابْتُغِيَ بِهِ وَجْهُهُ».

وَرَوَى الطَّبَرَانِيُّ مَرْفُوعًا: «الدُّنْيَا مَلْعُونَةٌ مَلْعُونٌ مَا فِيهَا إِلَّا مَا ابْتُغِيَ بِهِ وَجْهُ اللهِ».

وَرَوَى الْبَيْهَقِيُّ مَرْفُوعًا عَنْ عُبَادَةَ بْنِ الصَّامِتِ قَالَ: «يُجَاءُ بِالدُّنْيَا يَوْمَ الْقِيَامَةِ فَيُقَالُ مَيِّزُوا مَا كَانَ مِنْهَا لِلهِ عَزَّ وَجَلَّ فَيُمَتَازُوا وَيُرْمَى مَا عَدَاهُ فِي النَّارِ».

of it is for Allah ﷻ.' It will be separated, and the rest will be cast into the Fire."[4]

Al-Ḥāfiẓ Razīn al-ʿAbdarī narrated a *mursal* Prophetic Hadith: *"If someone is sincerely for Allah for forty days, the fountains of wisdom will appear from his heart and tongue."*[5]

Imam Aḥmad and al-Bayhaqī narrated the following Prophetic Hadith: *"Whoever believes sincerely and renders his heart serene, his tongue truthful, his soul content, his body steadfast, his ears alert, and his eyes acute, he will have succeeded."*

Al-Bukhārī, Muslim, and others have narrated the Prophetic Hadith: *"Indeed, actions are by the intention."* – or in another Hadith: *"Indeed, actions are by intentions."* – *"Each person will have that which they intended. Thus, if someone migrates to Allah and His Messenger, his migration is to Allah and His Messenger. However, if someone migrates to obtain a portion of this world, or to marry a woman, his migration is to that for which he migrated."*

With a sound chain, Ibn Mājah related a Prophetic Hadith: *"People will be resurrected upon"* – or in another Hadith: *"gathered according to"* – *"their intentions."*

Muslim narrated the following Prophetic Hadith: *"Indeed, Allah (Blessed and Exalted is He) does not look at your bodies or your forms. Rather, He looks at your hearts."*

Al-Ṭabarānī narrated the following Prophetic Hadith: *"When the end time approaches, my Ummah will be divided into three groups: one worshipping Allah sincerely, one worshipping Allah to show off, and another worshipping Allah to seek thereby that people feed them. Allah ﷻ will say about the sincere: 'Take*

---

(4) Al-Ḥāfiẓ al-Mundhirī said, "It may be said that statements like this are derived through opinion and legal judgement, so it is assumed to be a Prophetic tradition."

(5) Al-Ḥāfiẓ al-Mundhirī said, "I did not find any authentic or sound chain for this Hadith. Nor have I found it mentioned in any of the sources that Razīm gathered. And Allah knows best."

وَرَوَى الحَافِظُ رَزِينٌ العَبْدَرِيُّ مَرْفُوعًا مُرْسَلًا: «مَنْ أَخْلَصَ للهِ تَعَالَى أَرْبَعِينَ يَوْمًا ظَهَرَتْ يَنَابِيعُ الحِكْمَةِ مِنْ قَلْبِهِ عَلَى لِسَانِهِ».

وَرَوَى الإِمَامُ أَحْمَدُ وَالبَيْهَقِيُّ مَرْفُوعًا: «قَدْ أَفْلَحَ مَنْ أَخْلَصَ قَلْبَهُ لِلْإِيمَانِ، وَجَعَلَ قَلْبَهُ سَلِيمًا وَلِسَانَهُ صَادِقًا وَنَفْسَهُ مُطْمَئِنَّةً وَخَلِيقَتَهُ مُسْتَقِيمَةً، وَجَعَلَ أُذُنَهُ مُسْتَمِعَةً وَعَيْنَهُ نَاظِرَةً» الحَدِيثَ.

وَرَوَى الشَّيْخَانِ وَغَيْرُهُمَا مَرْفُوعًا: «إِنَّمَا الأَعْمَالُ بِالنِّيَّةِ» وَفِي رِوَايَةٍ: «بِالنِّيَّاتِ، وَإِنَّمَا لِكُلِّ امْرِىءٍ مَا نَوَى، فَمَنْ كَانَتْ هِجْرَتُهُ إِلَى اللهِ وَرَسُولِهِ فَهِجْرَتُهُ إِلَى اللهِ وَرَسُولِهِ، وَمَنْ كَانَتْ هِجْرَتُهُ إِلَى دُنْيَا يُصِيبُهَا أَوِ امْرَأَةٍ يَنْكِحُهَا فَهِجْرَتُهُ إِلَى مَا هَاجَرَ إِلَيْهِ».

وَرَوَى ابْنُ مَاجَهْ بِإِسْنَادٍ حَسَنٍ مَرْفُوعًا: «إِنَّمَا يُبْعَثُ النَّاسُ عَلَى نِيَّاتِهِمْ» وَفِي رِوَايَةٍ: «إِنَّمَا يُحْشَرُ النَّاسُ عَلَى نِيَّاتِهِمْ».

وَرَوَى مُسْلِمٌ مَرْفُوعًا: «إِنَّ اللهَ تَبَارَكَ وَتَعَالَى لَا يَنْظُرُ إِلَى أَجْسَامِكُمْ وَلَا إِلَى صُوَرِكُمْ وَلَكِنْ يَنْظُرُ إِلَى قُلُوبِكُمْ».

وَرَوَى الطَّبَرَانِيُّ وَالبَيْهَقِيُّ مَرْفُوعًا: «إِذَا كَانَ آخِرُ الزَّمَانِ صَارَتْ أُمَّتِي ثَلَاثَ فِرَقٍ: فِرْقَةٌ يَعْبُدُونَ اللهَ خَالِصًا، وَفِرْقَةٌ يَعْبُدُونَ اللهَ رِيَاءً، وَفِرْقَةٌ يَعْبُدُونَ اللهَ تَعَالَى لِيَسْتَأْكِلُوا بِهِ النَّاسَ، فَيَقُولُ اللهُ عَزَّ وَجَلَّ لِلْمُخْلِصِينَ: اذْهَبُوا بِهِمْ إِلَى الجَنَّةِ، وَيَقُولُ لِلْآخَرِينَ: امْضُوا بِهِمْ إِلَى النَّارِ» الحَدِيثَ.

them to Paradise.' He will say about the others: 'Drag them to Hell.'"

Abū Nuʿaym narrated that ʿĀʾishah ﷺ used to say, "If someone sees himself as among the sincere, he is among those who show off. If someone sees himself as among those who show off, he is among the sincere."

The *aḥādīth* to this effect are many and well known. In the first parts of the section of the book dedicated to the prohibitions, we will bring a good portion of traditions that have been narrated regarding showing off and insincerity in actions and knowledge – so, review that. And Allah knows best.

I say: It should have become clear to you that the one insincere in action and knowledge will be among those whose acts are destroyed. This has also been indicated by the context in which the *aḥādīth* were stated. All of what has been narrated regarding the excellence of knowledge is in the case of those sincere in it. Thus, beware, O brother, of becoming deluded, for the Judge sees you. In this time, the people who do not act upon their knowledge have multiplied. And when people oppose them in their claims – that is, when they say, "We are people of knowledge." – they support themselves by mentioning what has been narrated regarding the seeker of knowledge in an absolute sense, without stipulating sincerity. It should be said to such people: "Why have you not mentioned the verses and traditions that have been narrated regarding one who does not act upon his knowledge or one who seeks it without sincerity?" So, do not be deluded, O brother, in claiming sincerity in knowledge and action without introspection – for by that, you will be deceived.

Furthermore, I have heard Sīdī ʿAlī al-Khawwāṣ ﷺ say, regarding the meaning of the Hadith "*Indeed, Allah (Exalted is He) will aid this religion by a sinful man.*": "This is a man who learns knowledge to show off and for a position. Thus, he teaches people the matters of their religion, causes them to

وَرَوَى الْحَافِظُ أَبُو نُعَيمٍ عَنْ عَائِشَةَ رَضِيَ اللَّهُ عَنْهَا أَنَّهَا كَانَتْ تَقُولُ: مَنْ رَأَى نَفْسَهُ مِنَ الْمُخْلِصِينَ كَانَ مِنَ الْمُرَائِينَ، وَ مَنْ رَأَى نَفْسَهُ مِنَ الْمُرَائِينَ كَانَ مِنَ الْمُخْلِصِينَ.

وَالْأَحَادِيثُ فِي ذَلِكَ كَثِيرَةٌ مَشْهُورَةٌ، وَسَيَأْتِي فِي أَوَائِلِ قِسْمِ الْمَنْهِيَّاتِ نُبْذَةٌ صَالِحَةٌ فِيمَا جَاءَ فِي الرِّيَاءِ وَعَدَمِ الْإِخْلَاصِ فِي الْعَمَلِ وَالْعِلْمِ فَرَاجِعْهُ، وَاللَّهُ أَعْلَمُ.

قُلْتُ: فَقَدْ بَانَ لَكَ أَنَّ مَنْ لَمْ يُخْلِصْ فِي عَمَلِهِ وَعِلْمِهِ فَهُوَ مِنَ الْأَخْسَرِينَ أَعْمَالًا، وَيَشْهَدُ لِذَلِكَ أَيْضًا قَرَائِنُ الْأَحْوَالِ الَّتِي جَاءَتْ بِهَا الْأَحَادِيثُ فِي سِيَاقِهَا، وَجَمِيعُ مَا وَرَدَ فِي فَضْلِ الْعِلْمِ وَالْعَمَلِ إِنَّمَا هُوَ فِي حَقِّ الْمُخْلِصِينَ فِيهِ.

فَإِيَّاكَ يَا أَخِي وَالْغَلَطَ؛ فَإِنَّ النَّاقِدَ بَصِيرٌ، وَقَدْ كَثُرَ فِي هَذَا الزَّمَانِ أَقْوَامٌ لَا يَعْمَلُونَ بِعِلْمِهِمْ، وَإِذَا نَازَعَهُمْ إِنْسَانٌ فِي دَعْوَاهُمْ فِي قَوْلِهِمْ نَحْنُ مِنْ أَهْلِ الْعِلْمِ اسْتَدَلُّوا بِمَا جَاءَ فِي فَضْلِ طَلَبِ الْعِلْمِ مُطْلَقًا مِنْ غَيْرِ شَرْطِ إِخْلَاصٍ، فَيُقَالُ لِمِثْلِ هَؤُلَاءِ فَأَيْنَ الْآيَاتُ وَالْأَخْبَارُ وَالْآثَارُ الْوَارِدَةُ فِي حَقِّ مَنْ لَمْ يَعْمَلْ بِعِلْمِهِ وَلَمْ يُخْلِصْ؟

فَلَا تُغَالِطْ يَا أَخِي وَتَدَّعِي الْإِخْلَاصَ فِي عِلْمِكَ وَعَمَلِكَ مِنْ غَيْرِ تَفْتِيشٍ فَإِنَّهُ غِشٌّ.

وَقَدْ سَمِعْتُ سَيِّدِي عَلِيًّا الْخَوَّاصَ رَحِمَهُ اللَّهُ يَقُولُ فِي مَعْنَى حَدِيثِ: «إِنَّ اللَّهَ تَعَالَى لَيُؤَيِّدُ هَذَا الدِّينَ بِالرَّجُلِ الْفَاجِرِ».

هَذَا الرَّجُلُ يَتَعَلَّمُ الْعِلْمَ رِيَاءً وَسُمْعَةً، فَيُعَلِّمُ النَّاسَ أُمُورَ دِينِهِمْ وَيُفَقِّهُهُمْ

understand it, and watches over them. He even helps the religion when its influence has become weak. Despite all these, Allah (Exalted is He) will enter him into the Fire because of his insincerity."

وَيُحْرِسُهُمْ، وَيَنْصُرُ الدِّينَ إِذَا ضَعُفَ جَانِبُهُ، ثُمَّ يُدْخِلُهُ اللهُ تَعَالَى بَعْدَ ذَلِكَ النَّارَ لِعَدَمِ إِخْلَاصِهِ اهـ .

Encouragement to Act in Accordance with the Muhammadan Sunnah

A general covenant was taken from us by the Messenger of Allah ﷺ that we follow the Muhammadan Sunnah in all our statements, actions, and beliefs. If we do not know an evidence from the Book, the Sunnah, consensus, or analogy, we should refrain from acting upon it until we investigate whether that act has been deemed good by one of the scholars – then, out of *adab* with that scholar, we seek permission from the Messenger of Allah ﷺ and act upon it. This is out of fear of innovating in the purified Sacred Law, thereby becoming one of the Imams of misguidance.

However, it is not hidden that seeking permission from the Messenger of Allah ﷺ occurs according to the station the slave finds himself at the time of performing that act. If he is from among those who meet with him ﷺ directly in a wakeful state, as is the station of the people of unveiling, he should seek his permission at that time. If not, he should seek permission with his heart: inspect what Allah (Exalted is He) tells him in his heart – of whether that act is good or he should leave it.

I heard Sīdī ʿAlī al-Khawwāṣ ؓ say:

> The only intent that the distinguished saints have, in their drive to conform with the Book and the Sunnah, is the company of Allah and His Messenger ﷺ in that act, and nothing else. For they know that the Real (Exalted is He) only accompanies them in acts that He or His Messenger ﷺ have legislated. As for acts that have been innovated, neither the Real (Exalted is He) nor His Messenger ﷺ will ever accompany him – he will only be accompanied by the scholar or the ignorant one who innovated the act.

أُخِذَ عَلَيْنَا الْعَهْدُ الْعَامُّ مِنْ رَسُولِ اللهِ ﷺ أَنْ نَتَّبِعَ السُّنَّةَ الْمُحَمَّدِيَّةَ فِي جَمِيعِ أَقْوَالِنَا وَأَفْعَالِنَا وَعَقَائِدِنَا، فَإِنْ لَمْ نَعْرِفْ لِذَلِكَ الْأَمْرِ دَلِيلًا مِنَ الْكِتَابِ وَالسُّنَّةِ أَوِ الْإِجْمَاعِ أَوِ الْقِيَاسِ تَوَقَّفْنَا عَنِ الْعَمَلِ بِهِ، ثُمَّ نَنْظُرُ.. فَإِنْ كَانَ ذَلِكَ الْأَمْرُ قَدِ اسْتَحْسَنَهُ بَعْضُ الْعُلَمَاءِ اسْتَأْذَنَّا رَسُولَ اللهِ صلى الله عليه وسلم فِيهِ ثُمَّ فَعَلْنَاهُ أَدَبًا مَعَ ذَلِكَ الْعَالِمِ، وَذَلِكَ كُلُّهُ خَوْفُ الِابْتِدَاعِ فِي الشَّرِيعَةِ الْمُطَهَّرَةِ فَنَكُونُ مِنْ جُمْلَةِ الْأَئِمَّةِ الْمُضِلِّينَ، وَقَدْ شَاوَرْتُهُ ﷺ فِي قَوْلِ بَعْضِهِم: إِنَّهُ يَنْبَغِي أَنْ يَقُولَ الْمُصَلِّي فِي سُجُودِ السَّهْوِ: سُبْحَانَ مَنْ لَا يَنَامُ وَلَا يَسْهُو، فَقَالَ ﷺ هُوَ حَسَنٌ، ثُمَّ لَا يَخْفَى أَنَّ الِاسْتِئْذَانَ لِرَسُولِ اللهِ ﷺ يَكُونُ بِحَسَبِ الْمَقَامِ الَّذِي فِيهِ الْعَبْدُ حَالَ إِرَادَتِهِ الْفِعْلَ، فَإِنْ كَانَ مِنْ أَهْلِ الِاجْتِمَاعِ بِهِ ﷺ يَقَظَةً وَمُشَافَهَةً كَمَا هُوَ مَقَامُ أَهْلِ الْكَشْفِ اسْتَأْذَنَهُ كَذَلِكَ، وَإِلَّا اسْتَأْذَنَهُ بِالْقَلْبِ وَانْتَظَرَ مَا يُحْدِثُهُ اللهُ تَعَالَى فِي قَلْبِهِ مِنِ اسْتِحْسَانِ الْفِعْلِ أَوِ التَّرْكِ.

وَسَمِعْتُ سَيِّدِي عَلِيًّا الْخَوَّاصَ رَحِمَهُ اللهُ يَقُولُ: لَيْسَ مُرَادُ الْأَكَابِرِ مِنْ حَثِّهِمْ عَلَى الْعَمَلِ عَلَى مُوَافَقَةِ الْكِتَابِ وَالسُّنَّةِ إِلَّا مُجَالَسَةَ اللهِ وَرَسُولِهِ ﷺ فِي ذَلِكَ الْأَمْرِ لَا غَيْرُ، فَإِنَّهُمْ يَعْلَمُونَ أَنَّ الْحَقَّ تَعَالَى لَا يُجَالِسُهُمْ إِلَّا فِي عَمَلٍ شَرَعَهُ هُوَ وَرَسُولُهُ ﷺ، أَمَّا مَا ابْتُدِعَ فَلَا يُجَالِسُهُمُ الْحَقُّ تَعَالَى وَلَا رَسُولُهُ ﷺ فِيهِ أَبَدًا، وَإِنَّمَا يُجَالِسُونَ فِيهِ مَنِ ابْتَدَعَهُ مِنْ عَالِمٍ أَوْ جَاهِلٍ،

So, you should know that the objective of the people of Allah (Exalted is He) in their worship is not to obtain a reward or anything else in the Hereafter. In both abodes, they are slaves, and in both abodes, the slave does not own anything along-side his master. Rather, the wealth of his master feeds, clothes, and entertains him; his honour and reputation are from the master's blessings. If the Real (Exalted is He) were to give the slave anything, he would need to exonerate himself of own-ership and attribute it to his Lord – he is not permitted to claim ownership, not even for the blink of an eye. Through such a witnessing, they remove all their acts of worship from the realm of egotistical works. Thus, they are completely satis-fied with their Lord, and He is completely satisfied with them: "That is the grace of Allah. He gives it to whomever he wills. And Allah is the Owner of immense grace."[6]

You should know, O brother, that if someone achieves acting in this manner, he will be among the heads of the Ahl al-Sun-nah wa al-Jamāʿah in his time. If someone refuses to call him as such, he will have wronged him. However, I do not know, in our time, anyone in Egypt who has achieved this – of lim-iting his words, acts, and beliefs to the Book and the Sunnah – except a few individuals from among the scholars, such as Shaykh ʿAbd al-Raḥmān al-Tajūrī al-Maghribī and those like him ﷺ.

I say: Allah (Exalted is He) has blessed me to act upon this in some of my words and actions. So, by Allah, whoever levels false accusations against me, of innovation that contradicts the majority of Ahl al-Sunnah wa al-Jamāʿah, has lied. For that is in itself innovation – unless he means, of course, innovation in one of the matters permitted by the Sacred Law, according to one of the universal principles. There is no harm for him in

(6) *Al-Ḥadīd*, 21.

فَعُلِمَ أَنَّهُ لَيْسَ قَصْدُ أَهْلِ اللهِ تَعَالَى بِعِبَادَتِهِمْ حُصُولَ ثَوَابٍ وَلَا غَيْرِهِ فِي الْآخِرَةِ، لِأَنَّهُمْ فِي الدَّارَيْنِ عَبِيدٌ وَالْعَبْدُ لَا يَمْلِكُ شَيْئًا مَعَ سَيِّدِهِ فِي الدُّنْيَا وَالْآخِرَةِ، إِنَّمَا يَأْكُلُ وَيَلْبَسُ وَيَتَمَتَّعُ بِمَالِ سَيِّدِهِ، وَسَدَاهُ وَلُحْمَتُهُ مِنْ نِعْمَتِهِ، وَلَوْ أَنَّ الْحَقَّ تَعَالَى أَعْطَاهُ شَيْئًا لَوَجَبَ عَلَيْهِ التَّبَرِّي مِنْهُ إِلَى رَبِّهِ، وَلَا يَجُوزُ لَهُ أَنْ يَشْهَدَ مِلْكَهُ لَهُ طَرْفَةَ عَيْنٍ، فَلِهَذَا الْمَشْهَدِ خَرَجُوا فِي جَمِيعِ عِبَادَاتِهِمْ عَنِ الْعِلَلِ النَّفْسَانِيَّةِ.. فَرَضُوا عَنْ رَبِّهِمْ رِضًا مُطْلَقًا، وَرَضِيَ عَنْهُمْ رِضًا مُطْلَقًا:

﴿ذَٰلِكَ فَضْلُ ٱللَّهِ يُؤْتِيهِ مَن يَشَآءُۚ وَٱللَّهُ ذُو ٱلْفَضْلِ ٱلْعَظِيمِ﴾ [الجمعة: ٤١] اهـ.

وَاعْلَمْ يَا أَخِي؛ أَنَّ مَنْ تَحَقَّقَ بِالْعَمَلِ بِهَذَا الْعَهْدِ صَارَ مِنْ رُؤُوسِ أَهْلِ السُّنَّةِ وَالْجَمَاعَةِ فِي عَصْرِهِ؛ وَمَنْ لَمْ يُلَقِّبْهُ بِذَلِكَ فَقَدْ ظَلَمَهُ، وَلَا أَعْلَمُ الْآنَ أَحَدًا فِي مِصْرَ تَحَقَّقَ بِالْعَمَلِ بِهَذَا الْعَهْدِ وَتَقَيَّدَ فِي أَقْوَالِهِ وَأَفْعَالِهِ وَعَقَائِدِهِ بِالْكِتَابِ وَالسُّنَّةِ إِلَّا بَعْضَ أَفْرَادٍ مِنَ الْعُلَمَاءِ، كَالشَّيْخِ عَبْدِ الرَّحْمَنِ التَّاجُورِيِّ الْمَغْرِبِيِّ وَأَضْرَابِهِ رَضِيَ اللهُ عَنْهُمْ أَجْمَعِينَ.

قُلْتُ: وَقَدْ مَنَّ اللهُ تَعَالَى عَلَيَّ بِالْعَمَلِ بِهِ فِي بَعْضِ أَقْوَالِي وَأَفْعَالِي، فَكَذَبَ وَاللهِ؛ وَافْتَرَى مَنْ نَسَبَنِي إِلَى الْبِدْعَةِ الْمُخَالِفَةِ لِجُمْهُورِ أَهْلِ السُّنَّةِ وَالْجَمَاعَةِ، فَإِنَّ هَذَا مَا هُوَ نَفَسُ مُبْتَدِعٍ، اللَّهُمَّ إِلَّا أَنْ يُرِيدَ الِابْتِدَاعَ فِي شَيْءٍ مِنَ الْمُبَاحَاتِ فِي الشَّرِيعَةِ بِحُكْمِ الْعُمُومَاتِ.. فَهَذَا لَا يُحْرَجُ عَلَيْهِ فِي ذَلِكَ، لِأَنَّ هَذَا الْأَمْرَ قَلَّ مَنْ سَلِمَ مِنْهُ مِنَ الْعُلَمَاءِ فَضْلًا عَنْ

that because it is a matter from which few of the scholars are safe, much less anyone else, as is evident.

Know this, and protect your hearing and sight regarding the scholars! Never follow the statements of the envious among them, until you meet with one and discuss that particular innovation with him. If you find him practising an innovation, and insisting on it even after being informed of its innovation, only then should you warn people about him, out of kindness to him and to the Muslims, that is, so that none among them fall into sin – neither the innovator nor anyone who follows him. However, beware of warning people from following one of the scholars based on the words of such enviers without having met him, for he may be free of what is attributed to him. In that case, you will bear the sin of cutting off the disciples from the path to the Sacred Law; in that instant, you will be warning people of following the Muhammadan Sunnah. This is very common among the groups of this age; you will see them warning each of the other, believing that they alone hail from the People of the Sunnah and the Jamāʿah. Thus, the affair may disintegrate to the point that none of them are followed. May Allah protect us and our companions from such a fate by His grace and generosity. *Āmīn*!

Sīdī Abū al-Ḥasan al-Shādhilī ﷺ used to say, "A faqir's worship is incomplete until he witnesses the Legislator in each act of worship. In other words, he performs each act in his presence – with unveiling and witnessing, not with veiled faith." Then he said, "If someone were to say, 'What's your evidence for that?' we would respond: I have seen the Prophet ﷺ in one of our experiences. I asked him, 'O Messenger of Allah! What is it to truly follow you in acts that correspond to your Sacred Law?' He said, '*It is to perform the act while witnessing the Legislator while within and after it.*'"

If someone wants to act in accordance with this covenant, he needs to know the evidences of all the *madhāhib*, both those

غَيْرِهِمْ كَمَا هُوَ مُشَاهَدٌ، فَاعْلَمْ ذَلِكَ وَاحْمِ سَمْعَكَ وَبَصَرَكَ فِي حَقِّ الْعُلَمَاءِ، وَلَا تُصْغِ إِلَى قَوْلِ حَاسِدٍ لَهُمْ قَطُّ إِلَّا إِنِ اجْتَمَعْتَ بِأَحَدِهِمْ وَفَاوَضْتَهُ فِي الْكَلَامِ فِي تِلْكَ الْبِدْعَةِ، فَإِذَا رَأَيْتَهُ مُتَخَلِّقًا بِهَا وَعَرَفْتَهُ بِأَنَّهَا بِدْعَةٌ وَصَمَّمَ عَلَى الْعَمَلِ بِهَا فَهُنَاكَ حَذِّرِ النَّاسَ مِنْهُ شَفَقَةً عَلَيْهِ وَعَلَى الْمُسْلِمِينَ، حَتَّى لَا يَقَعَ أَحَدٌ مِنْهُمْ فِي إِثْمٍ لَا الْمُبْتَدِعُ وَلَا مَنْ تَبِعَهُ. وَإِيَّاكَ أَنْ تُحَذِّرَ مِنِ اتِّبَاعِ أَحَدٍ مِنَ الْعُلَمَاءِ بِقَوْلِ أَحَدٍ مِنْ حُسَّادِهِمْ مِنْ غَيْرِ اجْتِمَاعٍ بِهِ فَرُبَّمَا يَكُونُ بَرِيئًا مِمَّا نُسِبَ إِلَيْهِ، فَيَكُونُ عَلَيْكَ إِثْمُ قَاطِعِ الطَّرِيقِ عَلَى الْمُرِيدِينَ لِاتِّبَاعِ الشَّرِيعَةِ، فَإِنَّكَ حِينَئِذٍ تُحَذِّرُ مِنِ اتِّبَاعِ السُّنَّةِ الْمُحَمَّدِيَّةِ، وَهَذَا وَاقِعٌ كَثِيرًا فِي الْأَقْرَانِ فِي هَذَا الزَّمَانِ، فَتَرَى كُلَّ وَاحِدٍ يُحَذِّرُ النَّاسَ عَنِ الْآخَرِ وَكُلٌّ مِنْهُمَا يَزْعُمُ أَنَّهُ مِنْ أَهْلِ الطَّرِيقِ وَالسُّنَّةِ وَالْجَمَاعَةِ، فَيَخْتَلُّ الْأَمْرُ إِلَى عَدَمِ الِاقْتِدَاءِ بِوَاحِدٍ مِنْهُمَا، فَاللهُ يَحْمِينَا وَأَصْحَابَنَا مِنْ مِثْلِ ذَلِكَ بِمَنِّهِ وَكَرَمِهِ آمِينَ.

وَكَانَ سَيِّدِي أَبُو الْحَسَنِ الشَّاذِلِيُّ رضى الله عنه يَقُولُ: لَا تَكْمُلُ عِبَادَةُ فَقِيرٍ حَتَّى يَصِيرَ يُشَاهِدُ الشَّرْعَ فِي كُلِّ عِبَادَةٍ عَمِلَهَا، يَعْنِي يَعْمَلُهَا بِحَضْرَتِهِ عَلَى الْكَشْفِ وَالْمُشَاهَدَةِ، لَا عَلَى الْإِيمَانِ وَالْحِجَابِ، ثُمَّ قَالَ: فَإِنْ قَالَ قَائِلٌ مَا دَلِيلُكَ عَلَى ذَلِكَ؟ قُلْنَا لَهُ: قَدْ رَأَيْتُ النَّبِيَّ ﷺ فِي وَاقِعَةٍ مِنَ الْوَقَائِعِ، فَقُلْتُ لَهُ: يَا رَسُولَ اللهِ؛ مَا حَقِيقَةُ مُتَابَعَتِكَ فِي الْعَمَلِ عَلَى مُوَافَقَةِ شَرِيعَتِكَ؟ فَقَالَ: «هِيَ أَنْ تَعْمَلَ الْعَمَلَ مَعَ شُهُودِكَ لِلشَّرْعِ حَالَ الْعَمَلِ وَبَعْدَ الْعَمَلِ» اهـ.

that are used and those that have been abandoned, along with the opinions of the scholars, until none of the evidences nor the opinions regarding legislated, forbidden, or licit matters are hidden from him. Then, he must have a true *shaykh,* who submits him to spiritual exercises until the struggle removes from him all blameworthy traits and fills him with praiseworthy ones so that he will be worthy of the company of Allah (Exalted is He) and His Messenger ﷺ.

Indeed, the majority of people have claimed the company of Allah (Exalted is He) and His Messenger ﷺ, despite being stained with evil traits that prevent them from entering their presence. Thus, they are increased in abomination and rejection.

Hence, O brother, work on cleaning the mirror of your heart from rust and grime and purifying yourself from evil traits until not one remains within that would prevent you from entering the presence of Allah (Exalted is He) or of the Messenger of Allah ﷺ. If you were to send copious prayers and salutations upon him ﷺ, you may arrive at the station of witnessing the Messenger ﷺ. That is the path of Shaykh Nūr al-Dīn al-Shūnī, Shaykh Aḥmad al-Zawāwī, Shaykh Muhammad ibn Dāwūd al-Munzalāwī, and a group of the *shuyūkh* of Yemen; they all continue to send prayers upon the Prophet of Allah ﷺ in abundant amounts until they are purified of all sin and then begin to meet him ﷺ directly in a wakeful state any time they wish. Someone who has not attained to that meeting has not yet reached the level of sending the amount of abundant prayers and salutations required to achieve that station.

Shaykh Aḥmad al-Zawāwī informed me that he did not reach the station of meeting with the Prophet ﷺ in a wakeful state until he had been steadfast in sending prayers upon him for an entire year – fifty thousand times, day and night. Likewise, Shaykh Nūr al-Dīn al-Shūnī informed me that he had

وَيَحْتَاجُ مَنْ يُرِيدُ الْعَمَلَ بِهَذَا الْعَهْدِ إِلَى الْإِحَاطَةِ بِأَدِلَّةِ جَمِيعِ الْمَذَاهِبِ الْمُسْتَعْمَلَةِ وَالْمُنْدَرِسَةِ وَأَقْوَالِ عُلَمَائِهَا، حَتَّى لَا يَكَادَ يَخْفَى عَلَيْهِ دَلِيلٌ مِنْ أَدِلَّتِهِمْ وَلَا قَوْلٌ مِنْ أَقْوَالِهِمْ فِي مَأْمُورٍ بِهِ أَوْ مَنْهِيٍّ عَنْهُ أَوْ مُبَاحٍ، ثُمَّ بَعْدَ ذَلِكَ لَا بُدَّ لَهُ مِنْ شَيْخٍ صَادِقٍ يُسَلِّمُ إِلَيْهِ نَفْسَهُ يَتَصَرَّفُ فِيهَا بِالرِّيَاضَاتِ وَالْمُجَاهَدَاتِ حَتَّى يُزِيلَ عَنْهُ سَائِرَ الصِّفَاتِ الْمَذْمُومَةِ وَيُحَلِّيَهُ بِالصِّفَاتِ الْمَحْمُودَةِ لِيَصْلُحَ لِمُجَالَسَةِ اللهِ تَعَالَى وَرَسُولِهِ ﷺ؛ فَإِنَّ غَالِبَ النَّاسِ قَدِ ادَّعَوْا مُجَالَسَةَ اللهِ تَعَالَى وَرَسُولِهِ ﷺ مَعَ تَلَطُّخِهِمْ بِالْقَاذُورَاتِ الْمَانِعَةِ مِنْ دُخُولِ حَضْرَةِ اللهِ وَحَضْرَةِ رَسُولِهِ فَازْدَادُوا مَقْتًا وَطَرْدًا. فَاعْمَلْ يَا أَخِي عَلَى جَلَاءِ مِرْآةِ قَلْبِكَ مِنَ الصَّدَأِ وَالْغُبَارِ، وَعَلَى تَطَهُّرِكَ مِنْ سَائِرِ الرَّذَائِلِ حَتَّى لَا يَبْقَى فِيكَ خَصْلَةٌ وَاحِدَةٌ تَمْنَعُكَ مِنْ دُخُولِ حَضْرَةِ اللهِ تَعَالَى أَوْ حَضْرَةِ رَسُولِ اللهِ ﷺ، فَإِنْ أَكْثَرْتَ مِنَ الصَّلَاةِ وَالسَّلَامِ عَلَيْهِ ﷺ فَرُبَّمَا تَصِلُ إِلَى مَقَامِ مُشَاهَدَتِهِ ﷺ، وَهِيَ طَرِيقُ الشَّيْخِ نُورِ الدِّينِ الشُّونِيِّ، وَالشَّيْخِ أَحْمَدَ الزَّوَاوِيِّ، وَالشَّيْخِ مُحَمَّدِ بْنِ دَاوُدَ الْمَنْزِلَاوِيِّ، وَجَمَاعَةٍ مِنْ مَشَايِخِ الْيَمَنِ، فَلا يَزَالُ أَحَدُهُمْ يُصَلِّي عَلَى رَسُولِ اللهِ ﷺ وَيُكْثِرُ مِنْهَا حَتَّى يَتَطَهَّرَ مِنْ كُلِّ الذُّنُوبِ، وَيَصِيرَ يَجْتَمِعُ بِهِ يَقَظَةً أَيَّ وَقْتٍ شَاءَ وَمُشَافَهَةً، وَمَنْ لَمْ يَحْصُلْ لَهُ هَذَا الِاجْتِمَاعُ فَهُوَ إِلَى الْآنَ لَمْ يُكْثِرْ مِنَ الصَّلَاةِ وَالتَّسْلِيمِ عَلَى رَسُولِ اللهِ ﷺ الْإِكْثَارَ الْمَطْلُوبَ لِيَحْصُلَ لَهُ هَذَا الْمَقَامُ.

وَأَخْبَرَنِي الشَّيْخُ أَحْمَدُ الزَّوَاوِيُّ أَنَّهُ لَمْ يَحْصُلْ لَهُ الِاجْتِمَاعُ بِالنَّبِيِّ ﷺ يَقَظَةً حَتَّى وَاظَبَ عَلَى الصَّلَاةِ عَلَيْهِ سَنَةً كَامِلَةً يُصَلِّي كُلَّ يَوْمٍ وَلَيْلَةٍ خَمْسِينَ أَلْفَ مَرَّةٍ، وَكَذَلِكَ أَخْبَرَنِي الشَّيْخُ نُورُ الدِّينِ الشُّونِيُّ أَنَّهُ وَاظَبَ عَلَى الصَّلَاةِ عَلَى النَّبِيِّ ﷺ كَذَا وَكَذَا سَنَةً يُصَلِّي كُلَّ يَوْمٍ ثَلَاثِينَ أَلْفَ صَلَاةٍ.

been steadfast in offering prayers upon the Prophet ﷺ for a number of years – thirty thousand times daily.

I heard Sīdī ʿAlī al-Khawwāṣ ﵁ saying, "The slave is not complete in the station of *maʿrifah* until he begins meeting the Messenger of Allah ﷺ any time he wants." He also said, "Among the predecessors about whom it reached us that they would meet with the Prophet ﷺ directly in a wakeful state are Shaykh Abū Madyan (the *shaykh* of the community), Shaykh ʿAbd al-Raḥīm al-Qenāwī, Shaykh Mūsā al-Zūlī, Shaykh Abū al-Ḥasan al-Shādhilī, Shaykh Abū al-ʿAbbās al-Mursī, Shaykh Abū al-Suʿūd ibn Abī al-ʿAshāʾir, Sīdī Ibrāhīm al-Matbūlī, and Shaykh Jalāl al-Dīn al-Suyūṭī. The latter used to say, 'I saw the Prophet ﷺ and met with him in a wakeful state over seventy times.' As for Ibrāhīm al-Matbūlī, the times that he met with him cannot be counted because he would meet with him in all his states. He used to say, 'I do not have a *shaykh* other than the Messenger of Allah ﷺ.' Abū al-ʿAbbās al-Mursī used to say, 'If the Messenger of Allah ﷺ had been hidden from me for an hour, I would not consider myself as being among the believers.'"

However, you should know the utter rarity that is the station of keeping company with the Messenger of Allah ﷺ. One day, a man came to Sīdī ʿAlī al-Mursafī while I was present. He said, "My master! I have reached the station where I have begun to see the Messenger of Allah ﷺ in a wakeful state whenever I want." The latter replied, "My son, between the slave and that station are two hundred and forty-seven stations – we want you to speak to us about only ten of them." However, that claimant did not know what he was saying and was exposed. So recognize that *Allah guides whomever He wills to a Straight Path.*[7]

---

(7) *Al-Nūr*, 46.

وَسَمِعْتُ سَيِّدِي عَلِيًّا الْخَوَّاصَ رَحِمَهُ اللهُ يَقُولُ: لَا يَكْمُلُ عَبْدٌ فِي مَقَامِ الْعِرْفَانِ حَتَّى يَصِيرَ يَجْتَمِعُ بِرَسُولِ اللهِ ﷺ أَيَّ وَقْتٍ شَاءَ، قَالَ: وَمِمَّنْ بَلَغَنَا أَنَّهُ كَانَ يَجْتَمِعُ بِالنَّبِيِّ ﷺ يَقَظَةً وَمُشَافَهَةً مِنَ السَّلَفِ، الشَّيْخُ أَبُو مَدْيَنَ شَيْخُ الْجَمَاعَةِ، وَالشَّيْخُ عَبْدُ الرَّحِيمِ الْقِنَاوِيُّ، وَالشَّيْخُ مُوسَى الزُّولِيُّ، وَالشَّيْخُ أَبُو الْحَسَنِ الشَّاذِلِيُّ، وَالشَّيْخُ أَبُو الْعَبَّاسِ الْمُرْسِيُّ، وَالشَّيْخُ أَبُو السُّعُودِ بْنُ أَبِي الْعَشَائِرِ، وَسَيِّدِي إِبْرَاهِيمُ الْمَتْبُولِيُّ وَالشَّيْخُ جَلَالُ الدِّينِ الْأَسْيُوطِيُّ، كَانَ يَقُولُ: رَأَيْتُ النَّبِيَّ ﷺ وَاجْتَمَعْتُ بِهِ يَقَظَةً نَيِّفًا وَسَبْعِينَ مَرَّةً.

وَأَمَّا سَيِّدِي إِبْرَاهِيمُ الْمَتْبُولِيُّ فَلَا يُحْصَى اجْتِمَاعُهُ بِهِ؛ لِأَنَّهُ كَانَ يَجْتَمِعُ بِهِ فِي أَحْوَالِهِ كُلِّهَا وَيَقُولُ: لَيْسَ لِي شَيْخٌ إِلَّا رَسُولُ اللهِ ﷺ، وَكَانَ الشَّيْخُ أَبُو الْعَبَّاسِ الْمُرْسِيُّ يَقُولُ: لَوِ احْتَجَبَ عَنِّي رَسُولُ اللهِ ﷺ سَاعَةً مَا عَدَدْتُ نَفْسِي مِنْ جُمْلَةِ الْمُؤْمِنِينَ.

وَاعْلَمْ أَنَّ مَقَامَ مُجَالَسَةِ رَسُولِ اللهِ ﷺ عَزِيزَةٌ جِدًّا، وَقَدْ جَاءَ شَخْصٌ إِلَى سَيِّدِي عَلِيٍّ الْمَرْصِفِيِّ وَأَنَا حَاضِرٌ فَقَالَ: يَا سَيِّدِي؛ قَدْ وَصَلْتُ إِلَى مَقَامٍ صِرْتُ أَرَى رَسُولَ اللهِ ﷺ يَقَظَةً أَيَّ وَقْتٍ شِئْتُ، فَقَالَ لَهُ: يَا وَلَدِي؛ بَيْنَ الْعَبْدِ وَبَيْنَ هَذَا الْمَقَامِ مِائَتَا أَلْفِ مَقَامٍ؛ وَسَبْعَةٌ وَأَرْبَعُونَ أَلْفَ مَقَامٍ، وَمُرَادُنَا [أَنْ] تَتَكَلَّمَ لَنَا يَا وَلَدِي عَلَى عَشْرِ مَقَامَاتٍ مِنْهَا، فَمَا دَرَى ذَلِكَ الْمُدَّعِي مَا يَقُولُ وَافْتَضَحَ، فَاعْلَمْ ذَلِكَ:

﴿وَٱللَّهُ يَهۡدِي مَن يَشَآءُ إِلَىٰ صِرَٰطٖ مُّسۡتَقِيمٍ﴾ [النور: ٤٦].

We will now mention a portion of the *aḥādīth* that exhort one to act upon the Book and the Sunnah. We say – and Allah facilitates:

Abū Dāwūd, al-Tirmidhī, and Ibn Mājah, along with Ibn Ḥibbān, narrate the following[8]: Al-ʿIrbāḍ ibn Sāriyah ﵁ said, "The Messenger of Allah ﷺ gave us a sermon that caused our hearts to tremble and our eyes to shed tears. So we said, 'O Messenger of Allah! It is as if it is a farewell sermon, so advise us.' He said, '*I advise you to have fear of Allah, to act, hear, and obey, even if an Abyssinian slave with a deformed head is put in charge of you. For indeed, anyone among you who lives some time will see much discord. Nevertheless, it is incumbent upon you to adhere to my Sunnah and the Sunnah of the rightly guided khulafāʾ after me – bite down on it with your molars.*[9] *Beware of newly invented matters, for every innovation is misguidance, and every misguidance is in the Fire.*'"

Ibn Abī al-Dunyā and al-Ḥākim both narrated the following Prophetic Hadith, declaring its chain authentic: "*If someone eats what is pure, acts on the Sunnah, and keeps people safe from his evil deeds, he will enter Paradise.*" The people said, "O Messenger of Allah! They are many in your Ummah today." He replied, "*And they will be among a people after me.*"[10] Al-Bayhaqī also narrated the following Prophetic Hadith: "*If someone adheres to my Sunnah when my Ummah has become corrupted, he will have the reward of one hundred shuhadāʾ.*"

Al-Ḥākim narrated the following Prophetic Hadith, declaring its chain authentic according to the conditions of al-Bukhārī

(8) Al-Mundhirī declared the Hadith to be *ḥasan al-ṣaḥīḥ*.

(9) The meaning of "bite down on it with your molars" is to struggle to efface innovation and to persevere in sticking to the Sunnah just as a biting dog clenches onto something with its canines out of fear of its loss or escape.

(10) Meaning that they will be few.

وَلْنَشْرَعْ فِي بَيَانِ جُمْلَةٍ مِنَ الْأَحَادِيثِ الْحَاثَّةِ عَلَى اتِّبَاعِ الْكِتَابِ وَالسُّنَّةِ فَنَقُولُ، وَبِاللهِ التَّوْفِيقُ:

رَوَى أَبُو دَاوُدَ وَالتِّرمِذِيُّ وَابْنُ مَاجه وَابْنُ حِبَّانَ فِي «صَحِيحِهِ»، قَالَ الْمُنْذِرِيُّ: وَهَذَا حَدِيثٌ حَسَنٌ صَحِيحٌ عَنِ الْعِرْبَاضِ بْنِ سَارِيَةَ رَضِيَ اللهُ عَنْهُ قَالَ:

وَعَظَنَا رَسُولُ اللهِ ﷺ مَوْعِظَةً وَجِلَتْ مِنْهَا الْقُلُوبُ وَذَرَفَتْ مِنْهَا الْعُيُونُ، فَقُلْنَا يَا رَسُولَ اللهِ؛ كَأَنَّهَا مَوْعِظَةُ مُوَدِّعٍ فَأَوْصِنَا، فَقَالَ: «أُوصِيكُمْ بِتَقْوَى اللهِ وَالْعَمَلِ وَالسَّمْعِ وَالطَّاعَةِ، وَإِنْ تَأَمَّرَ عَلَيْكُمْ عَبْدٌ حَبَشِيٌّ مُجَدَّعُ الْأَطْرَافِ؛ فَإِنَّ مَنْ يَعِشْ مِنْكُمْ فَسَيَرَى اخْتِلَافًا كَثِيرًا، فَعَلَيْكُمْ بِسُنَّتِي وَسُنَّةِ الْخُلَفَاءِ الرَّاشِدِينَ الْمَهْدِيِّينَ مِنْ بَعْدِي عَضُّوا عَلَيْهَا بِالنَّوَاجِذِ، وَإِيَّاكُمْ وَمُحْدَثَاتِ الْأُمُورِ، فَإِنَّ كُلَّ بِدْعَةٍ ضَلَالَةٌ وَكُلَّ ضَلَالَةٍ فِي النَّارِ».

وَمَعنَى «عَضُّوا عَلَيْهَا بِالنَّوَاجِذِ»: أَيِ اجْتَهِدُوا عَلَى وَجْهِ الْبِدْعَةِ، وَالْزَمُوا السُّنَّةَ وَاحْرِصُوا عَلَيْهَا، كَمَا يَلْزَمُ العَاضُّ عَلَى الشَّيءِ بِنَوَاجِذِهِ خَوْفًا مِنْ ذَهَابِهِ وَتَفَلُّتِهِ، وَالنَّوَاجِذُ: هِيَ الْأَنْيَابُ، وَقِيلَ: هِيَ الْأَضْرَاسُ.

وَرَوَى ابْنُ أَبِي الدُّنيَا وَالْحَاكِمُ وَقَالَا: صَحِيحُ الْإِسْنَادِ مَرْفُوعًا:

«مَنْ أَكَلَ طَيِّبًا وَعَمِلَ فِي سُنَّةٍ وَأَمِنَ النَّاسُ بَوَائِقَهُ.. دَخَلَ الْجَنَّةَ، قَالُوا: يَا رَسُولَ اللهِ؛ إِنَّ هَذَا الْيَوْمَ فِي أُمَّتِكَ كَثِيرٌ؟ قَالَ: وَسَيَكُونُ فِي قَوْمٍ بَعْدِي». يَعنِي: قَلَائِلَ.

وَرَوَى الْبَيْهَقِيُّ مَرْفُوعًا: «مَنْ تَمَسَّكَ بِسُنَّتِي عِنْدَ فَسَادِ أُمَّتِي فَلَهُ أَجْرُ مِائَةِ شَهِيدٍ».

and Muslim: "*Moderation in following the Sunnah is better than great effort in innovation.*"

Al-Bukhārī, Muslim, and others narrated that ʿUmar ibn al-Khaṭṭāb ﷺ kissed the Black Stone and said, "I know that you are only a stone, and that you neither harm nor benefit. If it weren't for the fact that I had seen the Messenger of Allah ﷺ kiss you, I would not have kissed you."

Ibn Mājah and Ibn Ḥibbān narrated from Muʿāwiyah ibn Qurrah that his father said, "I met the Messenger of Allah ﷺ in a caravan; we pledged our allegiance to him. He was wearing an unbuttoned shirt." ʿUrwah ibn ʿAbdullāh said, "I never saw Muʿāwiyah nor his father at all, even in winter, except that they wore unbuttoned shirts."[11]

Ibn Khuzayma in his *Ṣaḥīḥ* and al-Bayhaqī narrated that Zayd ibn Aslam said, "I saw Ibn ʿUmar praying with his buttons unfastened. So, I asked him about that. He said, 'I saw the Messenger of Allah ﷺ do it.'" Imam Aḥmad and al-Bazzār narrated that Mujāhid and others said, "We were with Ibn ʿUmar on a journey. We passed by a place which he turned away from.[12] He was asked why he had done that, and he responded, 'I saw the Messenger of Allah ﷺ doing that, so I did it.'"

Al-Bazzār narrated that Ibn ʿUmar used to go to a tree between Makkah and Madinah and nap under it; he narrated the Prophet ﷺ used to do the same. Imam Aḥmad and others also narrated that Ibn ʿUmar made his camel kneel in a place and used its restroom; he narrated that the Prophet ﷺ would use the very same restroom: "I desired to use the restroom in the same place that the Messenger of Allah ﷺ had used."

---

(11) Or in another narration: "except with their buttons unfastened."

(12) The phrase "turned away from" means that he turned either to the right or the left from that place.

وَرَوَى الْحَاكِمُ وَقَالَ: صَحِيحُ الْإِسْنَادِ عَلَى شَرْطِ الشَّيْخَيْنِ مَرْفُوعًا: «الِاقْتِصَادُ فِي السُّنَّةِ أَحْسَنُ مِنَ الِاجْتِهَادِ فِي الْبِدْعَةِ».

وَرَوَى الشَّيْخَانِ وَغَيْرُهُمَا مَرْفُوعًا، عَنْ عُمَرَ بْنِ الْخَطَّابِ رَضِيَ اللهُ عَنْهُ أَنَّهُ قَبَّلَ الْحَجَرَ الْأَسْوَدَ وَقَالَ: إِنِّي لَأَعْلَمُ أَنَّكَ حَجَرٌ لَا تَضُرُّ وَلَا تَنْفَعُ، وَلَوْلَا أَنِّي رَأَيْتُ رَسُولَ اللهِ صلى الله عليه وسلم يُقَبِّلُكَ مَا قَبَّلْتُكَ.

وَرَوَى ابْنُ مَاجَهْ وَابْنُ حِبَّانَ فِي «صَحِيحَيْهِمَا» عَنْ مُعَاوِيَةَ بْنِ قُرَّةَ عَنْ أَبِيهِ قَالَ: لَقِيتُ رَسُولَ اللهِ ﷺ فِي رَهْطٍ فَبَايَعْنَاهُ وَإِنَّهُ لَمُطْلَقُ الْأَزْرَارِ. قَالَ عُرْوَةُ بْنُ عَبْدِ اللهِ: فَمَا رَأَيْتُ مُعَاوِيَةَ وَلَا ابْنَهُ قَطُّ فِي شِتَاءٍ وَلَا صَيْفٍ، إِلَّا مُطْلَقَ الْأَزْرَارِ، وَفِي رِوَايَةٍ: إِلَّا مُطْلَقَةً أَزْرَارُهُمَا.

وَرَوَى ابْنُ خُزَيْمَةَ فِي «صَحِيحِهِ»، وَالْبَيْهَقِيُّ عَنْ زَيْدِ بْنِ أَسْلَمَ قَالَ: رَأَيْتُ ابْنَ عُمَرَ يُصَلِّي مَحْلُولَةً أَزْرَارُهُ، فَسَأَلْتُهُ عَنْ ذَلِكَ فَقَالَ: رَأَيْتُ رَسُولَ اللهِ ﷺ يَفْعَلُهُ. وَرَوَى الْإِمَامُ أَحْمَدُ وَالْبَزَّارُ عَنْ مُجَاهِدٍ وَغَيْرِهِ قَالَ: كُنَّا مَعَ ابْنِ عُمَرَ فِي سَفَرٍ فَمَرَّ بِمَكَانٍ فَحَادَ عَنْهُ، فَسُئِلَ: لِمَ فَعَلْتَ ذَلِكَ؟ فَقَالَ: رَأَيْتُ رَسُولَ اللهِ ﷺ فَعَلَ هَذَا.. فَفَعَلْتُهُ. وَقَوْلُهُ حَادَ: أَيْ: تَنَحَّى عَنْهُ وَأَخَذَ يَمِينًا أَوْ شِمَالًا.

وَرَوَى الْبَزَّارُ عَنِ ابْنِ عُمَرَ أَنَّهُ كَانَ يَأْتِي شَجَرَةً بَيْنَ مَكَّةَ وَالْمَدِينَةِ فَيُقِيلُ تَحْتَهَا، وَيُخْبِرُ أَنَّ النَّبِيَّ صلى الله عليه وسلم كَانَ يَفْعَلُ مِثْلَ ذَلِكَ. وَرَوَى الْإِمَامُ أَحْمَدُ وَغَيْرُهُ أَنَّ ابْنَ عُمَرَ أَنَاخَ رَاحِلَتَهُ فِي مَكَانٍ فَقَضَى حَاجَتَهُ، وَأَخْبَرَ أَنَّ النَّبِيَّ صلى الله عليه وسلم قَضَى حَاجَتَهُ فِي ذَلِكَ الْمَكَانِ، وَقَالَ: أَحْبَبْتُ أَنْ أَقْضِيَ حَاجَتِي فِي مَوْضِعٍ قَضَى فِيهِ رَسُولُ اللهِ ﷺ حَاجَتَهُ.

I (al-Shaʿrānī) say: Ibn ʿUmar only followed the Messenger of Allah ﷺ in that because the perfected souls are careful when they use the restroom in any land, out of fear that it is a noble piece of land in which one should not use the restroom. However, when he saw the Messenger of Allah ﷺ do it, he said to himself, "If the Messenger of Allah ﷺ had not known that this piece of land is good for us to use the restroom, he would not have gone on it."

Al-Ḥāfiẓ said, "The narrations about the Companions ﷺ in their following him and emulating his Sunnah are numerous. And Allah knows best."

قُلْتُ: وَإِنَّمَا تَبِعَ ابْنُ عُمَرَ النَّبِيَّ ﷺ فِي ذَلِكَ لِأَنَّ الْكَمَلَةَ يَسْتَحْيُونَ مِنَ الْأَرْضِ إِذَا قَضَوْا عَلَيْهَا الْحَاجَةَ خَوْفًا أَنْ تَكُونَ تِلْكَ الْبُقْعَةُ مُشْرِفَةً لَا تَصْلُحُ لِقَضَاءِ الْحَاجَةِ، فَلَمَّا رَأَى رَسُولَ اللهِ ﷺ فَعَلَ ذَلِكَ، قَالَ فِي نَفْسِهِ: لَوْلَا أَنَّ رَسُولَ اللهِ صلى الله عليه وسلم عَلِمَ أَنَّ تِلْكَ الْبُقْعَةَ تَصْلُحُ لِذَلِكَ.. مَا فَعَلَ النَّبِيُّ ﷺ ذَلِكَ.

قَالَ الْحَافِظُ: وَالْآثَارُ عَنِ الصَّحَابَةِ رَضِيَ اللهُ عَنْهُمْ فِي اتِّبَاعِهِمْ لَهُ وَاقْتِفَائِهِمْ سُنَنَهُ كَثِيرَةٌ جِدًّا، وَاللهُ أَعْلَمُ.

Encouragement to Manifest Good

A general covenant was taken from us by the Messenger of Allah ﷺ that we would be among the foremost of people in doing good. We should race towards good and set an example for the people. For example, if we see a man begging for money and no one gives him anything, we should give him something publicly – and not give it secretly – to encourage the people to give.

Likewise, we should be eager to stand for *tahajjud*, from the first appearance of the manifestation of the Real (Exalted is He) calling out, *"Is there anyone asking so that I may give him? Is there anyone seeking forgiveness so that I may forgive him? Is there anyone who is afflicted so that I may grant him relief?"* to the end of what has been related regarding this. We should stand during the same third part of the night as when the Messenger of Allah ﷺ would perform *tahajjud*[13] so that one of our brethren would perhaps rise and perform *tahajjud* when he sees us, and thereby a reward will be recorded for him and for us.

Another example of this is to manifest the outward signs of patience with the trials of this age so that people will be inspired by us to have patience and not be upset (by the Decree). If we see that patience reaching its limit, we should show weakness until the affliction is lifted, as was the case with Ayyūb ﷺ. For it is known that every actor should conceal his works as much as he can, except those in which he may be emulated in his act and method.

I heard Sīdī ʿAlī al-Khawwāṣ ﷺ say:

(13) As alluded to in Allah's (Exalted is He) words [*al-Muzzammil*, 20]: "Indeed, your Lord knows that you stand less than a third of the night, half of it, or a third of it."

أُخِذَ عَلَيْنَا الْعَهْدُ الْعَامُّ مِنْ رَسُولِ اللهِ ﷺ أَنْ نَكُونَ فِي أَعْمَالِ الْخَيْرِ مِنْ أَهْلِ الرَّعِيلِ الْأَوَّلِ.. فَنَبْدَأُ بِفِعْلِ الْخَيْرِ قَبْلَ النَّاسِ مُسَارَعَةً لِلْخَيْرِ وَيَسْتَنُّ بِنَا النَّاسُ، وَذَلِكَ كَمَا إِذَا رَأَيْنَا إِنْسَانًا يَسْأَلُ النَّاسَ وَلَا أَحَدٌ يُعْطِيهِ شَيْئًا.. فَنُعْطِيهِ أَمَامَ النَّاسِ تَحْرِيضًا لَهُمْ عَلَى الْعَطَاءِ وَلَا نُعْطِيهِ سِرًّا، وَكَذَلِكَ نَحْرِصُ عَلَى أَنْ نَقُومَ مِنَ اللَّيْلِ مِنْ أَوَّلِ مَا يَقَعُ التَّجَلِّي وَيُنَادِي الْحَقُّ تَعَالَى: «هَلْ مِنْ سَائِلٍ فَأُعْطِيَهُ سُؤْلَهُ، هَلْ مِنْ مُسْتَغْفِرٍ فَأَغْفِرَ لَهُ، هَلْ مِنْ مُبْتَلًى فَأُعَافِيَهُ».

إِلَى آخِرِ مَا وَرَدَ فِي ذَلِكَ مِنْ أَوَّلِ الثُّلُثِ الْأَخِيرِ مِنَ اللَّيْلِ فِي أَغْلَبِ التَّجَلِّيَاتِ الَّتِي كَانَ ﷺ يَتَهَجَّدُ وَقْتَهَا، كَمَا أَشَارَ إِلَيْهِ قَوْلُهُ تَعَالَى: ﴿إِنَّ رَبَّكَ يَعْلَمُ أَنَّكَ تَقُومُ أَدْنَىٰ مِن ثُلُثَيِ ٱلَّيْلِ وَنِصْفَهُۥ وَثُلُثَهُۥ﴾ [المزمل: ٢٠].

وَذَلِكَ لِيَتَأَسَّى بِنَا إِخْوَانُنَا وَجِيرَانُنَا، فَرُبَّمَا قَامَ أَحَدُهُمْ يَتَهَجَّدُ حِينَ يَرَانَا.. فَيُكْتَبُ لَنَا وَلَهُ الْأَجْرُ.

وَمِنْ هَذَا الْبَابِ أَيْضًا إِظْهَارُ التَّصَبُّرِ عَلَى الْبَلَايَا وَالْمِحَنِ فِي هَذَا الزَّمَانِ؛ لِيَتَأَسَّى النَّاسُ بِنَا فِي الصَّبْرِ وَعَدَمِ التَّسَخُّطِ، فَإِنْ رَأَيْنَا الصَّبْرَ بَلَغَ حَدَّهُ أَظْهَرْنَا الضَّعْفَ حَتَّى يَرْتَفِعَ كَمَا وَقَعَ لِأَيُّوبَ عليه السلام، فَعُلِمَ أَنَّهُ يَنْبَغِي لِكُلِّ عَامِلٍ أَنْ يَسْتُرَ عَمَلَهُ مَا اسْتَطَاعَ إِلَّا فِي مَحَلٍّ يُقْتَدَى بِهِ فِي فِعْلِهِ وَفِي كَيْفِيَّتِهِ، وَاللهُ تَعَالَى أَعْلَمُ.

وَسَمِعْتُ سَيِّدِي عَلِيًّا الْخَوَّاصَ رضى الله عنه يَقُولُ: لَا يَنْبَغِي إِظْهَارُ الْأَعْمَالِ إِلَّا لِلْأَكَابِرِ مِنَ الْعُلَمَاءِ وَالصَّالِحِينَ الْغَوَّاصِينَ عَلَى دَسَائِسِ النُّفُوسِ، وَأَمَّا أَمْثَالُنَا فَرُبَّمَا يُظْهِرُ الْوَاحِدُ مِنَّا أَعْمَالَهُ رِيَاءً وَسُمْعَةً وَتَلَبَّسَ

> It does not befit anyone to reveal their works, save the greatest scholars and the utmost in piety, deeply aware as they are of the soul's defects. As for the likes of us, we would instead boast our actions to be noticed, whereupon our souls would deceive us by saying, "You are – all praise is due to Allah – among those sincere in worship; surely your display of worship is only for people to follow!" Such a person, examining his soul, should imagine someone else doing the same act and being followed by as many people as him, or much more. If he is happy with that, he is sincere; if the thought disturbs him, then he has a subtle inclination towards showing off. Had he been sincere, he would have been immensely elated at the fact that Allah (Exalted is He) assigned someone to relieve his burden. If your soul were to then say, "You're only confused because you're losing out on great good", say to it: "I depend on the grace of Allah, not acts – if I enter Paradise, it will be by the mercy of Allah (Exalted is He)." Thus, it is imperative that the slave never agrees with what the soul claims. The *shaykh* should also examine himself with the same thought of his gathering fleeing to one of his peers, leaving him alone without anyone to teach. If he is happy with that, he is sincere; if discomfort arises with that thought, it is imperative that he take a *shaykh* who will bring him out of the darkness of showing off. Otherwise, he will die in disobedience, and proceed to the Hereafter bereft of all good, because Allah will not have accepted any of his acts.

I also heard him say:

> It is imperative for any scholar who gives lessons, for example in the Jāmiʿ al-Azhar, to first purify his inten-

عَلَيهِ نَفْسُهُ وَتقُولُ لَهُ أَنْتَ بِحَمْدِ اللهِ مِنَ الْمُخْلِصِينَ، وَإِنَّمَا تُظْهِرُ هَذِهِ الْعِبَادَةَ لِيَقْتَدِيَ بِكَ النَّاسُ.. فَيَنْبَغِي لِمِثْلِ هَذَا أَنْ يَمْتَحِنَ نَفْسَهُ بِمَا لَوْ جَاءَ أَحَدٌ يَفْعَلُ ذَلِكَ الخَيْرَ وَتَنْقَادُ النَّاسُ لَهُ مِثْلَهُ أَوْ أَكْثَرَ مِنْهُ، فَإِنِ انْشَرَحَ لِذَلِكَ فَهُوَ مُخْلِصٌ، وَإِنِ انْقَبَضَ خَاطِرُهُ فَهُوَ مُرَاءٍ دَقَّ الْمِطْرَقَةَ، وَلَوْ أَنَّهُ كَانَ مُخْلِصًا لَفَرِحَ بِذَلِكَ أَشَدَّ الْفَرَحِ الَّذِي قَيَّضَ اللهُ تَعَالَى لَهُ مَنْ كَفَاهُ الْمُؤْنَةَ، ثُمَّ إِنْ قَالَتْ لَهُ نَفْسُهُ: إِنَّمَا تَشَوَّشْتَ لِفَوَاتِ الخَيْرِ الْعَظِيمِ الَّذِي كَانَ يَحْصُلُ لَكَ مِنْ حَيْثُ هُوَ خَيْرٌ، فَلْيَقُلْ لَهَا: إِنِّي مُعْتَمِدٌ عَلَى فَضْلِ اللهِ.. لاَ عَلَى الأَعْمَالِ، فَإِنْ دَخَلْتُ الْجَنَّةَ فَإِنَّمَا هُوَ بِرَحْمَةِ اللهِ تَعَالَى.. لاَ بِعَمَلِي، فَيَنْبَغِي لِلْعَبْدِ أَنْ لاَ يُصْغِيَ لِدَعْوَى نَفْسِهِ فِي الإِخْلاَصِ، وَلْيَمْتَحِنِ الشَّيْخُ أَوِ الْمُدَرِّسُ نَفْسَهُ بِمَا إِذَا فَرَّتْ جَمَاعَتُهُ كُلُّهُمْ مِنْهُ إِلَى شَخْصٍ مِنْ أَقْرَانِهِ.. وَبَقِيَ وَحْدَهُ لاَ يَجِدُ أَحَدًا يَتَمَشْيَخُ عَلَيْهِ، فَإِنِ انْشَرَحَ لِذَلِكَ فَهُوَ مُخْلِصٌ، وَإِنْ حَصَلَ فِي نَفْسِهِ حَزَازَةٌ.. فَالْوَاجِبُ عَلَيْهِ أَنْ يَتَّخِذَ لَهُ شَيْخًا يُخْرِجُهُ مِنْ ظُلُمَاتِ الرِّيَاءِ، وَإِلاَّ مَاتَ عَاصِيًا وَذَهَبَ إِلَى الآخِرَةِ صِفْرَ الْيَدَيْنِ مِنَ الْخَيْرِ؛ لِأَنَّ اللهَ تَعَالَى لَمْ يَقْبَلْ لَهُ عَمَلاً اهـ.

وَسَمِعْتُهُ أَيْضًا يَقُولُ: يَنْبَغِي لِلْعَالِمِ إِذَا دَرَّسَ فِي مِثْلِ جَامِعِ الأَزْهَرِ أَنْ يُحَرِّرَ نِيَّتَهُ قَبْلَ ذَلِكَ، وَلَوْ مَكَثَ سِنِينَ بِلاَ إِقْرَاءٍ حَتَّى يَجِدَ لَهُ نِيَّةً صَالِحَةً وَذَلِكَ لِغَلَبَةِ دُخُولِ الأَكَابِرِ الَّذِينَ تَمِيلُ النُّفُوسُ إِلَى مُرَاآتِهِمْ مِنَ الأُمَرَاءِ وَالأَغْنِيَاءِ إِلَى الْجَامِعِ، وَكَانَ النَّوَوِيُّ إِذَا دَرَّسَ فِي الْمَدْرَسَةِ الأَشْرَفِيَّةِ بِدِمَشْقَ يُوصِي الطَّلَبَةَ أَنْ لاَ يَجِيئُوا دَفْعَةً وَاحِدَةً خَوْفًا مِنْ كِبَرِ الْحَلْقَةِ.

وَكَانَ إِذَا دَرَّسَ جَلَسَ فِي عَطْفَةِ الْمَسْجِدِ وَيَقُولُ: إِنَّ النَّفْسَ تَسْتَحْلِي رُؤْيَةَ النَّاسِ لَهَا وَهِيَ تُدَرِّسُ فِي صَحْنِ الْمَسْجِدِ أَوْ صَدْرِهِ.

tion – even if many years pass without his teaching anything – until he finds his intention pure. That is because the senior officials and rich people, by whom the souls wish to be noticed, frequently visit the *jāmiʿ*. When al-Nawawī would teach in the Ashrafiyyah madrasah in Damascus, he would tell his students not to come all at once, for fear of having a large circle. When teaching, he would sit in the corner of the mosque, saying, "The soul desires to be seen by people while teaching in the front or the middle of the mosque." While he was teaching in the Jāmiʿ Banu Umayyah, it once reached him that the king, al-Ẓāhir, had planned to pray in the *jāmiʿ*. He then abandoned teaching or attending that mosque for a year. So beware, O brother, that you do not organize a gathering of knowledge, remembrance of Allah (Exalted is He), or prayers upon the Messenger of Allah ﷺ in a way that people will see you, unless you are free of all these defects and faults. Once, I was present when the *shaykh* and scholar who acts upon his knowledge, Shaykh Shams al-Dīn al-Laqqānī, the Mufti of the Malikis in the Jāmiʿ al-Azhar, said to Shaykh Nūr al-Dīn al-Shūnī, our *shaykh* who led a gathering of prayers upon the Messenger ﷺ: "By Allah, O brother, I fear for your heading this gathering in the *jāmiʿ* on the night or day of *Jumuʿah* while the governors and dignitaries are in attendance, such that they see you, make you believe something about yourself, and speak about you. May Allah protect you – for perhaps the soul will incline towards liking that manner of elation, thereby losing its portion in this world and the Hereafter."

On another occasion, I heard him say, "When the people finish praying the *Jumuʿah* prayer, wait a while before you recite

وَبَلَغَهُ يَوْمًا وَهُوَ يُدَرِّسُ فِي جَامِعِ بَنِي أُمَيَّةَ.. أَنَّ الْمَلِكَ الظَّاهِرَ عَازِمٌ عَلَى الصَّلَاةِ فِي الْجَامِعِ، فَتَرَكَ التَّدْرِيسَ وَحُضُورَ الْمَسْجِدِ ذَلِكَ الْيَوْمَ. فَإِيَّاكَ يَا أَخِي؛ أَنْ تُعْقَدَ لَكَ مَجْلِسُ عِلْمٍ أَوْ ذِكْرِ اللهِ تَعَالَى أَوْ صَلَاةٍ عَلَى رَسُولِ اللهِ ﷺ بِحَيْثُ يَرَاكَ النَّاسُ إِلَّا أَنْ تَكُونَ سَالِمًا مِنْ هَذِهِ الْعِلَلِ وَالْآفَاتِ.

وَقَدْ حَضَرْتُ مَرَّةً الشَّيْخَ الْعَالِمَ الْعَامِلَ شَمْسَ الدِّينِ اللَّقَانِيَّ مُفْتِي الْمَالِكِيَّةِ بِالْجَامِعِ الْأَزْهَرِ وَهُوَ يَقُولُ لِشَيْخِنَا الشَّيْخِ نُورِ الدِّينِ الشُّونِيِّ شَيْخِ مَجْلِسِ الصَّلَاةِ عَلَى رَسُولِ اللهِ ﷺ: وَاللهِ يَا أَخِي؛ إِنِّي خَائِفٌ عَلَيْكَ مِنْ تَصَدُّرِكَ فِي الْجَامِعِ فِي هَذَا الْمَجْلِسِ لَيْلَةَ الْجُمُعَةِ وَيَوْمَهَا وَالْأُمَرَاءُ وَالْأَكَابِرُ يَنْظُرُونَ إِلَيْكَ، وَيَعْتَقِدُونَكَ عَلَى ذَلِكَ وَيَقُولُونَ شَيْءٌ لِلهِ الْمَدَدُ. فَرُبَّمَا مَالَتْ نَفْسُكَ إِلَى حُبِّ فَرَحِهَا بِذَلِكَ، فَخَسِرْتَ الدُّنْيَا وَالْآخِرَةَ.

وَسَمِعْتُهُ مَرَّةً أُخْرَى يَقُولُ: إِذَا فَرَغَ النَّاسُ مِنْ صَلَاةِ الْجُمُعَةِ فَاصْبِرْ عَلَى قِرَاءَةِ سُورَةِ الْكَهْفِ حَتَّى يَنْفَضَّ النَّاسُ، ثُمَّ اشْرَعْ فِي الْقِرَاءَةِ؛ فَإِنَّ النَّفْسَ تَسْتَحْلِي رُؤْيَةَ النَّاسِ لَهَا فِي ذَلِكَ الْمَحْفِلِ الْعَظِيمِ اهـ.

Sūrah al-Kahf, until people leave. Then start your recitation; the soul desires that people notice it in that great gathering."

So, O brother, you should know this and act upon it, and upon the guidance of the sincere. May Allah take charge of guiding you.

Muslim, al-Nasāʾī, Ibn Mājah, and others narrate that a people from Mudar came to the Messenger of Allah ﷺ wearing robes of sown wool. He ﷺ, seeing their neediness, became dismayed; he then entered his house, came out, and ordered Bilāl to give the *adhān*, which he did. Then, he stood and prayed. He then gave a sermon and said, "*O people! Fear your Lord who created you from a single soul*" until he reached "*Indeed, Allah is All-Knowing, Most Vigilant.*"[14] He also recited the verse from *al-Ḥashr*: "*Fear Allah, and let each soul look to what it has sent forth.*"[15] "*So, let a man give charity from his dinars, another from his dirhams, another from his clothes, another from a ṣāʿ of dates, and another from a ṣāʿ of wheat, or even half a date.*"

Once, a man came with a bundle of coins that his hands could not hold. People then followed him until there were two great piles of food and clothes, until the Messenger of Allah ﷺ said, "*If someone inaugurates a good practice in Islam, he will have its reward and the reward of all those who follow him afterwards without reducing their reward in the slightest.*"

In a *marfūʿ*[16] narration by Imam Aḥmad, al-Ḥākim, Ibn Mājah, and others: "*If someone inaugurates good and is followed in that by people, he will have its reward and a similar reward to those who follow him in it without reducing their reward at all.*"

In a *marfūʿ* narration by al-Ṭabarānī: "*If someone inaugurates a good practice, he will have its reward and the reward of whoever*

---

(14) *Al-Nisāʾ*, 1.

(15) *Al-Ḥashr*, 18.

(16) A narration attributed to the Prophet ﷺ.

فَاعْلَمْ يَا أَخِي ذَلِكَ وَاعْمَلْ بِهِ، وَبِهَدْيِ هُدَى الصَّادِقِينَ اقْتَدِ، وَاللهُ يَتَوَلَّى هُدَاكَ.

وَرَوَى مُسْلِمٌ وَالنَّسَائِيُّ وَابْنُ مَاجَهْ وَغَيْرُهُمْ أَنَّ رَسُولَ اللهِ ﷺ جَاءَهُ قَوْمٌ مِنْ مُضَرَ مُجْتَابِي النِّمَارِ: أَيْ: لَابِسِي الْعَبَاءِ الصُّوفِ الْمُخَطَّطِ، فَتَمَعَّرَ وَجْهُ رَسُولِ اللهِ ﷺ لِمَا رَأَى بِهِمْ مِنَ الْفَاقَةِ، فَدَخَلَ ثُمَّ خَرَجَ، فَأَمَرَ بِلَالًا فَأَذَّنَ وَأَقَامَ، فَصَلَّى ثُمَّ خَطَبَ فَقَالَ: ﴿يَٰٓأَيُّهَا ٱلنَّاسُ ٱتَّقُواْ رَبَّكُمُ ٱلَّذِي خَلَقَكُم مِّن نَّفۡسٖ وَٰحِدَةٖ﴾ إِلَى قَوْلِهِ: ﴿إِنَّ ٱللَّهَ كَانَ عَلَيۡكُمۡ رَقِيبٗا﴾ [النساء: ١]، وَالْآيَةَ الَّتِي فِي الْحَشْرِ: ﴿ٱتَّقُواْ ٱللَّهَ وَلۡتَنظُرۡ نَفۡسٞ مَّا قَدَّمَتۡ لِغَدٖ﴾ [الحشر: ١٨].

«تَصَدَّقَ رَجُلٌ مِنْ دِينَارِهِ، مِنْ دِرْهَمِهِ، مِنْ ثَوْبِهِ، مِنْ صَاعِ تَمْرٍ، مِنْ صَاعِ بُرٍّ - حَتَّى قَالَ - وَلَوْ بِشِقِّ تَمْرَةٍ».

قَالَ: فَجَاءَ رَجُلٌ مِنَ الْأَنْصَارِ بِصُرَّةٍ كَادَتْ كَفُّهُ تَعْجِزُ عَنْهَا، بَلْ قَدْ عَجَزَتْ، فَتَتَابَعَ النَّاسُ، حَتَّى صَارَ كَوْمَيْنِ مِنْ طَعَامٍ وَثِيَابٍ، حَتَّى تَهَلَّلَ وَجْهُ رَسُولِ اللهِ ﷺ، فَقَالَ رَسُولُ اللهِ ﷺ: «مَنْ سَنَّ فِي الْإِسْلَامِ سُنَّةً حَسَنَةً، فَلَهُ أَجْرُهَا وَأَجْرُ مَنْ عَمِلَ بِهَا مِنْ بَعْدِهِ، مِنْ غَيْرِ أَنْ يَنْقُصَ مِنْ أُجُورِهِمْ شَيْءٌ» الْحَدِيثَ.

وَفِي رِوَايَةٍ لِلْإِمَامِ أَحْمَدَ وَالْحَاكِمِ وَابْنِ مَاجَهْ وَغَيْرِهِمْ مَرْفُوعًا: «مَنْ سَنَّ خَيْرًا فَاسْتُنَّ بِهِ، كَانَ لَهُ أَجْرُهُ وَمِثْلُ أُجُورِ مَنْ تَبِعَهُ، مِنْ غَيْرِ أَنْ يَنْقُصَ مِنْ أُجُورِهِمْ شَيْءٌ» الْحَدِيثَ. وَفِي رِوَايَةٍ لِلطَّبَرَانِيِّ مَرْفُوعًا: «مَنْ سَنَّ سُنَّةً حَسَنَةً، فَلَهُ أَجْرُهَا مَا عَمِلَ بِهَا عَامِلٌ فِي حَيَاتِهِ وَبَعْدَ مَمَاتِهِ حَتَّى تُتْرَكَ» الْحَدِيثَ.

acts upon it as long as it is acted upon, in his life and after his death, until it is abandoned."

In a *marfūʿ* narration by Ibn Mājah and al-Tirmidhī, the latter of whom said it is a sound Hadith: *"If someone revives one of my Sunnahs that had died out after me, he will have the same reward of those who act upon it without that reducing their reward in anything. If someone innovates an act of misguidance with which Allah and His Messenger are not pleased*[17]*, he will have the same sin as those who act upon it without reducing the weight of their sin in the least."*

Ibn Mājah, al-Tirmidhī, and others narrated the following Prophetic Hadith: *"Indeed, there are treasures in this good. Those treasures have keys. Glad tidings to the slave for whom Allah has made a key to good and a lock to evil."*

(17) The meaning of *"with which Allah and His Messenger are not pleased"* is that the Book and the Sunnah don't uphold its validity.

وَرَوَى ابْنُ مَاجَهْ وَالتِّرْمِذِيُّ مَرْفُوعًا وَقَالَ حَدِيثٌ حَسَنٌ: «مَنْ أَحْيَا سُنَّةً مِنْ سُنَّتِي قَدْ أُمِيتَتْ بَعْدِي، كَانَ لَهُ مِنَ الْأَجْرِ مِثْلُ مَنْ عَمِلَ بِهَا، مِنْ غَيْرِ أَنْ يَنْقُصَ ذَلِكَ مِنْ أُجُورِهِمْ شَيْئًا، وَمَنِ ابْتَدَعَ بِدْعَةَ ضَلَالَةٍ لَا يَرْضَاهَا اللهُ وَرَسُولُهُ، كَانَ عَلَيْهِ مِثْلُ آثَامِ مَنْ عَمِلَ بِهَا، لَا يَنْقُصُ ذَلِكَ مِنْ أَوْزَارِ النَّاسِ شَيْئًا».

وَمَعْنَى لَا يَرْضَاهَا اللهُ وَرَسُولُهُ: أَيْ لَا يَشْهَدُ لَهَا كِتَابٌ وَلَا سُنَّةٌ بِالصِّحَّةِ.

وَرَوَى ابْنُ مَاجَهْ وَالتِّرْمِذِيُّ وَغَيْرُهُمَا مَرْفُوعًا: «إِنَّ لِهَذَا الْخَيْرِ خَزَائِنَ وَلِتِلْكَ الْخَزَائِنِ مَفَاتِيحُ، فَطُوبَى لِعَبْدٍ جَعَلَهُ اللهُ مِفْتَاحًا لِلْخَيْرِ مِغْلَاقًا لِلشَّرِّ» وَاللهُ تَعَالَى أَعْلَمُ.

Urging Pursuit and Review of Sacred Knowledge

A general covenant was taken from us by the Messenger of Allah ﷺ that, beyond the acts of worship stipulated at certain times and necessities, we are to continuously read the books of knowledge and teach them to people night and day. The school of our Imām al-Shāfiʿī ؓ deems seeking knowledge immensely superior to voluntary prayers.

You should know that the Lawgiver ﷺ only stipulated some acts of worship to be superior in reward as he knew that, inevitably, those who acted upon them would become bored, even of compulsory acts. Thus, they would move on to another compulsory or preferred act. Then, once bored of it, they would likewise move on to look for another preferred act, a superior act, or one more superior, as long as they do not find in themselves any boredom with it. You should, then, know the reason for the division in categories of commanded acts, which is the presence of boredom in them when practised perpetually. If it was conceivable that a man never tires of obligatory or superior acts, he ﷺ would order him to adhere to them (obligatory acts) and leave off extra acts completely, as those who draw near to Allah (Exalted is He) only do so through fulfilling that with which He has obligated them. However, since they do tire of obligatory acts – to the point where no inclination, humility, or sweetness of those acts of worship would remain in the soul of the one who acted upon it – the extra acts they are inclined towards, in which they find sweetness and humility, are thus more perfect and complete.

Imām al-Shāfiʿī ؓ used to divide the night into three parts: a part in which he would sleep, a part in which he would read *aḥādīth* and derive rulings, and a part in which he would pray *tahajjud*. He used to say, "If it were not for discussing knowledge with the brethren or praying *tahajjud,* I would not have desired to remain in this abode."

أُخِذَ عَلَيْنَا الْعَهْدُ الْعَامُّ مِنْ رَسُولِ اللهِ ﷺ أَنْ نَدْمِنَ مُطَالَعَةَ كُتُبِ الْعِلْمِ وَتَعْلِيمَهُ لِلنَّاسِ لَيْلًا وَنَهَارًا مَا عَدَا الْعِبَادَاتِ الْمُؤَقَّتَةَ وَالْحَوَائِجَ الضَّرُورِيَّةَ.

وَمَذْهَبُ إِمَامِنَا الشَّافِعِيِّ رضى الله عنه أَنَّ طَلَبَ الْعِلْمِ عَلَى وَجْهِ الْإِخْلَاصِ أَفْضَلُ مِنْ صَلَاةِ النَّافِلَةِ. وَاعْلَمْ أَنَّ الشَّارِعَ ﷺ مَا نَوَّعَ الْعِبَادَاتِ الْمُتَفَاضِلَةَ فِي الْأَجْرِ إِلَّا لِعِلْمِهِ ﷺ بِحُصُولِ الْمَلَلِ لِلْعَامِلِينَ وَلَوْ فِي الْأُمُورِ الْوَاجِبَةِ، فَإِذَا حَصَلَ الْمَلَلُ فِيهَا انْتَقَلُوا إِلَى وَاجِبٍ آخَرَ أَوْ إِلَى ذَلِكَ الْأَمْرِ الْمَفْضُولِ، فَإِذَا حَصَلَ الْمَلَلُ مِنْهُ كَذَلِكَ انْتَقَلُوا لِمَفْضُولٍ آخَرَ أَوْ فَاضِلٍ أَوْ أَفْضَلَ مَا لَمْ يَجِدُوا فِي نُفُوسِهِمْ مَلَلًا فِيهِ، فَعُلِمَ أَنَّ سَبَبَ تَنَوُّعِ الْمَأْمُورَاتِ إِنَّمَا هُوَ وُجُودُ الْمَلَلِ فِيهَا إِذَا دَامَتْ. فَلَوْ تُصُوِّرَ أَنَّ إِنْسَانًا لَمْ يَمَلَّ مِنَ الْوَاجِبَاتِ أَوْ مِمَّا هُوَ أَفْضَلُ لِأَمْرِهِ ﷺ بِمُلَازَمَتِهَا وَتَرْكِ الْأُمُورِ الْمَفْضُولَةِ جُمْلَةً، لِأَنَّهُ مَا تَقَرَّبَ الْمُتَقَرِّبُونَ إِلَى اللهِ تَعَالَى بِمِثْلِ أَدَاءِ مَا افْتَرَضَهُ عَلَيْهِمْ، وَلَكِنْ لَمَّا كَانَ يَحْصُلُ لَهُمْ مِنَ الْمَلَلِ فِي الْوَاجِبَاتِ حَتَّى لَا يَبْقَى فِي نَفْسِ الْعَامِلِ دَاعِيَةٌ وَلَا خُشُوعٌ وَلَا لَذَّةٌ بِتِلْكَ الْعِبَادَاتِ.. كَانَ الْعَمَلُ الْمَفْضُولُ الَّذِي لَهُ فِيهِ دَاعِيَةٌ وَلَذَّةٌ وَخُشُوعٌ أَتَمَّ وَأَكْمَلَ.

وَقَدْ كَانَ الْإِمَامُ الشَّافِعِيُّ رضى الله عنه يَقْسِمُ اللَّيْلَ ثَلَاثَةَ أَجْزَاءٍ، جُزْءًا يَنَامُ فِيهِ، وَجُزْءًا يُطَالِعُ الْحَدِيثَ وَيَسْتَنْبِطُ، وَجُزْءًا يَتَهَجَّدُ فِيهِ. وَكَانَ يَقُولُ: لَوْلَا مُذَاكَرَةُ الْإِخْوَانِ فِي الْعِلْمِ وَالتَّهَجُّدُ فِي اللَّيْلِ مَا أَحْبَبْتُ الْبَقَاءَ فِي هَذِهِ الدَّارِ، فَعُلِمَ أَنَّهُ لَا يَنْبَغِي لِطَالِبِ الْعِلْمِ أَنْ يَكُبَّ عَلَى مُطَالَعَةِ الْعِلْمِ لَيْلًا وَنَهَارًا إِلَّا إِذَا صَلُحَتِ النِّيَّةُ فِيهِ وَلَمْ يَقُمْ أَحَدٌ مَقَامَهُ فِي بَلَدِهِ أَوْ إِقْلِيمِهِ، فَإِنْ دَخَلَ نِيَّتَهُ حُبُّ رِيَاسَةٍ أَوْ طَلَبُ دُنْيَا أَوْ قَامَ أَحَدٌ مَقَامَهُ فِي نَشْرِ الْعِلْمِ.. فَالِاشْتِغَالُ بِكُلِّ مَا صَلُحَتْ فِيهِ النِّيَّةُ مِنَ الطَّاعَاتِ أَوْلَى، وَسَيَأْتِي فِي

Hence, it does not befit the seeker of knowledge to dedicate himself solely to teaching knowledge day and night, unless his intention in it is pure or if no one in his land is performing that duty. However, if the pursuit of worldly benefit pollutes his intention, or someone else in his land fulfils the duty of spreading knowledge, he should then occupy himself with every act of obedience in which his intention is pure.

Shortly, we will discuss, among the covenants, that part of acting upon knowledge to do with the slave's repentance and seeking forgiveness whenever he commits any act of disobedience. Contemplate over how, without knowledge, he would not know that it is an act of disobedience and would not repent from it. Dāwūd al-Ṭāʾī ﷺ said, "The seeker of knowledge is like a warrior. If he spends all his time teaching the method of fighting, when will he fight?" Thus, the intelligent one – seeing that he has acted upon all that he knows, and is in need of more knowledge – would give it precedence over all else that the Sacred Law has not commanded him such. He would just as well give precedence to acts of obedience upon seeing that he is in no need of knowledge, or that it is beyond what he needs, as was the practice of the Pious Predecessors. Thus, every person needs knowledge and action; to busy oneself with one over the other is a deficiency.

You should also know that everything that has been related regarding the excellence of knowledge and teaching it only applies to those sincere in it – so do not err in that, for the Examiner is All-Seeing. We have had much discord with the debaters on this matter. We see how, despite their claims to knowledge, they eagerly acquire the world night and day, and how they aggrandize themselves for their knowledge and skilful debate without ever rising to acting upon what they know. One of them will use as evidence (of his state) that which has been related regarding the excellence of knowledge, but they forget the *aḥādīth* censuring those who also do not act upon

الْعُهُودِ قَرِيبًا أَنَّ مِنْ جُمْلَةِ الْعَمَلِ بِالْعِلْمِ تَوْبَةُ الْعَبْدِ وَاسْتِغْفَارُهُ إِذَا وَقَعَ فِي مَعْصِيَةٍ، فَإِنَّهُ لَوْلَا الْعِلْمُ مَا عَرَفَ أَنَّهَا مَعْصِيَةٌ، وَلَا تَابَ مِنْهَا، فَتَأَمَّلْ.

وَقَدْ قَالَ دَاوُدُ الطَّائِيُّ رحمه الله تعالى: طَالِبُ الْعِلْمِ كَالْمُحَارِبِ؛ فَإِذَا أَفْنَى عُمْرَهُ فِي تَعْلِيمِ كَيْفِيَّةِ الْقِتَالِ، فَمَتَى يُقَاتِلُ؟ فَمِنْ عَقْلِ الْعَاقِلِ أَنَّهُ كُلَّمَا رَأَى نَفْسَهُ عَمِلَتْ بِكُلِّ مَا عَلِمَ وَاحْتَاجَتْ لِلْعِلْمِ أَنْ يُقَدِّمَهُ عَلَى سَائِرِ الطَّاعَاتِ الَّتِي لَمْ يَأْمُرْهُ الشَّارِعُ بِتَقْدِيمِهَا عَلَيْهِ، وَكُلَّمَا رَأَى نَفْسَهُ مُسْتَغْنِيَةً عَنِ الْعِلْمِ.. وَعِلْمُهَا زَائِدٌ عَلَى حَاجَتِهَا أَنْ يُقَدِّمَ غَيْرَهُ عَلَيْهِ كَمَا كَانَ عَلَيْهِ السَّلَفُ الصَّالِحُ، فَلَا بُدَّ لِكُلِّ إِنْسَانٍ مِنَ الْعِلْمِ وَالْعَمَلِ وَالِاشْتِغَالِ بِوَاحِدٍ مِنْهُمَا دُونَ الْآخَرِ نَقْصٌ.

وَاعْلَمْ أَنَّ جَمِيعَ مَا وَرَدَ فِي فَضْلِ الْعِلْمِ وَتَعْلِيمِهِ إِنَّمَا هُوَ فِي حَقِّ الْمُخْلِصِينَ فِي ذَلِكَ، فَلَا تُغَالِطْ فِي ذَلِكَ فَإِنَّ النَّاقِدَ بَصِيرٌ. وَقَدْ وَقَعَ لَنَا مَعَ الْمُجَادِلِينَ نِزَاعٌ كَثِيرٌ فِي ذَلِكَ، فَإِنَّا نَرَاهُمْ مُتَكَالِبِينَ عَلَى الدُّنْيَا لَيْلًا وَنَهَارًا مَعَ دَعْوَاهُمُ الْعِلْمَ وَتَعْظِيمِهِمْ نُفُوسَهُمْ بِالْعِلْمِ وَالْجِدَالِ مِنْ غَيْرِ أَنْ يَعْرُجُوا عَلَى الْعَمَلِ بِمَا عَلِمُوا، وَيَسْتَدِلُّ أَحَدُهُمْ بِمَا وَرَدَ فِي فَضْلِ الْعِلْمِ، وَيَنْسَى الْأَحَادِيثَ الَّتِي جَاءَتْ فِي ذَمِّ مَنْ لَمْ يَعْمَلْ بِعِلْمِهِ جُمْلَةً وَاحِدَةً، وَهَذَا كُلُّهُ غِشُّ النَّفْسِ، وَفِي الْقُرْآنِ الْعَظِيمِ: ﴿هَٰٓأَنتُمْ هَٰٓؤُلَآءِ جَٰدَلْتُمْ عَنْهُمْ فِى ٱلْحَيَوٰةِ ٱلدُّنْيَا فَمَن يُجَٰدِلُ ٱللَّهَ عَنْهُمْ يَوْمَ ٱلْقِيَٰمَةِ أَم مَّن يَكُونُ عَلَيْهِمْ وَكِيلًا ﴿١٠٩﴾﴾ [النساء: ١٠٩].

their knowledge: all of that is from the tricks of the ego. It was revealed in the Immense Qur'an: Here you are with those on whose behalf you argued in the life of this world. But who will dispute with Allah on their behalf on the Day of Judgement? Who will even be their advocate?[18]

So, O brother, you must travel by the hand of a *shaykh* who can take you out of all those states of heedlessness, obscurities, and claims, such that you begin to cry over your neglect of action until black lines develop on your face from the trail of tears. If you do not travel the road that we have described, your exhaustion will be intensified in the Hereafter – and what a loss is that self-exhaustion from obtaining this world!

I have heard Sīdī ʿAlī al-Khawwāṣ ﵁ say about the meaning of the Hadith, "*Indeed, Allah will assist this religion by a sinful person*": it means that people will benefit from the transgressor's knowledge, teachings, verdicts, and lessons until he begins to appear as one of the scholars who act upon their knowledge. However, as mentioned before, Allah will enter him into the Fire because of his insincerity – we ask Allah for His gentle mercy. So, know that, and may Allah take charge of your guidance.

The two Shaykhs and others have related the following Prophetic Hadith: "*If Allah wants good for a slave, He grants him understanding of the religion.*" In one narration, it was added: "*Among His servants, only the Scholars truly fear Allah*".[19]

Al-Bazzār and al-Ṭabarānī both narrated the following Hadith attributed to the Prophet ﷺ: "*When Allah wants good for a slave, He gives him understanding of the religion and inspires him with guidance.*" Al-Ṭabarānī also narrated the following, attributing it to the Prophet ﷺ: "*The best worship is*

(18) *Al-Nisā'*, 109.
(19) *Fāṭir*, 28.

فَاسْلُكْ يَا أَخِي عَلَى يَدِ شَيْخٍ يُخْرِجُكَ مِنْ هَذِهِ الرُّعُونَاتِ وَالظُّلُمَاتِ وَالدَّعَاوَى، وَتَصِيرُ تَبْكِي عَلَى تَفْرِيطِكَ فِي الْأَعْمَالِ حَتَّى يَصِيرَ لَكَ خَطَّانِ أَسْوَدَانِ فِي وَجْهِكَ مِنْ سَيَلَانِ الدُّمُوعِ، وَإِنْ لَمْ تَسْلُكْ كَمَا ذَكَرْنَا فَيَطُولُ تَعَبُكَ فِي الْآخِرَةِ، يَا خَسَارَةَ تَعَبِكَ فِي تَحْصِيلِكَ لِلدُّنْيَا.

وَقَدْ سَمِعْتُ سَيِّدِي عَلِيًّا الْخَوَّاصَ رَحِمَهُ اللهُ يَقُولُ فِي مَعْنَى حَدِيثِ: «إِنَّ اللهَ لَيُؤَيِّدُ هَذَا الدِّينَ بِالرَّجُلِ الْفَاجِرِ».

مَعْنَاهُ: أَنَّ النَّاسَ يَنْتَفِعُونَ بِعِلْمِ الْفَاجِرِ وَتَعْلِيمِهِ وَإِفْتَائِهِ وَتَدْرِيسِهِ حَتَّى يَكُونَ فِي الصُّورَةِ كَالْعُلَمَاءِ الْعَامِلِينَ، ثُمَّ يُدْخِلُهُ اللهُ بَعْدَ ذَلِكَ النَّارَ لِعَدَمِ إِخْلَاصِهِ كَمَا مَرَّ قَرِيبًا، نَسْأَلُ اللهَ اللُّطْفَ، فَاعْلَمْ ذَلِكَ، وَاللهُ يَتَوَلَّى هُدَاكَ.

وَرَوَى الشَّيْخَانِ وَغَيْرُهُمَا مَرْفُوعًا: «مَنْ يُرِدِ اللهُ بِهِ خَيْرًا يُفَقِّهْهُ فِي الدِّينِ»، زَادَ فِي رِوَايَةٍ: ﴿إِنَّمَا يَخْشَى ٱللَّهَ مِنْ عِبَادِهِ ٱلْعُلَمَٰٓؤُاْ﴾ [فاطر: ٢٨].

وَرَوَى الْبَزَّارُ وَالطَّبَرَانِيُّ مَرْفُوعًا: «إِذَا أَرَادَ اللهُ بِعَبْدٍ خَيْرًا فَقَّهَهُ فِي الدِّينِ وَأَلْهَمَهُ رُشْدَهُ».

وَرَوَى الطَّبَرَانِيُّ مَرْفُوعًا: «أَفْضَلُ الْعِبَادَاتِ الْفِقْهُ، وَأَفْضَلُ الدِّينِ الْوَرَعُ».

understanding, and the best of the religion is caution." Al-Bazzār and al-Ṭabarānī both narrated a Prophetic Hadith with a sound chain: *"The benefit of knowledge is better than the benefit of worship. And the best of your religion is caution."* Al-Ṭabarānī narrated the following Hadith attributed to the Prophet ﷺ: *"A little knowledge is better than a lot of worship."* He also narrated a lengthier version of the same Prophetic Hadith: *"A little knowledge is better than a lot of worship. It is sufficient understanding for a person that he worships Allah. And it is sufficient ignorance for a person that he is impressed with his own opinion."*[20]

Muslim, Abū Dāwūd, al-Tirmidhī, al-Nasāʾī, and others all narrated the following Prophetic Hadith: *"If someone travels a path in pursuit of knowledge, Allah (Exalted is He) will thereby facilitate for him a path to Paradise."* Abū Dāwūd, al-Tirmidhī, and Ibn Mājah all narrated the Prophetic Hadith: *"Indeed, the Angels lower their wings over the seeker of knowledge out of satisfaction with what he is doing. Indeed, those in the Heavens and those in the Earth, even the whales in the sea, all seek forgiveness for the scholar. The superiority of the scholar over the worshipper is like the superiority of the Moon to all the stars – indeed, the scholars are the inheritors of the Prophets. The Prophets do not bequeath any gold or silver: they only bequeath knowledge. Thus, if anyone takes it, he has taken an ample portion."*

Ibn Mājah and others narrated the following Prophetic Hadith: *"Seeking knowledge is an obligation on every Muslim. However, the one who gives knowledge to those unworthy is like a person who places a necklace of gems, pearls, or gold on swine."* Al-Ṭabarānī narrated the Prophetic Hadith: *"If someone's appointed time comes while he is seeking knowledge, he will meet*

(20) Al-Bayhaqī narrated the same narration with a sound, authentic chain, as a statement of al-Muṭarrif ibn ʿAbdullāh ibn al-Shikhkhīr ﵀.

وَرَوَى الطَّبَرَانِيُّ وَالْبَزَّارُ بِإِسْنَادٍ حَسَنٍ مَرْفُوعًا: «فَضلُ الْعِلْمِ خَيْرٌ مِنْ فَضْلِ الْعِبَادَةِ، وَخَيْرُ دِينِكُمُ الْوَرَعُ».

وَرَوَى الطَّبَرَانِيُّ مَرْفُوعًا: «قَلِيلُ الْعِلْمِ خَيْرٌ مِنْ كَثِيرِ الْعِبَادَةِ، وَكَفَى بِالْمَرْءِ فِقْهًا إِذَا عَبَدَ اللهَ، وَكَفَى بِالْمَرْءِ جَهْلًا إِذَا عَجِبَ بِرَأْيِهِ».

وَرَوَاهُ الْبَيْهَقِيُّ بِإِسْنَادٍ حَسَنٍ صَحِيحٍ مِنْ قَوْلِ مُطَرِّفِ بْنِ عَبْدِ اللهِ بْنِ الشِّخِّيرِ رَضِيَ اللهُ عَنْهُ.

وَرَوَى مُسْلِمٌ وَأَبُو دَاوُدَ وَالتِّرْمِذِيُّ وَالنَّسَائِيُّ وَغَيْرُهُمْ مَرْفُوعًا: «مَنْ سَلَكَ طَرِيقًا يَلْتَمِسُ فِيهِ عِلْمًا سَهَّلَ اللهُ تَعَالَى لَهُ بِهِ طَرِيقًا إِلَى الْجَنَّةِ».

وَرَوَى أَبُو دَاوُدَ وَالتِّرْمِذِيُّ وَابْنُ مَاجَهْ فِي «صَحِيحِهِ» مَرْفُوعًا: «إِنَّ الْمَلَائِكَةَ لَتَضَعُ أَجْنِحَتَهَا لِطَالِبِ الْعِلْمِ رِضًا بِمَا يَصْنَعُ، وَإِنَّ الْعَالِمَ يَسْتَغْفِرُ لَهُ مَنْ فِي السَّمَاوَاتِ وَمَنْ فِي الْأَرْضِ حَتَّى الْحِيتَانُ فِي الْمَاءِ، وَفَضْلُ الْعَالِمِ عَلَى الْعَابِدِ كَفَضْلِ الْقَمَرِ عَلَى سَائِرِ الْكَوَاكِبِ، وَإِنَّ الْعُلَمَاءَ وَرَثَةُ الْأَنْبِيَاءِ، إِنَّ الْأَنْبِيَاءَ لَمْ يُوَرِّثُوا دِينَارًا وَلَا دِرْهَمًا.. إِنَّمَا وَرَّثُوا الْعِلْمَ، فَمَنْ أَخَذَهُ أَخَذَ بِحَظٍّ وَافِرٍ».

وَرَوَى ابْنُ مَاجَهْ وَغَيْرُهُ مَرْفُوعًا: «طَلَبُ الْعِلْمِ فَرِيضَةٌ عَلَى كُلِّ مُسْلِمٍ، وَوَاضِعُ الْعِلْمِ عِنْدَ غَيْرِ أَهْلِهِ كَمُقَلِّدِ الْخَنَازِيرِ الْجَوْهَرَ وَاللُّؤْلُؤَ وَالذَّهَبَ».

وَرَوَى الطَّبَرَانِيُّ مَرْفُوعًا: «مَنْ جَاءَهُ أَجَلُهُ وَهُوَ يَطْلُبُ الْعِلْمَ، لَقِيَ اللهَ وَلَمْ يَكُنْ بَيْنَهُ وَبَيْنَ النَّبِيِّينَ إِلَّا دَرَجَةُ النُّبُوَّةِ».

Allah having no difference between him and the Prophets, except the degree of prophethood."

Ibn Mājah narrated with a sound chain that Abū Dharr said, "The Messenger of Allah ﷺ said to me, '*That you sit and study a verse of the Book of Allah (Exalted is He) is better for you than praying one hundred rakʿah. That you sit and study a chapter of knowledge, whether or not you act upon it, is better for you than praying one thousand rakʿah.*'" Al-Khaṭīb narrated the Prophetic Hadith with a sound chain: "*Knowledge is of two types: knowledge that settles in the heart and knowledge that is only on the tongue. The former is beneficial knowledge, while the latter is Allah's proof against the son of Adam.*"

Al-Daylamī narrated in his *Musnad*, Abū ʿAbd al-Raḥmān al-Sulamī in his collection of forty *aḥādīth* on *taṣawwuf*, and al-Ḥakīm al-Tirmidhī in *Nawādir al-Uṣūl*, that the Messenger of Allah ﷺ said, "*From knowledge is a hidden kind, known only by those who know by Allah (Exalted is He): when they speak it, only those who are heedless of Allah criticize them.*"

The *aḥādīth* on this matter are numerous. And Allah (Exalted is He) knows best.

وَرَوَى ابْنُ مَاجَهْ بِإِسْنَادٍ حَسَنٍ عَنْ أَبِي ذَرٍّ قَالَ: قَالَ لِي رَسُولُ اللهِ ﷺ: «لأَنْ تَغْدُوَ فَتَعَلَّمَ آيَةً مِنْ كِتَابِ اللهِ تَعَالَى، خَيْرٌ لَكَ مِنْ أَنْ تُصَلِّيَ مِائَةَ رَكْعَةٍ، وَلأَنْ تَغْدُوَ فَتَعَلَّمَ بَابًا مِنَ الْعِلْمِ عَمِلْتَ بِهِ أَوْ لَمْ تَعْمَلْ بِهِ، خَيْرٌ لَكَ مِنْ أَنْ تُصَلِّيَ أَلْفَ رَكْعَةٍ».

وَرَوَى الْخَطِيبُ بِإِسْنَادٍ حَسَنٍ مَرْفُوعًا: «الْعِلْمُ عِلْمَانِ: عِلْمٌ فِي الْقَلْبِ فَذَلِكَ الْعِلْمُ النَّافِعُ، وَعِلْمٌ فِي اللِّسَانِ وَذَلِكَ حُجَّةُ اللهِ عَلَى ابْنِ آدَمَ».

وَرَوَى الدَّيْلَمِيُّ فِي «مُسْنَدِهِ»، وَأَبُو عَبْدِ الرَّحْمَنِ السُّلَمِيُّ فِي الْأَرْبَعِينَ الَّتِي لَهُ فِي التَّصَوُّفِ، وَالْحَكِيمُ التِّرْمِذِيُّ فِي «نَوَادِرِ الْأُصُولِ» أَنَّ رَسُولَ اللهِ ﷺ قَالَ: «إِنَّ مِنَ الْعِلْمِ كَهَيْئَةِ الْمَكْنُونِ لَا يَعْلَمُهُ إِلَّا الْعُلَمَاءُ بِاللهِ تَعَالَى، فَإِذَا نَطَقُوا بِهِ.. لَا يُنْكِرُهُ إِلَّا أَهْلُ الْغِرَّةِ بِاللهِ عَزَّ وَجَلَّ».

وَالْأَحَادِيثُ فِي ذَلِكَ كَثِيرَةٌ، وَاللهُ تَعَالَى أَعْلَمُ.

Urging Travel in Search of Sacred Knowledge

A general covenant was taken from us by the Messenger of Allah ﷺ that we are to travel to a land in which there is knowledge, upon finding none in our land from whom to learn the knowledge of the Sacred Law. That migration is incumbent upon us, for if an obligation can only be completed with something, then that thing is also an obligation.

Suchwise, this covenant has been abandoned by many who died upon ignorance, despite having scholars in their land – they may have even been their neighbours. The scholars have said, "If someone prays while being ignorant of how to perform ablution or the prayer, or any other act (of which he is ignorant), then his worship is invalid, even if it does correspond to the correct way." This is supported by the Hadith: "*Every act that does not correspond to our command is rejected.*" So, if someone prays, marries, conducts business, fasts, or performs Hajj only based on how he sees people do them, his worship is invalid.

Contemplate the person who, doubtful over what Munkar and Nakīr ask him about his religion and his Prophet ﷺ, says, "I don't know. I heard people saying something, so I said it." Contemplate how they will whip him in such a manner that, as was narrated, a mountain would crumble if struck by it. Thus, you will know that the Legislator had obligated you to know the levels of worship, and that it is insufficient to follow people in what they do without knowledge. *And Allah guides whomever He wills to a Straight Path.*[21]

Al-Tirmidhī, along with Ibn Mājah, Ibn Ḥibbān, and al-Ḥākim narrated the following Hadith, attributing it to the Prophet ﷺ: "*No one exits his home in search of knowledge except*

(21) *Al-Baqarah*, 213.

أُخِذَ عَلَيْنَا الْعَهْدُ الْعَامُّ مِنْ رَسُولِ اللهِ ﷺ إِذَا لَمْ نَجِدْ أَحَدًا نَتَعَلَّمُ مِنْهُ الْعِلْمَ الشَّرْعِيَّ فِي بَلَدِنَا أَنْ نُسَافِرَ إِلَى بَلَدٍ فِيهَا الْعِلْمُ، وَهِيَ هِجْرَةٌ وَاجِبَةٌ عَلَيْنَا إِذًا؛ لِأَنَّ مَا لَا يَتِمُّ الْوَاجِبُ إِلَّا بِهِ فَهُوَ وَاجِبٌ، وَهَذَا الْعَهْدُ قَدْ أَخَلَّ بِهِ كَثِيرٌ مِنَ الْخَلْقِ، وَمَاتُوا عَلَى جَهْلِهِمْ، مَعَ أَنَّ الْعُلَمَاءَ فِي بَلَدِهِمْ وَرُبَّمَا كَانُوا جِيرَانًا لَهُمْ. وَقَدْ قَالَ الْعُلَمَاءُ: مَنْ صَلَّى جَاهِلًا بِكَيْفِيَّةِ الْوُضُوءِ وَالصَّلَاةِ يَعْنِي أَوْ غَيْرِهِمَا لَمْ تَصِحَّ عِبَادَتُهُ وَإِنْ وَافَقَ الصِّحَّةَ فِيهَا، وَيُؤَيِّدُهُ الْحَدِيثُ الصَّحِيحُ مَرْفُوعًا: «كُلُّ عَمَلٍ لَيْسَ عَلَيْهِ أَمْرُنَا، فَهُوَ رَدٌّ».

فَمَنْ صَلَّى وَنَكَحَ وَبَاعَ وَصَامَ وَحَجَّ عَلَى حَسَبِ مَا يَرَى النَّاسَ يَفْعَلُونَ فَقَطْ فَعِبَادَتُهُ فَاسِدَةٌ، وَتَأَمَّلْ مَنْ كَانَ عِنْدَهُ شَكٌّ لِمَا يَسْأَلُهُ مُنْكَرٌ وَنَكِيرٌ عَنْ دِينِهِ وَعَنْ نَبِيِّهِ ﷺ، فَيَقُولُ: لَا أَدْرِي، سَمِعْتُ النَّاسَ يَقُولُونَ شَيْئًا فَقُلْتُهُ، كَيْفَ يَضْرِبَانِهِ بِمِرْزَبَةٍ لَوْ ضُرِبَ بِهَا جَبَلٌ لَهُدِمَ كَمَا وَرَدَ، تَعْرِفُ أَنَّ الشَّارِعَ فَرَضَ عَلَيْكَ مَعْرِفَةَ مَرَاتِبِ الْعِبَادَاتِ، وَأَنَّهُ لَا يَكْفِيكَ أَنْ تَتَّبِعَ النَّاسَ عَلَى فِعْلِهِمْ مِنْ غَيْرِ مَعْرِفَةٍ: ﴿وَٱللَّهُ يَهْدِي مَن يَشَآءُ إِلَىٰ صِرَٰطٍ مُّسْتَقِيمٍ﴾ [البقرة: ٢١٣].

وَتَقَدَّمَ حَدِيثُ مُسْلِمٍ وَغَيْرِهِ مَرْفُوعًا: «مَنْ سَلَكَ طَرِيقًا يَلْتَمِسُ فِيهِ عِلْمًا، سَهَّلَ اللهُ تَعَالَى لَهُ بِهِ طَرِيقًا إِلَى الْجَنَّةِ».

وَرَوَى التِّرْمِذِيُّ، وَصَحَّحَهُ ابْنُ مَاجَهْ وَابْنُ حِبَّانَ فِي «صَحِيحِهِ»، وَالْحَاكِمُ وَقَالَ: صَحِيحُ الْإِسْنَادِ، وَاللَّفْظُ لِابْنِ مَاجَهْ مَرْفُوعًا: «مَا مِنْ خَارِجٍ خَرَجَ مِنْ بَيْتِهِ فِي طَلَبِ الْعِلْمِ، إِلَّا وَضَعَتْ لَهُ الْمَلَائِكَةُ أَجْنِحَتَهَا رِضًا بِمَا يَصْنَعُ».

that the Angels lower their wings over him out of satisfaction with what he is doing."[22]

Al-Ṭabarānī narrated a Prophetic Hadith with a non-problematic chain: "*If someone goes out in the morning to the mosque only wanting to learn or to teach good, he will have the reward of a pilgrim who has performed a perfect Hajj.*"

The *aḥādīth* on this subject are many. And Allah (Exalted is He) knows best.

---

(22) Both Ibn Mājah and Ibn Ḥibbān declared it authentic, with al-Ḥākim quoted as saying, "Its chain is authentic".

وَرَوَى الطَّبَرَانِيُّ بِإِسنَادٍ مَرفُوعٍ لَا بَأْسَ بِهِ: «مَنْ غَدَا إِلَى الْمَسْجِدِ لَا يُرِيدُ إِلَّا أَنْ يَتَعَلَّمَ خَيْرًا أَوْ يُعَلِّمَ، كَانَ لَهُ كَأَجْرِ حَاجٍّ تَامًّا حَجُّهُ».

وَالْأَحَادِيثُ فِي ذَلِكَ كَثِيرَةٌ، وَاللهُ تَعَالَى أَعْلَمُ.

Encouragement to Rehearse the Hadith Reports

A general covenant was taken from us by the Messenger of Allah ﷺ that we would recite the Hadith to people, except a few, and that we would convey it to lands that have no *aḥādīth*. That is accomplished through our writing the books of *aḥādīth* and sending them to the lands of Islam.

I have – and to Allah belongs all praise! – written a book that gathers the evidences of the different *madhāhib*. I sent it with some students of knowledge to the lands of Tukulor when they informed me that the books of *aḥādīth* can hardly be found with them – all they had were the books of the Malikis. I also sent a copy to the lands of the Maghrib. All of that was out of love for the Messenger ﷺ and working to satisfy him ﷺ.

Sufyān al-Thawrī, Ibn ʿUyaynah, and ʿAbdullāh ibn Sinān used to say, "If one of us were a judge, we would whip with palm branches the *faqīh* that does not learn Hadith and the *muḥaddith* that does not learn *fiqh*." Hence, it does not harm the *faqīh* to be a *muḥaddith* who knows the evidences for each of the chapters of *fiqh*.

In the writing of Hadith and rehearsing it with people lie great benefits. Among them is that the evidences of the Sacred Law will never be lost. If people are ignorant of all the evidences – and we seek refuge in Allah (Exalted is He) from that – they may be unable to defend their Sacred Legislation when others dispute with them – saying "We found our fathers upon that" would not suffice.

Among those benefits as well is repeating prayers and salutations of peace upon the Messenger of Allah ﷺ with each Hadith. Likewise, one repeats supplications for Allah's satisfaction and mercy upon the Companions and all the narrators that followed them until our time. Also among the benefits – indeed, the greatest one – is the blessing of obtaining his ﷺ supplication, where he said for the one conveying his words to

أُخِذَ عَلَيْنَا الْعَهْدُ الْعَامُّ مِنْ رَسُولِ اللهِ ﷺ أَنْ نُسْمِعَ النَّاسَ الْحَدِيثَ إِلَّا كُلَّ قَلِيلٍ، وَنُبَلِّغَهُ إِلَى الْبِلَادِ الَّتِي لَيْسَ فِيهَا أَحَادِيثُ، وَذَلِكَ بِكَتْبِنَا كُتُبَ الْحَدِيثِ وَإِرْسَالِهَا إِلَى بِلَادِ الْإِسْلَامِ.

وَقَدْ كَتَبْتُ بِحَمْدِ اللهِ كِتَابًا جَامِعًا لِأَدِلَّةِ الْمَذَاهِبِ، وَأَرْسَلْتُهُ مَعَ بَعْضِ طَلَبَةِ الْعِلْمِ إِلَى بِلَادِ التَّكْرُورِ حِينَ أَخْبَرُونِي أَنَّ كُتُبَ الْحَدِيثِ لَا تَكَادُ تُوجَدُ عِنْدَهُمْ.. إِنَّمَا عِنْدَهُمْ بَعْضُ كُتُبِ الْمَالِكِيَّةِ لَا غَيْرُ، وَأَرْسَلْتُ نُسْخَةً أُخْرَى إِلَى بِلَادِ الْمَغْرِبِ، كُلُّ ذَلِكَ مَحَبَّةً فِي رَسُولِ اللهِ ﷺ وَعَمَلًا عَلَى مَرْضَاتِهِ ﷺ.

وَكَانَ سُفْيَانُ الثَّوْرِيُّ وَابْنُ عُيَيْنَةَ وَعَبْدُ اللهِ بْنُ سِنَانٍ يَقُولُونَ: لَوْ كَانَ أَحَدُنَا قَاضِيًا لَضَرَبْنَا بِالْجَرِيدِ فَقِيهًا لَا يَتَعَلَّمُ الْحَدِيثَ، وَمُحَدِّثًا لَا يَتَعَلَّمُ الْفِقْهَ.

وَفِي كِتَابَةِ الْحَدِيثِ وَإِسْمَاعِهِ لِلنَّاسِ فَوَائِدُ عَظِيمَةٌ:

مِنْهَا: عَدَمُ انْدِرَاسِ أَدِلَّةِ الشَّرِيعَةِ، فَإِنَّ النَّاسَ لَوْ جَهِلُوا الْأَدِلَّةَ جُمْلَةً - وَالْعِيَاذُ بِاللهِ تَعَالَى - لَرُبَّمَا عَجَزُوا عَنْ نُصْرَةِ شَرِيعَتِهِمْ عِنْدَ خَصْمِهِمْ، وَقَوْلُهُمْ: إِنَّا وَجَدْنَا آبَاءَنَا عَلَى ذَلِكَ.. لَا يَكْفِي، وَمَاذَا يَضُرُّ الْفَقِيهَ أَنْ يَكُونَ مُحَدِّثًا يَعْرِفُ أَدِلَّةَ كُلِّ بَابٍ مِنْ أَبْوَابِ الْفِقْهِ.

وَمِنْهَا: تَجْدِيدُ الصَّلَاةِ وَالتَّسْلِيمِ عَلَى رَسُولِ اللهِ ﷺ فِي كُلِّ حَدِيثٍ، وَكَذَلِكَ تَجْدِيدُ التَّرَضِّي وَالتَّرَحُّمِ عَلَى الصَّحَابَةِ وَالتَّابِعِينَ مِنَ الرُّوَاةِ إِلَى وَقْتِنَا هَذَا.

وَمِنْهَا وَهُوَ أَعْظَمُهَا فَائِدَةً: الْفَوْزُ بِدُعَائِهِ ﷺ لِمَنْ بَلَّغَ كَلَامَهُ إِلَى أُمَّتِهِ فِي قَوْلِهِ: «نَضَّرَ اللهُ امْرَأً سَمِعَ مَقَالَتِي فَوَعَاهَا فَأَدَّاهَا كَمَا سَمِعَهَا».

his nation, "*May Allah beautify the person who hears my words, memorizes it, and then conveys it just as he heard it.*"

The following Hadith has been narrated by Abū Dāwūd, al-Tirmidhī, and Ibn Ḥibbān, with the wording attributed to the Prophet ﷺ: "*Naddar Allah.*"[23] In another narration by Ibn Ḥibbān, the wording is, "*May Allah have mercy on a person who hears something from me and then conveys it just as he heard it. For perhaps the person who receives will preserve it better than the one who heard it.*"

His words "*and conveys it just as he heard it*" give the meaning that his supplication is reserved for the one who conveys his ﷺ words as he heard it, letter by letter, and excludes those who convey it in meaning, such that they may not receive any part of his ﷺ supplication. That is why some scholars disliked transmitting *aḥādīth* in meaning, while others forbade it. His blessed ﷺ supplications are accepted without doubt, save where an exception has been made.[24] *But Allah is Most Forgiving, Most Merciful.*[25]

In a narration of al-Ṭabarānī, also attributed to the Messenger of Allah ﷺ: "*For perhaps someone conveys fiqh but is not a faqīh. And perhaps someone conveys fiqh to someone who has more understanding than him.*" In another of his narrations: "*O Allah! Raise my successors.*" The people asked, "Who are your successors?" He said, "*Those who will come after me and will narrate my ahādīth and teach them to people.*"

Al-Ḥāfiẓ ʿAbd al-ʿĀẓīm ﵀ said, "The writer of beneficial knowledge will have his reward and the reward of whoever

---

(23) The meaning of *naddar Allah* is a supplication for *nadarah*, which is blessing, handsomeness, and beauty. The meaning is: "May Allah adorn him with beautiful character and satisfactory actions." Other meanings have also been conveyed.

(24) Such as His not granting his ﷺ supplication that Allah (Exalted is He) forbid the Muslims from fighting one another, as has been narrated.

(25) *Al-Baqarah*, 216.

وَدُعَاؤُهُ ﷺ مَقْبُولٌ بِلَا شَكٍّ، إِلَّا مَا اسْتَثْنَى؛ كَعَدَمِ إِجَابَتِهِ ﷺ فِي أَنَّ اللّٰهَ تَعَالَى لَا يَجْعَلُ بَأْسَ أُمَّتِهِ فِيمَا بَيْنَهُمْ، كَمَا وَرَدَ.

وَقَوْلُهُ: «فَأَدَّاهَا كَمَا سَمِعَهَا»، يُفْهِمُ أَنَّ ذَلِكَ الدُّعَاءَ إِنَّمَا هُوَ خَاصٌّ بِمَنْ أَدَّى كَلَامَهُ ﷺ كَمَا سَمِعَهُ حَرْفًا بِحَرْفٍ بِخِلَافِ مَنْ يُؤَدِّيهِ بِالْمَعْنَى، فَرُبَّمَا لَا يُصِيبُهُ مِنْ ذَلِكَ الدُّعَاءِ شَيْءٌ. وَمِنْ هُنَا كَرِهَ بَعْضُهُمْ نَقْلَ الْحَدِيثِ بِالْمَعْنَى، وَبَعْضُهُمْ حَرَّمَهُ:

(وَاللّٰهُ غَفُورٌ رَحِيمٌ).

وَرَوَى أَبُو دَاوُدَ وَالتِّرْمِذِيُّ وَابْنُ حِبَّانَ فِي «صَحِيحِهِ» مَرْفُوعًا: «نَضَّرَ اللّٰهُ امْرَأً» وَفِي رِوَايَةِ ابْنِ حِبَّانَ: «رَحِمَ اللّٰهُ امْرَأً سَمِعَ مِنَّا شَيْئًا فَبَلَّغَهُ كَمَا سَمِعَهُ، فَرُبَّ مُبَلَّغٍ أَوْعَى مِنْ سَامِعٍ».

وَمَعْنَى «نَضَّرَ اللّٰهُ»: الدُّعَاءُ بِالنَّضَارَةِ، وَهِيَ النِّعْمَةُ وَالْبَهْجَةُ وَالْحُسْنُ، تَقْدِيرُهُ: جَمَّلَهُ اللّٰهُ وَزَيَّنَهُ بِالْأَخْلَاقِ الْحَسَنَةِ وَالْأَعْمَالِ الْمَرْضِيَّةِ، وَقِيلَ غَيْرُ ذَلِكَ.

وَفِي رِوَايَةٍ لِلطَّبَرَانِيِّ مَرْفُوعًا: «فَرُبَّمَا حَامِلُ فِقْهٍ لَيْسَ بِفَقِيهٍ، وَرُبَّ حَامِلِ فِقْهٍ إِلَى مَنْ هُوَ أَفْقَهُ مِنْهُ».

reads it, writes it, or acts upon it after him, as long as his writing remains and is acted upon. This is due to the Prophetic Hadith related in Muslim, '*When the son of Adam dies, all his works cease except three: a perpetual charity, knowledge by which people benefit, or a righteous son who supplicates for him.*' However, if someone records knowledge that is not beneficial, for which he incurs a sin[26], he will bear its weight and the weight of anyone who reads it, writes it, or acts upon it after him as long as his writing remains, as evidenced in the Hadith, '*If someone inaugurates an evil practice, he will bear the weight of it and the weight of all those who act upon it.*'"

Al-Ṭabarānī and others narrated the Prophetic Hadith, "*If someone prays upon me in a book, the Angels will continue to seek forgiveness for him as long as my name is in that book.*"

And Allah knows best.

(26) This refers to knowledge such as witchcraft, Brahman texts, alchemy, and other such sciences that harm its practitioner in this world and the Hereafter.

وَفِي رِوَايَةٍ لَهُ أَيْضًا مَرْفُوعًا: «اللَّهُمَّ؛ ارْفَعْ خُلَفَائِي»، قَالُوا: يَا رَسُولَ اللهِ؛ وَمَا خُلَفَاؤُكَ؟ قَالَ: «الَّذِينَ يَأْتُونَ مِنْ بَعْدِي، يَرْوُونَ أَحَادِيثِي وَيُعَلِّمُونَهَا النَّاسَ».

قَالَ الْحَافِظُ عَبْدُ الْعَظِيمِ رَحِمَهُ اللهُ: وَنَاسِخُ الْعِلْمِ النَّافِعِ لَهُ أَجْرُهُ، وَأَجْرُ مَنْ قَرَأَهُ أَوْ نَسَخَهُ أَوْ عَمِلَ بِهِ مِنْ بَعْدِهِ.. مَا بَقِيَ خَطُّهُ وَالْعَمَلُ بِهِ؛ لِحَدِيثِ مُسْلِمٍ مَرْفُوعًا: «إِذَا مَاتَ ابْنُ آدَمَ انْقَطَعَ عَمَلُهُ إِلَّا مِنْ ثَلَاثٍ: صَدَقَةٍ جَارِيَةٍ أَوْ عِلْمٍ يُنْتَفَعُ بِهِ» الْحَدِيثَ.

قَالَ: وَأَمَّا نَاسِخُ غَيْرِ الْعِلْمِ النَّافِعِ مِمَّا يُوجِبُ الْإِثْمَ عَلَيْهِ، فَعَلَيْهِ وِزْرُهُ وَوِزْرُ مَنْ قَرَأَهُ أَوْ نَسَخَهُ أَوْ عَمِلَ بِهِ مِنْ بَعْدِهِ.. مَا بَقِيَ خَطُّهُ وَالْعَمَلُ بِهِ؛ كَمَا يَشْهَدُ لَهُ حَدِيثُ: «وَمَنْ سَنَّ سُنَّةً سَيِّئَةً، فَعَلَيْهِ وِزْرُهَا وَوِزْرُ مَنْ عَمِلَ بِهَا».

وَذَلِكَ كَعُلُومِ السِّحْرِ وَالْبَرَاهِمَةِ وَعِلْمِ جَابِرٍ الْمُبَدِّلِ وَنَحْوِهَا، مِمَّا يَضُرُّ صَاحِبَهُ فِي الدُّنْيَا وَالْآخِرَةِ.

وَرَوَى الطَّبَرَانِيُّ وَغَيْرُهُ مَرْفُوعًا: «مَنْ صَلَّى عَلَيَّ فِي كِتَابٍ، لَمْ تَزَلِ الْمَلَائِكَةُ تَسْتَغْفِرُ لَهُ مَا دَامَ اسْمِي فِي ذَلِكَ الْكِتَابِ» وَاللهُ أَعْلَمُ.

Sticking to the Company of the People of Knowledge

A general covenant was taken from us by the Messenger of Allah ﷺ that we would not keep ourselves away from the gatherings of knowledge, even if we ourselves are scholars. For perhaps Allah has given them some knowledge that He has not given us. However, this covenant has been neglected by many of the *fuqahā'* and Sufis who claim to have whatever knowledge that is with other people. In fact, I have heard one of them say, when criticized for not frequenting the scholars, "By Allah, had I known anyone in Egypt who possessed knowledge that I did not have, I would carry his sandals. However, we praise Allah (Exalted is He) that He has given us enough knowledge to make us independent of all people." All of this is ignorance by proof of the statement of the Legislator ﷺ: *"If someone says, 'I am a scholar', he is an ignorant person."* The story of Mūsā with Khiḍr ﷺ is sufficient for anyone who takes heed.

Thus, O brother, gather often with the scholars, and imbibe the benefit they hold. Never be with those heedless of them, such that you are deprived of the blessing of all the people of your time because you believed yourself to be above them or their equal. For the ruling of divine assistance, whether in knowledge or anything else, is the same as the rule of water: water only flows towards the lowlands. Hence, no benefit will descend to the one who sees himself as above his contemporaries. If he believes himself their equal, their benefit will be prevented from him, akin to two slopes of equal size. Therefore, to obtain their benefit, the slave should regard himself as below the level of every Muslim he sits with, as was clarified for us in the first covenant regarding the *shuyūkh*. All good is to be found in this – *and Allah is All-Knowing, All-Wise.*[27]

---

(27) *Al-Nisā'*, 26.

أُخِذَ عَلَيْنَا الْعَهْدُ الْعَامُّ مِنْ رَسُولِ اللهِ ﷺ أَنْ لَا نُخَلِّيَ نُفُوسَنَا مِنْ مُجَالَسَةِ الْعُلَمَاءِ وَلَوْ كُنَّا عُلَمَاءَ، فَرُبَّمَا أَعْطَاهُمُ اللهُ مِنَ الْعِلْمِ مَا لَمْ يُعْطِنَا، وَهَذَا الْعَهْدُ يُخِلُّ بِالْعَمَلِ بِهِ كَثِيرٌ مِنَ الْفُقَهَاءِ وَالصُّوفِيَّةِ، فَيَدَّعُونَ أَنَّ عِنْدَهُمْ مِنَ الْعِلْمِ مَا عِنْدَ جَمِيعِ النَّاسِ، بَلْ سَمِعْتُ بَعْضَهُمْ يَقُولُ لَمَّا لُمْتُهُ عَلَى عَدَمِ التَّرَدُّدِ لِلْعُلَمَاءِ، وَاللهِ؛ لَوْ عَلِمْتُ أَنَّ أَحَدًا فِي مِصْرَ عِنْدَهُ عِلْمٌ زَائِدٌ عَلَى مَا عِنْدِي لَخَدَمْتُ نِعَالَهُ، وَلَكِنْ بِحَمْدِ اللهِ تَعَالَى قَدْ أَعْطَانَا اللهُ تَعَالَى مِنَ الْعِلْمِ مَا أَغْنَانَا بِهِ عَنِ النَّاسِ، وَهَذَا كُلُّهُ جَهْلٌ بِنَصِّ الشَّارِعِ كَمَا سَيَأْتِي فِي قَوْلِهِ ﷺ: «مَنْ قَالَ إِنِّي عَالِمٌ، فَهُوَ جَاهِلٌ».

وَفِي قِصَّةِ مُوسَى مَعَ الْخَضِرِ عليهما السلام كِفَايَةٌ لِكُلِّ مُعْتَبِرٍ. فَاجْتَمِعْ يَا أَخِي فِي كُلِّ قَلِيلٍ عَلَى الْعُلَمَاءِ وَاغْتَنِمْ فَوَائِدَهُمْ، وَلَا تَكُنْ مِنَ الْغَافِلِينَ عَنْهُمْ فَتُحْرَمَ بَرَكَةَ أَهْلِ عَصْرِكَ كُلِّهِمْ؛ لِكَوْنِكَ رَأَيْتَ نَفْسَكَ أَعْلَى مِنْهُمْ أَوْ مُسَاوِيًا لَهُمْ، فَإِنَّ الْإِمْدَادَاتِ الْإِلَهِيَّةَ مِنْ عِلْمٍ أَوْ غَيْرِهِ.. حُكْمُهَا حُكْمُ الْمَاءِ، وَالْمَاءُ لَا يَجْرِي إِلَّا فِي السُّفْلِيَّاتِ، فَمَنْ رَأَى نَفْسَهُ أَعْلَى مِنْ أَقْرَانِهِ لَمْ يَصْعَدْ لَهُ مِنْهُمْ مَدَدٌ، وَمَنْ رَأَى نَفْسَهُ مُسَاوِيًا لَهُمْ فَمَدَدُهُمْ وَاقِفٌ عَنْهُ كَالْحَوْضَيْنِ الْمُتَسَاوِيَيْنِ، فَمَا بَقِيَ الْخَيْرُ كُلُّهُ إِلَّا فِي شُهُودِ الْعَبْدِ أَنَّهُ دُونَ كُلِّ جَلِيسٍ مِنَ الْمُسْلِمِينَ؛ لِيَنْحَدِرَ لَهُ الْمَدَدُ مِنْهُمْ كَمَا أَوْضَحْنَا ذَلِكَ فِي أَوَّلِ عُهُودِ الْمَشَايِخِ:

(وَاللهُ عَلِيمٌ حَكِيمٌ).

Al-Ṭabarānī narrated[28] from Ibn ʿAbbās (may Allah be pleased with father and son) a Prophetic Hadith: "*When you pass by the gardens of Paradise, graze in them.*" The people asked, "O Messenger of Allah, what are the gardens of Paradise?" He replied, "*The gatherings of knowledge.*" On the authority of Abū Umāmah, he narrated another Prophetic Hadith[29] where Luqmān ﷺ said to his son, "*O my son! You must sit with the scholars and hear their words and wisdom. For surely Allah (Exalted is He) revives dead hearts with the light of wisdom, just as He revives dead earth with heavy rain.*"

Abū Yaʿlā narrated a Hadith[30] where Ibn ʿAbbās said, "It was said, 'O Messenger of Allah! Which of our sitting Companions is best?' He responded, '*Those whose sigh reminds you of Allah, whose speech increases you in knowledge, and whose knowledge reminds you of the Hereafter.*'"

And Allah (Exalted is He) knows best.

---

(28) Al-Ṭabarānī said that there is an unnamed narrator in its chain.

(29) Al-Ḥāfiẓ al-ʿAbdarī said, "This Hadith may be a saying of Abū Umāmah, the Companion."

(30) Its narrators – except one – are all narrators of the *ṣaḥīḥ* traditions.

وَرَوَى الطَّبَرَانِيُّ عَنِ ابْنِ عَبَّاسٍ رَضِيَ اللهُ عَنْهُمَا مَرْفُوعًا: «إِذَا مَرَرْتُمْ بِرِيَاضِ الْجَنَّةِ فَارْتَعُوا»، قَالُوا: يَا رَسُولَ اللهِ؛ وَمَا رِيَاضُ الْجَنَّةِ؟ قَالَ: «مَجَالِسُ الْعِلْمِ».

قَالَ: وَفِي سَنَدِهِ رَاوٍ لَمْ يُسَمَّ.

وَفِي رِوَايَةٍ لَهُ أَيْضًا عَنْ أَبِي أُمَامَةَ مَرْفُوعًا أَنَّ لُقْمَانَ عَلَيْهِ السَّلَامُ قَالَ لِابْنِهِ: يَا بُنَيَّ؛ عَلَيْكَ بِمُجَالَسَةِ الْعُلَمَاءِ، وَاسْمَعْ كَلَامَ الْحُكَمَاءِ؛ فَإِنَّ اللهَ تَعَالَى لَيُحْيِي الْقَلْبَ الْمَيِّتَ بِنُورِ الْحِكْمَةِ كَمَا يُحْيِي الْأَرْضَ الْمَيِّتَةَ بِوَابِلِ الْمَطَرِ.

قَالَ الْحَافِظُ الْعَبْدَرِيُّ: وَلَعَلَّ هَذَا الْحَدِيثَ مَوْقُوفٌ.

وَرَوَى أَبُو يَعْلَى وَرُوَاتُهُ رُوَاةُ الصَّحِيحِ إِلَّا وَاحِدًا عَنِ ابْنِ عَبَّاسٍ قَالَ:

قِيلَ: يَا رَسُولَ اللهِ؛ أَيُّ جُلَسَائِنَا خَيْرٌ؟ قَالَ: «مَنْ ذَكَّرَكُمُ اللهَ رُؤْيَتُهُ، وَزَادَ فِي عِلْمِكُمْ مَنْطِقُهُ، وَذَكَّرَكُمْ بِالْآخِرَةِ عِلْمُهُ». وَاللهُ تَعَالَى أَعْلَمُ.

Honouring the People of Knowledge

A general covenant was taken from us by the Messenger of Allah ﷺ that we would honour, venerate, and revere the people of knowledge. We should never believe that we can ever repay them, even if we gave up all that we own or spent our entire lives serving them. However, this covenant has been neglected by the majority of the seekers of knowledge and disciples in the path of the Sufis in this time – in fact, we hardly see any of them upholding the due right of their teacher. This is a great harm to the religion, which risks treating lightly both knowledge and his ﷺ command to venerate the scholars. Thus, they began showing pride before their *shuyūkh* until the latter are dimmed because of their excessive flattering. And there is neither might nor power save with Allah the Exalted, the Great.

It has reached us that Imam al-Nawawī was summoned one day by his complete Shaykh al-Irbilī in order to eat with him. However, he said, "My master, excuse me from it, for I have a legal excuse", and so, left him. One of his brethren asked him about that excuse, to which he said, "I fear that my *shaykh*'s eye may fall on a morsel of food, and I would eat it without knowing." He would also, when leaving for his lessons with his *shaykh*, give charity for the latter with whatever was easy for him, saying, "O Allah! Conceal from me the faults of my teacher, such that my eye does not fall on any deficiency, nor does anything reach me from anyone regarding his deficiency."

The smallest effect of your bad *adab* with your *shaykh*, O brother, is that it prevents you from the benefits he brings. That may be by his (intentionally) hiding them from you, out of anger with you, or, as a rebuke to you, he prevents his tongue from clarifying meanings for you so that you never receive any of what he had intended by his words. Then, when one of those who observes proper *adab* comes to him, he loosens his tongue because of his sincerity and *adab* with him.

أُخِذَ عَلَيْنَا الْعَهْدُ الْعَامُّ مِنْ رَسُولِ اللهِ ﷺ أَنْ نُكْرِمَ الْعُلَمَاءَ وَنُجِلَّهُمْ وَنُوَقِّرَهُمْ، وَلَا نَرَى لَنَا قُدْرَةً عَلَى مُكَافَأَتِهِمْ وَلَوْ أَعْطَيْنَاهُمْ جَمِيعَ مَا نَمْلِكُ، أَوْ خَدَمْنَاهُمُ الْعُمْرَ كُلَّهُ، وَهَذَا الْعَهْدُ قَدْ أَخَلَّ بِهِ غَالِبُ طَلَبَةِ الْعِلْمِ وَالْمُرِيدِينَ فِي طَرِيقِ الصُّوفِيَّةِ الْآنَ، حَتَّى لَا نَكَادَ نَرَى أَحَدًا مِنْهُمْ يَقُومُ بِوَاجِبِ حَقِّ مُعَلِّمِهِ، وَهَذَا دَاءٌ عَظِيمٌ فِي الدِّينِ مُؤْذِنٌ بِاسْتِهَانَةِ الْعِلْمِ وَبِأَمْرِ مَنْ أَمَرَنَا بِإِجْلَالِ الْعُلَمَاءِ ﷺ، فَصَارَ أَحَدُهُمْ يَفْخَرُ عَلَى شَيْخِهِ حَتَّى صَارَ شَيْخُهُ يُدَاهِنُهُ وَيُمَالِقُهُ حَتَّى يَسْكُتَ عَنْهُ، فَلَا حَوْلَ وَلَا قُوَّةَ إِلَّا بِاللهِ الْعَلِيِّ الْعَظِيمِ.

وَقَدْ بَلَغَنَا عَنِ الْإِمَامِ النَّوَوِيِّ أَنَّهُ دَعَاهُ يَوْمًا شَيْخُهُ الْكَمَالُ الْأَرْبَلِيُّ لِيَأْكُلَ مَعَهُ، فَقَالَ: يَا سَيِّدِي؛ أَعْفِنِي مِنْ ذَلِكَ؛ فَإِنَّ لِي عُذْرًا شَرْعِيًّا، فَتَرَكَهُ، فَسَأَلَهُ بَعْضُ إِخْوَانِهِ: مَا ذَلِكَ الْعُذْرُ؟ فَقَالَ: أَخَافُ أَنْ تَسْبِقَ عَيْنُ شَيْخِي إِلَى لُقْمَةٍ.. فَآكُلَهَا وَأَنَا لَا أَشْعُرُ.

وَكَانَ رضى الله عنه إِذَا خَرَجَ لِلدَّرْسِ لِيَقْرَأَ عَلَى شَيْخِهِ، يَتَصَدَّقُ عَنْهُ فِي الطَّرِيقِ بِمَا تَيَسَّرَ، وَيَقُولُ: اللَّهُمَّ؛ اسْتُرْ عَنِّي عَيْبَ مُعَلِّمِي، حَتَّى لَا تَقَعَ عَيْنِي لَهُ عَلَى نَقِيصَةٍ، وَلَا يَبْلُغَنِي ذَلِكَ عَنْهُ عَنْ أَحَدٍ رضى الله عنه.

ثُمَّ مِنْ أَقَلِّ آفَاتِ سُوءِ أَدَبِكَ يَا أَخِي مَعَ الشَّيْخِ؛ أَنَّكَ تُحْرَمُ فَوَائِدَهُ، فَإِمَّا بِكَتْمِهَا عَنْكَ بُغْضًا فِيكَ، وَإِمَّا أَنَّ لِسَانَهُ يَنْعَقِدُ عَنْ إِيضَاحِ الْمَعَانِي لَكَ، فَلَا تَتَحَصَّلُ مِنْ كَلَامِهِ عَلَى شَيْءٍ تَعْتَمِدُ عَلَيْهِ عُقُوبَةً لَكَ. فَإِذَا جَاءَهُ شَخْصٌ مِنَ الْمُتَأَدِّبِينَ مَعَهُ.. انْطَلَقَ لِسَانُهُ لَهُ لِمَوْضِعِ صِدْقِهِ وَأَدَبِهِ مَعَهُ، فَعُلِمَ أَنَّهُ يَنْبَغِي لِلطَّالِبِ أَنْ يُخَاطِبَ شَيْخَهُ بِالْإِجْلَالِ وَالْإِطْرَاقِ وَغَضِّ الْبَصَرِ.. كَمَا يُخَاطِبُ الْمُلُوكَ، وَلَا يُجَادِلُهُ قَطُّ بِعِلْمٍ اسْتَفَادَهُ مِنْهُ فِي وَقْتٍ

Thus, the seeker must speak to his *shaykh* with reverence, lowering his gaze as one addresses kings. He should never dispute with him in any knowledge that he had received from before, except by way of inquiry. For example, with an air of *adab*, he should say something like, "O my master, yesterday we heard you affirming something different than what you are affirming now. Which of your statements should we then rely on, so that we may preserve it?"

Likewise, he should not marry his *shaykh*'s wife, whether he has divorced her or she is his widow. He should never take possession of his office, his place of seclusion, or his house after his death – to say nothing of it during his life – except in the case of a legislated need, which returns to having etiquette with the *shaykh*. The seeker should also not betray any of his *shaykh*'s companions or neighbours – to say the least of his children – for he is obligated to guard himself from everything that would upset the *shaykh* in his absence and presence.

We will also discuss this later in the book throughout the covenants of business – so, review it. We also have spoken at length about it, transcribing from different scholars, in the covenants related to the *shuyūkh* – *and Allah is Almighty, Most Wise.*[31]

Both al-Ṭabarānī and al-Ḥākim narrated the Prophetic Hadith[32]: "*Blessing is found with your elders.*" Imam Aḥmad, al-Tirmidhī, and Ibn Ḥibbān all narrated the Prophetic Hadith: "*He who does not respect our elders and show mercy to our young is not of us.*" In another narration of Imam Aḥmad, al-Ṭabarānī, and al-Ḥākim, attributed to the Prophet ﷺ: "*He*

(31) *Al-Baqarah*, 228.
(32) Al-Ḥākim declared it authentic according to the conditions of Muslim.

آخرَ إلَّا عَلَى سَبِيلِ التَّعَرُّفِ؛ فَيَقُولُ: يَا سَيِّدِي؛ سَمِعْنَاكُمْ تُقَرِّرُونَ لَنَا أَمْسِ خِلَافَ هَذَا، فَمَاذَا تَعْتَمِدُونَ عَلَيْهِ مِنَ التَّقْرِيرَيْنِ الْآنَ حَتَّى نَحْفَظَهُ عَنْكُمْ؟ وَنَحْوَ ذَلِكَ الْأَلْفَاظِ الَّتِي فِيهَا رَائِحَةُ الْأَدَبِ، وَكَذَلِكَ يَنْبَغِي لَهُ أَنْ لَا يَتَزَوَّجَ امْرَأَةَ شَيْخِهِ سَوَاءٌ كَانَتْ مُطَلَّقَةً فِي حَيَاتِهِ أَوْ بَعْدَ مَمَاتِهِ، وَكَذَلِكَ لَا يَنْبَغِي لَهُ أَنْ يَسْعَى عَلَى وَظِيفَتِهِ أَوْ خَلْوَتِهِ أَوْ بَيْتِهِ بَعْدَ مَوْتِهِ فَضْلًا عَنْ حَيَاتِهِ.. إلَّا لِضَرُورَةٍ شَرْعِيَّةٍ تَرْجَحُ عَلَى الْأَدَبِ مَعَ الشَّيْخِ، وَكَذَلِكَ لَا يَنْبَغِي أَنْ يَسْعَى عَلَى أَحَدٍ مِنْ أَصْحَابِ شَيْخِهِ أَوْ جِيرَانِهِ فَضْلًا عَنْ أَوْلَادِهِ؛ فَإِنَّ الْوَاجِبَ عَلَى كُلِّ طَالِبٍ أَنْ يَحْفَظَ نَفْسَهُ عَنْ كُلِّ مَا يُغَيِّرُ خَاطِرَ شَيْخِهِ فِي غَيْبَتِهِ وَحُضُورِهِ.

وَسَيَأْتِي فِي هَذَا الْكِتَابِ أَيْضًا فِي أَثْنَاءِ عُهُودِ الْبَيْعِ فَرَاجِعْهُ، وَكَذَلِكَ بَسَطْنَا الْكَلَامَ بِنُقُولِ الْعُلَمَاءِ عَلَى ذَلِكَ فِي عُهُودِ الْمَشَايِخِ:

(وَاللهُ عَزِيزٌ حَكِيمٌ).

وَرَوَى الْبُخَارِيُّ: أَنَّ النَّبِيَّ ﷺ كَانَ يَجْمَعُ بَيْنَ الرَّجُلَيْنِ فِي قَتْلَى أُحُدٍ يَعْنِي فِي الْقَبْرِ، ثُمَّ يَقُولُ: «أَيُّهُمَا أَكْثَرُ أَخْذًا لِلْقُرْآنِ؟» فَإِذَا أُشِيرَ إِلَى أَحَدِهِمَا.. قَدَّمَهُ فِي اللَّحْدِ.

قُلْتُ: وَمَعْنَى كَوْنِهِ أَكْثَرَ أَخْذًا لِلْقُرْآنِ، أَيْ أَكْثَرُ عَمَلًا بِهِ مِنْ قِيَامِ لَيْلٍ، وَاجْتِنَابِ نَهْيٍ، وَنَحْوِ ذَلِكَ.

وَرَوَى الطَّبَرَانِيُّ وَالْحَاكِمُ وَقَالَ صَحِيحٌ عَلَى شَرْطِ مُسْلِمٍ مَرْفُوعًا: «الْبَرَكَةُ مَعَ أَكَابِرِكُمْ». وَرَوَى الْإِمَامُ أَحْمَدُ وَالتِّرْمِذِيُّ وَابْنُ حِبَّانَ فِي «صَحِيحِهِ» مَرْفُوعًا: «لَيْسَ مِنَّا مَنْ لَمْ يُوَقِّرِ الْكَبِيرَ وَيَرْحَمِ الصَّغِيرَ».

is not of my nation who does not venerate our elders, show mercy to our young, or recognize our scholars' due."[33]

Al-Ṭabarānī also narrated the Prophetic Hadith: "*Be humble before those from whom you learn.*" Al-Ṭabarānī also narrated the Prophetic Hadith: "*There are three things which only a hypocrite takes lightly: the one who grows old in Islam, the possessor of knowledge, and the just Imam.*" Imam Aḥmad and al-Ṭabarānī narrated, with a sound chain, that ʿAbdullāh ibn Bishr said, "I heard a Hadith some time ago: '*If you are in a group of less or more than twenty men, and you don't see in their faces anyone who is revered for the sake of Allah ﷻ, know that the affair has weakened.*'" Al-Ṭabarānī also narrated the Prophetic Hadith: "*I only fear three traits for my nation ...*" and mentioned among those traits the wasting of the opportunity to ask someone of knowledge, despite knowing that they possess it.

And Allah (Blessed and Exalted is He) knows best.

---

(33) In another narration: "*... who does not recognize our elders' rights ...*"

وَفِي رِوَايَةٍ لِلْإِمَامِ أَحْمَدَ وَالطَّبَرَانِيِّ وَالْحَاكِمِ مَرْفُوعًا: «لَيْسَ مِنْ أُمَّتِي مَنْ لَمْ يُجِلَّ كَبِيرَنَا وَيَرْحَمْ صَغِيرَنَا وَيَعْرِفْ لِعَالِمِنَا حَقَّهُ». وَفِي رِوَايَةٍ: «وَيَعْرِفْ شَرَفَ كَبِيرِنَا».

وَرَوَى الطَّبَرَانِيُّ مَرْفُوعًا: «تَوَاضَعُوا لِمَنْ تَعَلَّمُونَ مِنْهُ».

وَرَوَى الطَّبَرَانِيُّ أَيْضًا مَرْفُوعًا: «ثَلَاثَةٌ لَا يَسْتَخِفُّ بِهِمْ إِلَّا مُنَافِقٌ: ذُو الشَّيْبَةِ فِي الْإِسْلَامِ، وَذُو الْعِلْمِ، وَالْإِمَامُ الْمُقْسِطُ» الْحَدِيثَ.

وَرَوَى الْإِمَامُ أَحْمَدُ وَالطَّبَرَانِيُّ بِإِسْنَادٍ حَسَنٍ عَنْ عَبْدِ اللهِ بْنِ بِشْرٍ قَالَ: سَمِعْتُ حَدِيثًا مُنْذُ زَمَانٍ: «إِذَا كُنْتَ فِي قَوْمٍ عِشْرُونَ رَجُلًا أَوْ أَقَلَّ أَوْ أَكْثَرَ، فَتَصَفَّحْتَ وُجُوهَهُمْ فَلَمْ تَرَ فِيهِمْ رَجُلًا يُهَابُ فِي اللهِ عَزَّ وَجَلَّ، فَاعْلَمْ أَنَّ الْأَمْرَ قَدْ رَقَّ».

وَرَوَى الطَّبَرَانِيُّ مَرْفُوعًا: «لَا أَخَافُ عَلَى أُمَّتِي ثَلَاثَ خِصَالٍ؛ فَذَكَرَ مِنْهَا: وَأَنْ يَرَوْا ذَا عِلْمٍ فَيُضَيِّعُونَهُ وَلَا يَسْأَلُونَ عَلَيْهِ».

وَاللهُ سُبْحَانَهُ وَتَعَالَى أَعْلَمُ.

Transmitting Knowledge Even If We Fail to Act upon It

A general covenant was taken from us by the Messenger of Allah ﷺ that if we do not act upon our knowledge, we should teach it to a Muslim who will put it into practice. Among the public, there are those who have been allotted knowledge but do not act upon it, some who are allotted knowledge and act upon it, and some among them who are allotted neither.

I heard Sīdī ʿAlī al-Khawwāṣ say, "It is incumbent upon everyone who does not act upon his knowledge to teach it to people who he hopes will act upon it", even when that will not repair our deficiencies completely.

I heard him say another time:

> All the scholars act upon their knowledge one way or another, as long as they have their intellect. That is because if he acts upon the legislated commands and avoids the prohibitions, he will have acted upon his knowledge with certainty – if Allah gives him sincerity in that. If he does not act upon his knowledge in the way that we have described, he will recognize through knowledge that he has violated the command of Allah. So, he will repent and show remorse. In that case, he will have also acted upon his knowledge; if he did not have it, he would not have been guided to the fact that abandoning said acting is disobedience. Thus, knowledge always benefits. Whatever has been related regarding the punishment of those who do not act upon their knowledge is thus interpreted to refer to those who do not repent from their sin.

The summary of this immensely beneficial quote is that the condition for a person to be considered acting upon his knowledge, unlike what may be assumed, is not that he never falls

أُخِذَ عَلَيْنَا الْعَهْدُ الْعَامُّ مِنْ رَسُولِ اللهِ ﷺ إِذَا لَمْ نَعْمَلْ بِعِلْمِنَا أَنْ نَدُلَّ عَلَيْهِ مَنْ يَعْمَلُ بِهِ مِنَ الْمُسْلِمِينَ، وَإِنْ لَمْ يَكُنْ ذَلِكَ يُجْبِرُ خَلَلَنَا عَلَى التَّمَامِ؛ فَإِنَّ مِنَ النَّاسِ مَنْ قُسِمَ لَهُ الْعِلْمُ وَلَمْ يُقْسَمْ لَهُ عَمَلٌ بِهِ، وَمِنْهُمْ مَنْ قُسِمَ لَهُ الْعِلْمُ وَالْعَمَلُ بِهِ، وَمِنْهُمْ مَنْ لَمْ يُقْسَمْ لَهُ وَاحِدٌ مِنْهُمَا كَبَعْضِ الْعَوَامِّ.

وَسَمِعْتُ سَيِّدِي عَلِيًّا الْخَوَّاصَ رحمه الله تعالى يَقُولُ: يَتَعَيَّنُ عَلَى كُلِّ مَنْ لَمْ يَعْمَلْ بِعِلْمِهِ.. أَنْ يُعَلِّمَهُ النَّاسَ وَلِمَنْ يَرْجُو عَمَلَهُ بِهِ.

وَسَمِعْتُهُ مَرَّةً أُخْرَى يَقُولُ: مَا ثَمَّ عَالِمٌ إِلَّا وَهُوَ يَعْمَلُ بِعِلْمِهِ وَلَوْ بِوَجْهٍ مِنَ الْوُجُوهِ، مَا دَامَ عَقْلُهُ حَاضِرًا، وَذَلِكَ أَنَّهُ إِنْ عَمِلَ بِالْمَأْمُورَاتِ الشَّرْعِيَّةِ وَاجْتَنَبَ الْمَنْهِيَّاتِ فَقَدْ عَمِلَ بِعِلْمِهِ بِيَقِينٍ إِذَا رَزَقَهُ اللهُ الْإِخْلَاصَ فِيهِ، وَإِنْ لَمْ يَعْمَلْ بِعِلْمِهِ كَمَا ذَكَرْنَا فَيَعْرِفُ بِالْعِلْمِ أَنَّهُ خَالَفَ أَمْرَ اللهِ.. فَيَتُوبُ وَيَنْدَمُ، فَقَدْ عَمِلَ أَيْضًا بِعِلْمِهِ، لِأَنَّهُ لَوْلَا الْعِلْمُ مَا اهْتَدَى؛ لِكَوْنِ تَرْكِ الْعَمَلِ بِالْعِلْمِ مَعْصِيَةً، فَالْعِلْمُ نَافِعٌ عَلَى كُلِّ حَالٍ، وَيُحْمَلُ مَا وَرَدَ فِي عُقُوبَةِ مَنْ لَمْ يَعْمَلْ بِعِلْمِهِ عَلَى مَنْ لَمْ يَتُبْ مِنْ ذَنْبِهِ اهـ. وَهُوَ كَلَامٌ نَفِيسٌ.

وَمُلَخَّصُ ذَلِكَ أَنَّهُ لَا يُشْتَرَطُ فِي كَوْنِ الْإِنْسَانِ عَامِلًا بِعِلْمِهِ.. عَدَمُ وُقُوعِهِ فِي مَعْصِيَةٍ، كَمَا يَتَبَادَرُ إِلَى الْأَذْهَانِ، وَإِنَّمَا الشَّرْطُ عَدَمُ إِصْرَارِهِ عَلَى الذَّنْبِ، أَوْ عَدَمُ إِصْرَارِهِ عَلَى الْإِصْرَارِ وَهَكَذَا.

into disobedience. Rather, it is that he does not persist in sin – or that he does not persist in his persistence.

Ibn Mājah and Ibn Khuzayma narrated the Prophetic Hadith: "*The only part of a believer's knowledge, actions, and good deeds that reach him after his death is knowledge that he taught and spread.*" Al-Bazzār and al-Ṭabarānī narrated the Prophetic Hadith: "*The one who directs to good is like the one who acts upon it.*"

Muslim, Abū Dāwūd, and al-Tirmidhī narrated the Prophetic Hadith: "*If someone directs to good,*" – or "*whoever puts it into practice*" – "*he will have the reward of whoever acts upon it.*" Muslim and others also cite a variation of this Prophetic Hadith, which contains the following addition: "... *[he will have a reward] similar to the rewards of those who followed him without their rewards being decreased at all.*"

Al-Ḥākim narrated the Prophetic Hadith that ʿAlī ﷺ narrated about His words, Exalted is He, "Save yourselves and your families from the Fire"[34] that it means, "Teach your family good."

And Allah (Blessed and Exalted is He) knows best.

(34) *Al-Taḥrīm*, 6.

وَرَوَى ابْنُ مَاجَهْ وَابْنُ خُزَيْمَةَ مَرْفُوعًا: «إِنَّمَا يَلْحَقُ الْمُؤْمِنَ مِنْ عِلْمِهِ وَعَمَلِهِ وَحَسَنَاتِهِ بَعْدَ مَوْتِهِ، عِلْمٌ عَلَّمَهُ وَنَشَرَهُ».

وَرَوَى مُسْلِمٌ وَأَبُو دَاوُدَ وَالتِّرْمِذِيُّ مَرْفُوعًا: «مَنْ دَلَّ عَلَى خَيْرٍ، فَلَهُ مِثْلُ أَجْرِ فَاعِلِهِ»، أَوْ قَالَ: «عَامِلِهِ».

وَرَوَى الْبَزَّارُ وَالطَّبَرَانِيُّ مَرْفُوعًا: «الدَّالُّ عَلَى الْخَيْرِ كَفَاعِلِهِ».

وَرَوَى مُسْلِمٌ وَغَيْرُهُ مَرْفُوعًا: «مَنْ دَعَا إِلَى هُدًى، كَانَ لَهُ مِنَ الْأَجْرِ مِثْلُ أُجُورِ مَنْ تَبِعَهُ، لَا يَنْقُصُ ذَلِكَ مِنْ أُجُورِهِمْ شَيْئًا».

وَرَوَى الْحَاكِمُ مَرْفُوعًا عَنْ عَلِيٍّ رضى الله عنه فِي قَوْلِهِ تَعَالَى: ﴿قُوٓاْ أَنفُسَكُمْ وَأَهْلِيكُمْ نَارًا﴾ [التحريم: ٦]. قَالَ: «عَلِّمُوا أَهْلِيكُمُ الْخَيْرَ».

وَاللهُ سُبْحَانَهُ وَتَعَالَى أَعْلَمُ.

Things to Avoid The Prohibition of Taking Reprehensible Innovations as Part of One's Religious Practice

A general covenant was taken from us by the Messenger of Allah ﷺ that we would not employ in our religious practice any reprehensible innovation for which there is no support from the apparent meanings of the Book and the Sunnah. We should also avoid acting upon any opinion whose conformity with the Book and the Sunnah is not apparent to us, except where the matter is agreed upon.

However, if someone wishes to act upon this covenant, he needs to dive deeply into the knowledge of the Qur'an and traditional reports, and to encompass (in knowledge) all the evidences used by the schools of law, both those that have been abandoned and those put into use. In fact, only rarely should any of their evidence escape his knowledge. Such a person may indeed be excluded from following others in the majority of rulings. If someone has not reached this level, it is imperative upon him to follow a particular school of law. If not, he will fall into error.

Sīdī ʿAlī al-Khawwāṣ ؓ would know, by way of unveiling, if any issue had evidence from the speech of the Lawgiver ﷺ. He would say, "In our assessment, a person does not reach the station of completion until he knows with certainty that which is from a statement of the Lawgiver, a Companion, or from analogical reasoning and that which is from an opinion outside of what we have mentioned."[35]

He then said:

> As long as one has not reached this level of depth in the sciences of the Sacred Law and knowledge of the evi-

(35) Such an opinion should be thrown out, and no one should act upon it.

أُخِذَ عَلَيْنَا الْعَهْدُ الْعَامُّ مِنْ رَسُولِ اللهِ ﷺ أَنْ لَا نَتَدَيَّنَ بِفِعْلِ شَيْءٍ مِنَ الْبِدَعِ الْمَذْمُومَةِ الَّتِي لَا يَشْهَدُ لَهَا ظَاهِرُ كِتَابٍ وَلَا سُنَّةٍ، وَأَنْ نَجْتَنِبَ الْعَمَلَ بِكُلِّ رَأْيٍ لَمْ يَظْهَرْ لَنَا وَجْهُ مُوَافَقَتِهِ لِلْكِتَابِ وَالسُّنَّةِ، إِلَّا إِنْ أُجْمِعَ عَلَيْهِ.

وَيَحْتَاجُ مَنْ يُرِيدُ الْعَمَلَ بِهَذَا الْعَهْدِ إِلَى التَّبَحُّرِ فِي مَعْرِفَةِ الْأَحَادِيثِ وَالْآثَارِ وَالْإِحَاطَةِ بِجَمِيعِ أَدِلَّةِ الْمَذَاهِبِ الْمُنْدَرِسَةِ وَالْمُسْتَعْمَلَةِ، حَتَّى لَا يَكَادَ يَعْزُبُ عَنْ عِلْمِهِ مِنْ أَدِلَّتِهِمْ إِلَّا النَّادِرَ، وَلَعَلَّهُ يَخْرُجُ عَنِ التَّقْلِيدِ فِي أَكْثَرِ الْأَحْكَامِ، وَأَمَّا مَنْ لَمْ يَبْلُغْ هَذَا الْمَقَامَ فَيَجِبُ عَلَيْهِ التَّقْلِيدُ لِمَذْهَبٍ مُعَيَّنٍ، وَإِلَّا وَقَعَ فِي الضَّلَالِ.

وَقَدْ كَانَ سَيِّدِي عَلِيٌّ الْخَوَّاصُ رحمه الله تعالى يَعْرِفُ مِنْ طَرِيقِ كَشْفِهِ كُلَّ مَسْأَلَةٍ لَهَا دَلِيلٌ مِنْ كَلَامِ الشَّارِعِ وَيَقُولُ: لَا يَبْلُغُ الرَّجُلُ عِنْدَنَا مَقَامَ الْكَمَالِ حَتَّى يَعْرِفَ يَقِينًا مَا كَانَ مِنْ كَلَامِ الشَّارِعِ، وَمَا كَانَ مِنْ كَلَامِ الصَّحَابَةِ، وَمَا كَانَ مِنَ الْقِيَاسِ، وَمَا كَانَ رَأْيًا خَارِجًا عَنْ مُوَافَقَةِ مَا ذَكَرْنَاهُ. قَالَ: وَمِثْلُ هَذَا الرَّأْيِ هُوَ الَّذِي يُرْمَى بِهِ، وَلَيْسَ لِأَحَدٍ أَنْ يَعْمَلَ بِهِ. قَالَ: فَكُلُّ مَنْ لَمْ يَبْلُغْ مَرْتَبَةَ التَّبَحُّرِ فِي عُلُومِ الشَّرِيعَةِ وَمَعْرِفَةِ أَدِلَّةِ الْمَذَاهِبِ.. فَمِنْ لَازِمِهِ الْوُقُوعُ فِي التَّدَيُّنِ بِالْآرَاءِ الَّتِي لَا يَكَادُ يَشْهَدُ لَهَا كِتَابٌ وَلَا سُنَّةٌ.

> dences of the schools of law, he will inevitably act upon opinions that hardly have any support from the Book and the Sunnah. So, dive deeply, O brother, into the sciences of the Sacred Law! Give great personal effort in reading and memorizing the *aḥādīth* of the Sacred Law, the books of their exegetes, and their statements so that you will become a knower of all the schools of law. That is because they are, in essence, the entirety of the pure Sacred Law.

It is possible that in the school of law that he adheres to, a follower would put into practice the statement of his Imam that was derived from mere opinion, while the authentic *aḥādīth* support another school in opposition to that opinion. If he were to follow his school of law in that action, he will miss out on acting on authentic *aḥādīth* and will deviate from the path of the Sunnah. The statement by some followers that "If my Imam had not seen evidence (for his opinion), he would not have stated it" is rejected and deficient, not to mention the fact that the very Imam had exonerated himself of acting upon mere opinion and forbade others from following him in that.

My brother, Afḍal al-Dīn, used to say:

> The context in which one would act upon the opinion of an Imam that is ambiguous in its support is when one has not come upon an evidence that contradicts his statement. In that case, it is proper to have a good opinion of his statement, saying, "If he hadn't seen any evidence for his statement, he would not have said it." However, if we come upon evidence (that contradicts him), we must give precedence to acting upon it over acting upon the statement of the *mujtahid*. The statement of that Imam is then interpreted as his not having

فَتَبَحَّرْ يَا أَخِي فِي عُلُومِ الشَّرِيعَةِ وَأَعْطِ الْجِدَّ مِنْ نَفْسِكَ فِي الْمُطَالَعَةِ وَالْحِفْظِ لِأَحَادِيثِ الشَّرِيعَةِ وَكُتُبِ شُرَّاحِهَا وَحِفْظِ مَقَالَاتِهِمْ، حَتَّى تَكُونَ عَارِفًا بِجَمِيعِ الْمَذَاهِبِ، لِأَنَّهَا بِعَيْنِهَا هِيَ مَجْمُوعُ الشَّرِيعَةِ الْمُطَهَّرَةِ، وَرُبَّمَا تَدَيَّنَ مُقَلِّدٌ فِي مَذْهَبٍ بِقَوْلِ إِمَامِهِ مِنْ طَرِيقِ الرَّأْيِ، فَصَحَّتِ الْأَحَادِيثُ فِي مَذْهَبٍ آخَرَ بِضِدِّ ذَلِكَ الرَّأْيِ، فَوَقَفَ مَعَ مَذْهَبِهِ فَفَاتَهُ الْعَمَلُ بِالْأَحَادِيثِ الصَّحِيحَةِ فَأَخْطَأَ طَرِيقَ السُّنَّةِ. قَالَ: وَقَوْلُ بَعْضِ الْمُقَلِّدِينَ: لَوْلَا أَنْ رَأَى إِمَامِي دَلِيلًا مَا قَالَ بِهِ.. جُمُودٌ وَقُصُورٌ مَعَ أَنَّ نَفْسَ إِمَامِهِ قَدْ تَبَرَّأَ مِنَ الْعَمَلِ بِالرَّأْيِ وَنَهَى غَيْرَهُ عَنِ اتِّبَاعِهِ عَلَيْهِ اهـ.

وَكَانَ أَخِي أَفْضَلُ الدِّينِ يَقُولُ: مَحَلُّ الْعَمَلِ بِرَأْيِ الْإِمَامِ الَّذِي لَا يُعْرَفُ لِقَوْلِهِ مُسْتَنَدٌ مَا إِذَا لَمْ نَطَّلِعْ عَلَى دَلِيلٍ يُخَالِفُهُ، فَهُنَاكَ يَنْبَغِي لَنَا إِحْسَانُ الظَّنِّ بِقَوْلِهِ وَنَقُولُ: لَوْلَا أَنَّهُ رَأَى لِقَوْلِهِ دَلِيلًا مَا قَالَهُ، أَمَّا إِذَا اطَّلَعْنَا عَلَى دَلِيلٍ فَلَنَا تَقْدِيمُ الْعَمَلِ بِهِ عَلَى كَلَامِ الْمُجْتَهِدِ إِذَا كَانَ مِثْلُنَا مِنْ أَهْلِ النَّظَرِ الصَّحِيحِ، وَيُحْمَلُ كَلَامُ ذَلِكَ الْإِمَامِ عَلَى أَنَّهُ لَمْ يَظْفَرْ بِذَلِكَ الدَّلِيلِ، وَلَوْ ظَفِرَ بِهِ.. لَعَمِلَ بِهِ اهـ.

> come upon that evidence, and that if he had come upon it, he would have acted upon it.

I heard Sīdī ʿAlī al-Khawwāṣ ﷺ say:

> If someone wishes to restrict himself to acting upon the Book and the Sunnah and to avoid acting upon mere opinion, he needs to dive deeply into the science of Arabic, the science of meanings, the science of figurative speech, and the grammar of the Arabic language so that he would know the various modes of deriving rulings as well as the customary speech of the Arabs, their metaphors and similes, and (thereby) which rulings accept various interpretations and which do not.

I say: Allah (Exalted is He) has blessed me in that I have come upon all the evidence of each school of law, the four Imams and others, and I recognized the support for their statements in all the chapters of *fiqh*. There is not one statement of theirs except that I have seen its supporting evidence returning either to a verse of the Qur'an, a Hadith, a traditional report, or a valid analogy to an authentic source. Thus, I began to see the schools of the four Imams as a quilt, its borders and patterns woven from the pure Sacred Law – and all praise is due to Allah. Anyone who carefully reads my summary of *al-Sunan al-Kubrā* by Imam al-Bayhaqī ﷺ will likewise recognize this.

If someone does not examine the proof of the schools of law in the way that we have described, he will not know how to distinguish issues that arise from opinion from those that arise from textual evidence. He may even fall into wayward beliefs and act upon false methodologies, unless he issues rulings restricted to a single school of law. Imam Abū al-Qāsim al-Junayd ﷺ used to say, "According to us, a man does not become complete in the path of Allah ﷻ until he becomes an Imam in

وَسَمِعْتُ سَيِّدِي عَلِيًّا الْخَوَّاصَ رَحِمَهُ اللهُ يَقُولُ: يَحْتَاجُ مَنْ يُرِيدُ التَّقَيُّدَ عَلَى الْعَمَلِ بِالْكِتَابِ وَالسُّنَّةِ وَيَجْتَنِبُ الْعَمَلَ بِالرَّأْيِ إِلَى التَّبَحُّرِ فِي عِلْمِ الْعَرَبِيَّةِ وَعِلْمِ الْمَعَانِي وَالْبَيَانِ وَالنَّحْوِ فِي لُغَةِ الْعَرَبِ، حَتَّى يَعْرِفَ مَوَاطِنَ طُرُقِ الِاسْتِنْبَاطِ، وَيَعْرِفَ أَقْوَالَ الْعَرَبِ وَمَجَازَاتِهَا وَاسْتِعَارَاتِهَا، وَيَعْرِفَ مَا يَقْبَلُ التَّأْوِيلَ مِنَ الْأَدِلَّةِ وَمَا لَا يَقْبَلُهَا ا هـ.

قُلْتُ: وَقَدْ مَنَّ اللهُ تَعَالَى عَلَيَّ بِالِاطِّلَاعِ عَلَى أَدِلَّةِ مَذَاهِبِ الْأَئِمَّةِ الْأَرْبَعَةِ وَغَيْرِهَا، وَعَرَفْتُ مُسْتَنَدَ أَقْوَالِهِمْ فِي جَمِيعِ أَبْوَابِ الْفِقْهِ، فَمَا مِنْ قَوْلٍ مِنْ أَقْوَالِهِمْ إِلَّا وَرَأَيْتُهُ مُسْتَنِدًا إِلَى دَلِيلٍ؛ إِمَّا إِلَى آيَةٍ وَإِمَّا إِلَى حَدِيثٍ وَإِمَّا إِلَى أَثَرٍ وَإِمَّا إِلَى قِيَاسٍ صَحِيحٍ عَلَى أَصْلٍ صَحِيحٍ، وَصَارَتْ مَذَاهِبُ الْأَئِمَّةِ الْأَرْبَعَةِ بِحَمْدِ اللهِ الْآنَ عِنْدِي كَأَنَّهَا مَنْسُوجَةٌ مِنَ الشَّرِيعَةِ الْمُطَهَّرَةِ سَدَاهَا وَلُحْمَتُهَا، كَمَا يَعْرِفُ ذَلِكَ مَنْ طَالَعَ كِتَابِي «مُخْتَصَرَ السُّنَنِ الْكُبْرَى» لِلْإِمَامِ الْبَيْهَقِيِّ رَحِمَهُ اللهُ، وَكُلُّ مَنْ لَمْ يَطَّلِعْ عَلَى أَدِلَّةِ الْمَذَاهِبِ -كَمَا ذَكَرْنَا- فَلَا يَعْرِفُ يُمَيِّزُ مَسَائِلَ الرَّأْيِ مِنَ النَّصِّ، وَرُبَّمَا وَقَعَ فِي الْعَقَائِدِ الزَّائِغَةِ وَعَمِلَ بِالْمَذَاهِبِ الْبَاطِلَةِ.. إِلَّا أَنْ يُحْكِمَ التَّقَيُّدَ بِمَذْهَبٍ مُحَرَّرٍ.

وَقَدْ كَانَ الْإِمَامُ أَبُو الْقَاسِمِ الْجُنَيْدُ رَحِمَهُ اللهُ يَقُولُ: لَا يَكْمُلُ الرَّجُلُ عِنْدَنَا فِي طَرِيقِ اللهِ عَزَّجَلَّ حَتَّى يَكُونَ إِمَامًا فِي الْفِقْهِ وَالْحَدِيثِ وَالتَّصَوُّفِ، وَيُحَقِّقَ هَذِهِ الْعُلُومَ عَلَى أَهْلِهَا ا هـ.

fiqh, Hadith, and *taṣawwuf*, and verifies those sciences for its people."

Thus, it does not befit the one claiming knowledge of the Sacred Law to suffice himself with his own understanding without a *shaykh*, as had occurred with one of the people of our time. He busied himself with recording only that which he had understood while abandoning reading works with the scholars. Thus, he began to be on one side and the scholars were on the other. He was distanced from knowing the correct statements according to the scholars of his time; hence, he contradicted them (the correct statements), and no one benefitted from his knowledge. If he had made himself patient in studying with the *shuyūkh* until they had given him licenses to issue verdicts and to teach, they would have purified him, and people would have turned to him after his *shuyūkh*.

I heard our Shaykh, the Shaykh al-Islām, Zakariyyā al-Anṣārī ﵀ say:

> It is rare in any time that (the mastery of) the sciences of *fiqh*, Hadith, and *taṣawwuf* are joined in a single person. It has not reached us that (the mastery of) these three sciences joined in anyone from the time of al-Ṭībī, the author of *Ḥāshiyah al-Kashshāf*, to our time. If these three sciences are joined in a single person, he is the one who deserves to be called the Shaykh of the Ahl al-Sunnah wa al-Jamāʿah of his time. If someone refuses to call him that, he will have wronged him.

Thus, read, O brother, the books of the people of the Muhammadan Sunnah, the books of their scholars, the books of the jurisprudents (*uṣūliyyīn*), and the letters of the Sufis. It would be much better for you to travel the path of a *shaykh* out of fear that your tongue would slip and reveal something of the sciences of the inward domain, such that the scholars would

فَعُلِمَ أَنَّهُ لَا يَنْبَغِي لِمَنْ يَدَّعِي الْعِلْمَ بِالشَّرِيعَةِ أَنْ يَكْتَفِيَ بِمَا فَهِمَهُ هُوَ مِنْهَا بِغَيْرِ شَيْخٍ كَمَا وَقَعَ لِبَعْضِ أَهْلِ عَصْرِنَا، فَإِنَّهُ بِمُجَرَّدِ مَا صَارَ يُفْهَمُ اشْتَغَلَ بِالتَّأْلِيفِ وَتَرْكِ الْقِرَاءَةَ عَلَى الْعُلَمَاءِ.. فَصَارَ فِي جَانِبٍ وَالْعُلَمَاءُ فِي جَانِبٍ، وَبَعُدَ عَنْ مَعْرِفَةِ الرَّاجِحِ عِنْدَ عُلَمَاءِ زَمَانِهِ فَخَالَفُوهُ وَلَمْ يَنْتَفِعْ أَحَدٌ بِعِلْمِهِ، وَلَوْ أَنَّهُ صَبَرَ فِي الْقِرَاءَةِ عَلَى الْأَشْيَاخِ.. حَتَّى أَجَازُوهُ بِالْفَتْوَى وَالتَّدْرِيسِ لَزَكَّوْهُ، وَأَقْبَلَتِ النَّاسُ عَلَيْهِ بَعْدَ مَشَايِخِهِ، فَاعْلَمْ ذَلِكَ.

وَسَمِعْتُ شَيْخَنَا شَيْخَ الْإِسْلَامِ زَكَرِيَّا الْأَنْصَارِيَّ رَحِمَهُ اللهُ يَقُولُ: قَلَّ أَنْ يَجْتَمِعَ فِي شَخْصٍ فِي عَصْرٍ مِنَ الْأَعْصَارِ عِلْمُ الْفِقْهِ وَالْحَدِيثِ وَالتَّصَوُّفِ، قَالَ: وَلَمْ يَبْلُغْنَا أَنَّهَا اجْتَمَعَتْ فِي أَحَدٍ بَعْدَ الطِّيبِيِّ صَاحِبِ حَاشِيَةِ الْكَشَّافِ إِلَى وَقْتِنَا هَذَا، وَمَنِ اجْتَمَعَتْ فِيهِ هَذِهِ الْعُلُومُ الثَّلَاثَةُ.. فَهُوَ الَّذِي يَنْبَغِي أَنْ يُلَقَّبَ بِشَيْخِ أَهْلِ السُّنَّةِ وَالْجَمَاعَةِ فِي عَصْرِهِ، وَمَنْ لَمْ يُلَقِّبْهُ بِذَلِكَ.. فَقَدْ ظَلَمَهُ.

فَطَالِعْ يَا أَخِي كُتُبَ أَهْلِ السُّنَّةِ الْمُحَمَّدِيَّةِ وَكُتُبَ عُلَمَائِهَا وَكُتُبَ الْأُصُولِيِّينَ وَرَسَائِلَ الصُّوفِيَّةِ، وَلَوْ سَلَكْتَ الطَّرِيقَ عَلَى يَدِ شَيْخٍ خَوْفًا مِنْ أَنْ يَزِلَّ لِسَانُكَ بِشَيْءٍ مِنْ عُلُومِ الدَّائِرَةِ الْبَاطِنَةِ فَيُنْكِرَهُ عَلَيْكَ الْعُلَمَاءُ..

criticize you for it and (because of that) your benefit to people would be diminished.

However, if you know the limits of the scholars, only bring out to them those sciences which they will accept, and conceal from them that which they reject. For the rejection of the Sufis by the scholars is only due to the obscurity of the former's knowledge to the latter – their rejection of them does not therefore necessitate their statements as corrupt. It is like what Imam al-Ghazālī ﵀ said, "We used to criticize some people for certain matters until we found the truth with them. Allah (Exalted is He) said, "Rather, they rejected them for that which their knowledge had not encompassed and whose interpretation had not come to them."[36] He (Exalted is He) also said, "And if they are not guided by it, they say, 'This is an old lie.'"[37]

Imam al-Ghazālī's statement is supported by Imam Abū al-Qāsim al-Junayd ﵀: "I used to doubt their statement of 'The one who performs remembrance may reach a level in his remembrance where if he were to be struck in his face with a sword, he would not feel it', until I found the matter as they had stated it."

So, you should know that the soul always inclines, in action, towards that which is done by the majority because of the general prevalence of blind following. They give precedence to acting upon something because the vast majority of people are doing it, and they are at odds with that which only some people do. For the latter is like a path only a few people have taken. The traveller will not find anyone to accompany him in that action – hence, in his assessment, it will become lonely.

I heard Sīdī ʿAlī al-Khawwāṣ ﵀ say, "It is related that Sīdī Ibrāhīm al-Matbūlī ﵀ used to say, 'According to us, a person

---

(36) *Yūnus*, 39.
(37) *Al-Aḥqāf*, 11.

فَيَقِلُّ نفْعُكَ لِلنَّاسِ، بِخِلَافِ مَا إِذَا عَرَفْتَ سِيَاجَ الْعُلَمَاءِ فَتَصِيرَ تُخْرِجُ لَهُمْ مِنَ الْعُلُومِ مَا يَقْبَلُونَهُ، وَتَكْتُمَ عَنْهُمْ مَا لَا يَقْبَلُونَهُ؛ فَإِنَّ رَدَّ الْعُلَمَاءِ عَلَى الصُّوفِيَّةِ إِنَّمَا هُوَ لِدِقَّةِ مَدَارِكِ الصُّوفِيَّةِ عَلَيْهِمْ لَا غَيْرُ، فَلَا يَلْزَمُ مِنَ الرَّدِّ عَلَيْهِمْ فَسَادُ قَوْلِهِمْ فِي نَفْسِ الْأَمْرِ، كَمَا قَالَ الْغَزَالِيُّ رضي الله عنه: كُنَّا نُنْكِرُ عَلَى الْقَوْمِ أُمُورًا.. حَتَّى وَجَدْنَا الْحَقَّ مَعَهُمْ، قَالَ تَعَالَى: ﴿بَلْ كَذَّبُواْ بِمَا لَمْ يُحِيطُواْ بِعِلْمِهِۦ وَلَمَّا يَأْتِهِمْ تَأْوِيلُهُۥ﴾ [يونس: ٣٩]، وَقَالَ تَعَالَى: ﴿وَإِذْ لَمْ يَهْتَدُواْ بِهِۦ فَسَيَقُولُونَ هَٰذَآ إِفْكٌ قَدِيمٌ﴾ [الأحقاف: ١١] اهـ.

وَمِمَّا يُؤَيِّدُ كَلَامَ الْغَزَالِيِّ رَحِمَهُ اللَّهُ قَوْلُ الْإِمَامِ أَبِي الْقَاسِمِ الْجُنَيْدِ رَحِمَهُ اللَّهُ: كَانَ عِنْدِي وَقْفَةٌ فِي قَوْلِهِمْ (يَبْلُغُ الذَّاكِرُ فِي الذِّكْرِ إِلَى حَدٍّ لَوْ ضُرِبَ وَجْهُهُ بِالسَّيْفِ لَمْ يُحِسَّ)، إِلَى أَنْ وَجَدْنَا الْأَمْرَ كَمَا قَالُوا، فَعُلِمَ أَنَّ النُّفُوسَ لَمْ تَزَلْ تَحْتَجُّ وَتَمِيلُ فِي الْعَمَلِ إِلَى مَا عَلَيْهِ الْأَكْثَرُ بِحُكْمِ التَّقْلِيدِ، وَتَقَدَّمَ الْعَمَلُ بِهِ لِكَثْرَةِ الْعَامِلِينَ بِهِ بِخِلَافِ مَا عَلَيْهِ الْبَعْضُ، فَإِنَّهُ كَالطَّرِيقِ الَّتِي سَالِكُهَا قَلِيلٌ.. فَلَا يَجِدُ السَّالِكُ فِيهَا مَنْ يَسْتَأْنِسُ بِهِ فِي الْعَمَلِ، فَتَصِيرَ عِنْدَهُ وَحْشَةٌ، فَتَأَمَّلْ.

وَسَمِعْتُ سَيِّدِي عَلِيًّا الْخَوَّاصَ رَحِمَهُ اللَّهُ يَقُولُ: يُحْكَى عَنْ سَيِّدِي إِبْرَاهِيمَ الْمَتْبُولِيِّ رضي الله عنه أَنَّهُ كَانَ يَقُولُ: لَا يَكْمُلُ الرَّجُلُ عِنْدَنَا.. حَتَّى يَعْلَمَ حِكْمَةَ كُلِّ حَرْفٍ تَكَرَّرَ فِي الْقُرْآنِ، وَيُخْرِجَ مِنْهُ سَائِرَ الْأَحْكَامِ الشَّرْعِيَّةِ إِذَا شَاءَ.

does not become complete until he knows the wisdom of each letter that is repeated in the Qur'an and is able to extract from it all the rulings of the Sacred Law if he wished.'"

I also heard him ﷺ say:

> The slave does not reach the station of completion until he becomes an Imam in *tafsīr*, *fiqh*, and Hadith and [until he] travels the path of a *shaykh* who is a Knower of Allah (Exalted is He) so that he will know the path through experience, not by description and hearsay. At that point, he will enter into the Muhammadan Presence and know the rulings of the pure Sacred Law, distinguishing them from every heresy, for among the conditions of the Complete Saint is that his every movement and stillness, by night and by day, is weighed according to the Sacred Law.

I also heard him say, "Among the conditions of a Complete Saint is that he knows, by way of unveiling, all the statements of the *mujtahidūn*, distinguishing their statements that are only opinions from those that correspond in and of themselves to what is correct and what does not." I also heard him say, "The *shuyūkh* of earlier times used to say, 'It is not possible for the slave to lead in the Path until he knows that he has restricted himself to the Book and the Sunnah, and his outward is protected from all innovations. That is for him not to fall into any innovation and be followed in that by the disciples, misguiding himself and others. For in that case, he will be recorded as one of the Imams of misguidance.'"

I heard Sīdī ʿAlī al-Nabatītī ﷺ say to a *faqīh*:

> O my son, beware of acting upon any opinion that you find contradicts the authentic *aḥādīth* by saying, "This is the school of my Imam." For all the Imams have ex-

وَسَمِعْتُهُ رضي الله عنه يَقُولُ: لَا يَبْلُغُ الْعَبْدُ مَقَامَ الْكَمَالِ حَتَّى يَكُونَ إِمَامًا فِي التَّفْسِيرِ وَالْفِقْهِ وَالْحَدِيثِ، وَيَسْلُكُ الطَّرِيقَ عَلَى يَدِ شَيْخٍ عَارِفٍ بِاللهِ تَعَالَى.. حَتَّى يَصِيرَ يَعْرِفُ الطَّرِيقَ بِالذَّوْقِ لَا بِالْوَصْفِ وَالسَّمَاعِ، وَهُنَاكَ يَدْخُلُ الْحَضَرَاتِ الْمُحَمَّدِيَّةَ وَيَعْرِفُ أَحْكَامَ الشَّرِيعَةِ الْمُطَهَّرَةِ، وَيُمَيِّزُهَا مِنْ سَائِرِ الْبِدَعِ؛ لِأَنَّ الْكَامِلَ مِنْ شَرْطِهِ أَنْ لَا يَكُونَ لَهُ حَرَكَةٌ وَلَا سُكُونٌ فِي لَيْلٍ أَوْ نَهَارٍ، إِلَّا عَلَى الْمِيزَانِ الشَّرْعِيِّ.

وَسَمِعْتُهُ يَقُولُ أَيْضًا: مِنْ شَرْطِ الْكَامِلِ الاطِّلَاعُ مِنْ طَرِيقِ كَشْفِهِ عَلَى جَمِيعِ أَقْوَالِ الْمُجْتَهِدِينَ، وَيُمَيِّزُ الرَّأْيَ مِنْ أَقْوَالِهِمْ، وَيَعْرِفُ مَا وَافَقَ الصَّوَابَ فِي نَفْسِ الْأَمْرِ مِنْ أَقْوَالِهِمْ وَمَا خَالَفَهُ.

وَسَمِعْتُهُ أَيْضًا يَقُولُ: كَانَ الْأَشْيَاخُ الْمُتَقَدِّمُونَ يَقُولُونَ: لَا يَجُوزُ لِعَبْدٍ أَنْ يَتَصَدَّرَ لِلطَّرِيقِ إِلَّا إِنْ عَلِمَ مِنْ نَفْسِهِ التَّقَيُّدَ عَلَى الْكِتَابِ وَالسُّنَّةِ، وَيَكُونُ ظَاهِرُهُ مَحْفُوظًا مِنْ سَائِرِ الْبِدَعِ، وَذَلِكَ لِئَلَّا يَقَعَ فِي شَيْءٍ مِنَ الْبِدَعِ.. فَيَتَّبِعَهُ الْمُرِيدُونَ عَلَيْهِ فَيَضِلَّ فِي نَفْسِهِ وَيُضِلَّ غَيْرَهُ وَيُكْتَبَ مِنْ أَئِمَّةِ الضَّلَالِ. وَقَدْ بَسَطْنَا الْكَلَامَ عَلَى ذَمِّ الرَّأْيِ فِي أَوَائِلِ كِتَابِنَا «مُخْتَصَرِ السُّنَنِ الْكُبْرَى» لِلْبَيْهَقِيِّ رَحِمَهُ اللهُ، فَرَاجِعْهُ.

وَسَمِعْتُ سَيِّدِي عَلِيًّا النَّبْتِيتِيَّ رضي الله عنه يَقُولُ لِفَقِيهٍ: إِيَّاكَ يَا وَلَدِي؛ أَنْ تَعْمَلَ بِرَأْيٍ رَأَيْتَهُ مُخَالِفًا لِمَا صَحَّ فِي الْأَحَادِيثِ، وَتَقُولَ هَذَا مَذْهَبُ إِمَامِي، فَإِنَّ الْأَئِمَّةَ كُلَّهُمْ قَدْ تَبَرَّءُوا مِنْ أَقْوَالِهِمْ إِذَا خَالَفَتْ صَرِيحَ السُّنَّةِ، وَأَنْتَ مُقَلِّدٌ لِأَحَدِهِمْ بِلَا شَكٍّ، فَمَا لَكَ لَا تُقَلِّدُهُمْ فِي هَذَا الْقَوْلِ وَتَعْمَلُ بِالدَّلِيلِ؟ كَمَا تَقُولُ بِقَوْلِ إِمَامِكَ: (الِاحْتِمَالُ أَنْ يَكُونَ لَهُ دَلِيلٌ لَمْ تَطَّلِعْ أَنْتَ عَلَيْهِ)، وَذَلِكَ حَتَّى لَا تُعَطِّلَ الْعَمَلَ بِوَاحِدٍ مِنْهُمَا.

onerated themselves of their statements if they differ with the explicit Sunnah. Undoubtedly you follow one of them – so why do you not follow him in this statement and act upon the evidence, just as you say that your Imam's statement should be interpreted as having an evidence that you are unaware of? That will not deprive you of acting upon one of your statements.

The meaning of a blameworthy opinion, as coined by the People of the Sunnah, is that which does not conform to the principles of the pure Sacred Law. The meaning is not simply any opinion which is additional to the explicit Sunnah, such that it would include statements supported by the principles and evidence of the Sacred Law. No intelligent person would say that, as it would result in rejecting all the statements of the *mujtahidūn* that are not explicitly stated in the Sacred Law. As Imam al-Bayhaqī narrated in the chapter on legal verdicts in *al-Sunan al-Kubrā*: blameworthy opinions, when scholars use them, are everything that do not resemble a source.[38]

We have explained in detail the blameworthiness of opinion in the first part of our summary of *al-Sunan al-Kubrā* of al-Bayhaqī ﷺ – so, review that.

From that which we have related regarding the *mujtahid* Imams exonerating themselves of statements according to mere opinion in the religion of Allah is what Ibn ʿAbbās and ʿAtāʾ used to say, and were followed in that by Imam Mālik: "Everyone's statement can either be accepted or rejected, except the statement of the Messenger of Allah ﷺ."

Imam Abū Ḥanīfah ﷺ used to say, "It is impermissible for someone who does not know my evidence to give verdicts

(38) He then said, "Everything related to blameworthy opinions is interpreted in this meaning."

ثُمَّ إِنَّ الْمُرَادَ بِالرَّأْيِ الْمَذْمُومِ حَيْثُ أُطْلِقَ فِي كَلَامِ أَهْلِ السُّنَّةِ أَنْ لَا يُوَافِقَ قَوَاعِدَ الشَّرِيعَةِ الْمُطَهَّرَةِ، وَلَيْسَ الْمُرَادُ بِهِ كُلَّ مَا زَادَ عَلَى صَرِيحِ السُّنَّةِ مُطْلَقًا، حَتَّى يَشْمَلَ مَا شَهِدَتْ لَهُ قَوَاعِدُ الشَّرِيعَةِ وَأَدِلَّتُهَا؛ فَإِنَّ ذَلِكَ لَا يَقُولُ بِهِ عَاقِلٌ وَيَلْزَمُ مِنْهُ رَدُّ جَمِيعِ أَقْوَالِ الْمُجْتَهِدِينَ الَّتِي لَمْ تُصَرِّحْ بِهَا الشَّرِيعَةُ، وَلَا قَائِلَ بِذَلِكَ.

وَرَوَى الْإِمَامُ الْبَيْهَقِيُّ فِي بَابِ الْقَضَاءِ مِنَ «السُّنَنِ الْكُبْرَى» أَنَّ الرَّأْيَ الْمَذْمُومَ حَيْثُ أُطْلِقَ.. فَهُوَ كُلُّ مَا لَا يَكُونُ مُشَبَّهًا بِأَصْلٍ. قَالَ: وَعَلَى ذَلِكَ يُحْمَلُ كُلُّ مَا وَرَدَ فِي ذَمِّ الرَّأْيِ اهـ.

وَمِمَّا رَوَيْنَاهُ عَنِ الْأَئِمَّةِ الْمُجْتَهِدِينَ فِي تَبَرُّئِهِمْ مِنَ الْقَوْلِ بِالرَّأْيِ فِي دِينِ اللهِ، أَنَّ ابْنَ عَبَّاسٍ وَعَطَاءً وَتَبِعَهُمَا عَلَى ذَلِكَ الْإِمَامُ مَالِكٌ، كَانُوا يَقُولُونَ: كُلُّ أَحَدٍ مَأْخُوذٌ مِنْ كَلَامِهِ وَمَرْدُودٌ عَلَيْهِ إِلَّا رَسُولَ اللهِ ﷺ.

وَكَانَ الْإِمَامُ أَبُو حَنِيفَةَ رضى الله عنه يَقُولُ: حَرَامٌ عَلَى مَنْ لَا يَعْرِفُ دَلِيلِي أَنْ يُفْتِيَ بِكَلَامِي، وَكَانَ إِذَا أَفْتَى أَحَدًا بِفَتْوَى يَقُولُ: هَذَا رَأْيُ أَبِي حَنِيفَةَ، وَهُوَ أَحْسَنُ مَا قَدَرْنَا عَلَيْهِ، فَمَنْ جَاءَ بِأَحْسَنَ مِنْهُ فَهُوَ أَوْلَى بِالصَّوَابِ.

according to my statements." Whenever someone would transmit his verdict (regarding a matter), he would say, "That is the opinion of Abū Ḥanīfah. And it is the best of which we are capable. If someone comes up with better than it, he is closer to what is correct."

Imam al-Shāfiʿī ﵀ used to say, "When a Hadith is authentic, that is my opinion." He also used to say, "If you see any of my words contradicting the words of the Messenger ﷺ, act upon the statement of the Messenger of Allah ﷺ and part ways with mine." When al-Muzanī followed him in a matter, al-Shāfiʿī said to him, "Do not follow me in everything that I say, O Ibrāhīm; rather, investigate for yourself, for this is religion."

He also used to say on an issue, "If you see that its evidence is weak, yet there is an authentic Hadith on it, we will follow it. That would be more beloved to us than analogy."

In another narration, "If something is confirmed from the Prophet ﷺ – my mother and father be ransomed for him – it is not permitted for us to leave it. Nor is anyone else's statement a proof alongside it."

In another narration, he said, "No one – even if they are many – has any right to say anything when there is a statement of the Messenger of Allah ﷺ. There is also to be no evidence in analogical reasoning or anything else with it. For Allah (Exalted is He) did not allow anyone to speak alongside him – rather, He made his statement supersede all others."[39]

As for Imam Aḥmad ibn Ḥanbal ﵀, his situation in following the Sunnah is well known – in fact, he hid for three days during his trial. When he came out, it was said to him, "They are looking for you", to which he replied, "Indeed, the Messen-

(39) We have gathered all the Imam's statements regarding this in the introduction to our book *al-Manhaj al-Mubīn*.

وَكَانَ الْإِمَامُ الشَّافِعِيُّ رضى الله عنه يَقُولُ: إِذَا صَحَّ الْحَدِيثُ فَهُوَ مَذْهَبِي.

وَكَانَ يَقُولُ: إِذَا رَأَيْتُمْ كَلَامِي يُخَالِفُ كَلَامَ رَسُولِ اللهِ ﷺ، فَاعْمَلُوا بِكَلَامِ رَسُولِ اللهِ ﷺ وَاضْرِبُوا بِكَلَامِي الْحَائِطَ.

وَقَالَ لِلْمُزَنِيِّ حِينَ قَلَّدَهُ فِي مَسْأَلَةٍ: لَا تُقَلِّدْنِي يَا أَبَا إِبْرَاهِيمَ فِي كُلِّ مَا أَقُولُ، وَانْظُرْ لِنَفْسِكَ فَإِنَّهُ دِينٌ، وَكَانَ يَقُولُ فِي الْمَسْأَلَةِ إِذَا رَأَى دَلِيلَهَا ضَعِيفًا: لَوْ صَحَّ الْحَدِيثُ.. لَقُلْنَا بِهِ، وَكَانَ أَحَبَّ إِلَيْنَا مِنَ الْقِيَاسِ.

وَفِي رِوَايَةٍ: إِذَا ثَبَتَ عَنِ النَّبِيِّ ﷺ - بِأَبِي هُوَ وَأُمِّي - شَيْءٌ.. لَمْ يَحِلَّ لَنَا تَرْكُهُ، وَلَا حُجَّةَ لِأَحَدٍ مَعَهُ.

وَفِي رِوَايَةٍ: لَا حُجَّةَ لِأَحَدٍ مَعَ قَوْلِ رَسُولِ اللهِ ﷺ وَإِنْ كَثُرُوا.. لَا فِي قِيَاسٍ وَلَا فِي شَيْءٍ؛ فَإِنَّ اللهَ تَعَالَى لَمْ يَجْعَلْ لِأَحَدٍ مَعَهُ كَلَامًا، وَجَعَلَ قَوْلَهُ يَقْطَعُ كُلَّ قَوْلٍ.

وَقَدْ جَمَعْنَا كَلَامَ الْإِمَامِ كُلَّهُ فِي ذَلِكَ فِي مُقَدِّمَةِ كِتَابِنَا الْمُسَمَّى بِـ «الْمَنْهَجِ الْمُبِينِ».

وَأَمَّا الْإِمَامُ أَحْمَدُ بْنُ حَنْبَلٍ رَحِمَهُ اللهُ.. فَحَالُهُ مَعْلُومٌ فِي اتِّبَاعِ السُّنَّةِ، حَتَّى إِنَّهُ اخْتَفَى أَيَّامَ الْمِحْنَةِ ثَلَاثَةَ أَيَّامٍ ثُمَّ خَرَجَ، فَقِيلَ لَهُ: إِنَّهُمُ الْآنَ يَطْلُبُونَكَ، فَقَالَ: إِنَّ رَسُولَ اللهِ ﷺ لَمْ يَمْكُثْ فِي الْغَارِ حِينَ اخْتَفَى مِنَ الْكُفَّارِ أَكْثَرَ مِنْ ثَلَاثٍ.

ger of Allah ﷺ did not stay in the cave more than three days when he hid from the disbelievers."

It has also reached me that none of his legal statements were recorded, out of fear that his opinion would contradict the statement of the Lawgiver ﷺ.[40] He would say, "Can anyone say anything alongside the statement of Allah and His Messenger?" He also used to say, "Hardly anyone looks into the books of opinion except that there is some corruption in his heart." He had said as well, "If you are in a land in which the people of Hadith cannot distinguish the authentic *aḥādīth* from the defective, and they are of the people of opinion, ask the people of Hadith – and never ask the people of opinion about any matter."

He also used to say, "Do not follow anyone in your religion, for it is ugly for someone who has been given a lamp, by which he can light the way, to put it out and walk in darkness."[41]

He also used to say, "Do not follow me. Do not follow Mālik, nor al-Awzāʿī, nor al-Nakhaʿī, or anyone else. Rather, take your rulings from where they took theirs."

I say: This is interpreted to refer to one who has strong analytical skills. Otherwise, the scholars have explicitly stated that following a school of law is better for the one whose analytical skills are weak. Know that – and Allah knows best.

Imam Mālik narrated, conveying that the Messenger of Allah ﷺ said, "*I have left among you two matters. As long as you adhere to them, you will not go astray: the Book of Allah and the Sunnah of His Messenger.*"

Al-Tirmidhī narrated the Prophetic Hadith: "*I have left among you that which, if you adhere to them, you will never go*

(40) The entirety of his school has been built from the memory of his students.

(41) Perhaps he was alluding to the intellect, which Allah made a tool for distinguishing between matters and for insight into His religion.

وَبَلَغَنَا أَنَّهُ لَمْ يُدَوِّنْ لَهُ فِي الْفِقْهِ كَلَامًا قَطُّ خَوْفًا أَنْ يُخَالِفَ رَأْيُهُ كَلَامَ الشَّارِعِ ﷺ.

وَكَانَ يَقُولُ: أَوَ لِأَحَدٍ كَلَامٌ مَعَ اللهِ وَرَسُولِهِ؟ وَجَمِيعُ مَذْهَبِهِ مُلَفَّقٌ مِنْ صُدُورِ أَصْحَابِهِ.

وَكَانَ يَقُولُ: لَا يَكَادُ أَحَدٌ يَنْظُرُ فِي كُتُبِ الرَّأْيِ إِلَّا وَفِي قَلْبِهِ دَغَلٌ. وَكَانَ يَقُولُ: إِذَا رَأَيْتُمْ فِي بَلَدٍ صَاحِبَ حَدِيثٍ لَا يَدْرِي صَحِيحَهُ مِنْ سَقِيمِهِ وَهُنَاكَ صَاحِبُ رَأْيٍ، فَاسْأَلُوا مِنْ صَاحِبِ الْحَدِيثِ وَلَا تَسْأَلُوا مِنْ صَاحِبِ الرَّأْيِ.

وَكَانَ يَقُولُ: لَا تُقَلِّدُوا فِي دِينِكُمْ؛ فَإِنَّهُ قَبِيحٌ عَلَى مَنْ أُعْطِيَ شَمْعَةً يَسْتَضِيءُ بِهَا أَنْ يُطْفِئَهَا وَيَمْشِيَ فِي الظَّلَامِ، وَلَعَلَّهُ يُشِيرُ بِهِ إِلَى الْعَقْلِ الَّذِي جَعَلَهُ اللهُ آلَةً يُمَيِّزُ بِهَا بَيْنَ الْأُمُورِ وَيَسْتَبْصِرُ بِهَا فِي دِينِهِ.

وَكَانَ يَقُولُ: لَا تُقَلِّدُونِي وَلَا تُقَلِّدُوا مَالِكًا وَلَا الْأَوْزَاعِيَّ وَلَا النَّخَعِيَّ وَلَا غَيْرَهُمْ، وَخُذُوا الْأَحْكَامَ مِنْ حَيْثُ أَخَذُوا ا هـ .

قُلْتُ: وَهُوَ مَحْمُولٌ عَلَى مَنْ كَانَ فِيهِ قُوَّةُ النَّظَرِ، وَإِلَّا فَقَدْ صَرَّحَ الْعُلَمَاءُ بِأَنَّ التَّقْلِيدَ أَوْلَى لِضَعِيفِ النَّظَرِ. فَاعْلَمْ ذَلِكَ، وَاللهُ أَعْلَمُ.

وَرَوَى الْإِمَامُ مَالِكٌ بَلَاغًا أَنَّ رَسُولَ اللهِ ﷺ قَالَ: «تَرَكْتُ فِيكُمْ أَمْرَيْنِ لَنْ تَضِلُّوا مَا تَمَسَّكْتُمْ بِهِمَا: كِتَابَ اللهِ، وَسُنَّةَ رَسُولِهِ».

وَرَوَى التِّرْمِذِيُّ مَرْفُوعًا: «إِنِّي تَرَكْتُ فِيكُمْ مَا إِنْ أَخَذْتُمْ بِهِ لَنْ تَضِلُّوا: كِتَابَ اللهِ، وَعِتْرَتِي أَهْلَ بَيْتِي».

astray: [i] the Book of Allah and [ii] my descendants, the People of my House."[42] In another narration, he ﷺ said further, "*So, take care of how you treat them both after me.*"

In another Hadith from Abū Dāwūd and others, he ﷺ said, "*You must adhere to my Sunnah and the Sunnah of the rightly guided khulafāʾ. Adhere to them, and bite down on them with your canine teeth. Beware of newly invented matters, for every newly invented matter is an innovation, and every innovation is misguidance.*"

Al-Bukhārī narrated from Ibn Masʿūd that the Messenger of Allah ﷺ said, "*Indeed, the best of speech is the Book of Allah, and the best of guidance is the guidance of Muhammad ﷺ. The worst of matters are those newly invented.*"

He also narrated, "*Learn religion before the assumers.*"[43] He mentioned this narration in the beginning of *Kitāb al-Farāʾiḍ*, with a chain that stops at Ibn Masʿūd.

Al-Bukhārī, Muslim, and others narrated the following Prophetic Hadith: "*If someone introduces into this affair of ours that which is not from it, it will be rejected.*" Abū Dāwūd also narrated a Prophetic Hadith related to it: "*If someone parts from the assembly of Muslims a handspan, he will have removed the yoke of Islam from his neck.*"

We will mention a good number of *aḥādīth* narrated on boasting one's knowledge in the covenant after this, if Allah (Exalted is He) so wills. And Allah (Exalted is He) knows best.

---

(42) The meaning of 'the People of his House' are the scholars among them, such as ʿAlī, Ibn ʿAbbās, al-Ḥasan and al-Ḥusayn. And Allah knows best.

(43) By "assumers", he meant those who speak about the religion of Allah based on assumptions.

زَادَ فِي رِوَايَةٍ: «فَانْظُرُوا كَيْفَ تَخْلُفُونِي فِيهِمَا».

وَالْمُرَادُ بِأَهْلِ بَيْتِهِ؛ الْعُلَمَاءُ مِنْهُمْ.. كَعَلِيٍّ وَابْنِ عَبَّاسٍ وَالْحَسَنِ وَالْحُسَيْنِ. وَاللهُ أَعْلَمُ.

وَفِي حَدِيثِ أَبِي دَاوُدَ وَغَيْرِهِ مَرْفُوعًا: «فَعَلَيْكُمْ بِسُنَّتِي وَسُنَّةِ الْخُلَفَاءِ الرَّاشِدِينَ الْمَهْدِيِّينَ، تَمَسَّكُوا بِهَا وَعَضُّوا عَلَيْهَا بِالنَّوَاجِذِ، وَإِيَّاكُمْ وَمُحْدَثَاتِ الْأُمُورِ؛ فَإِنَّ كُلَّ مُحْدَثٍ بِدْعَةٌ، وَكُلَّ بِدْعَةٍ ضَلَالَةٌ».

وَرَوَى الْبُخَارِيُّ عَنِ ابْنِ مَسْعُودٍ أَنَّ رَسُولَ اللهِ ﷺ قَالَ: «إِنَّ أَحْسَنَ الْحَدِيثِ كِتَابُ اللهِ، وَأَحْسَنُ الْهَدْيِ هَدْيُ مُحَمَّدٍ ﷺ، وَشَرَّ الْأُمُورِ مُحْدَثَاتُهَا».

وَرَوَى أَيْضًا: «تَعَلَّمُوا الْعِلْمَ قَبْلَ الظَّانِّينَ». أَيِ: الَّذِينَ يَتَكَلَّمُونَ فِي دِينِ اللهِ بِالظَّنِّ، ذَكَرَهُ فِي أَوَّلِ كِتَابِ الْفَرَائِضِ مَوْقُوفًا عَلَى ابْنِ مَسْعُودٍ.

وَرَوَى الشَّيْخَانِ وَغَيْرُهُمَا مَرْفُوعًا: «مَنْ أَحْدَثَ فِي أَمْرِنَا هَذَا مَا لَيْسَ فِيهِ فَهُوَ رَدٌّ».

وَرَوَى أَبُو دَاوُدَ مَرْفُوعًا: «مَنْ فَارَقَ الْجَمَاعَةَ شِبْرًا فَقَدْ خَلَعَ رِبْقَةَ الْإِسْلَامِ مِنْ عُنُقِهِ».

وَسَيَأْتِي جُمْلَةٌ مِنَ الْأَحَادِيثِ الْوَارِدَةِ فِي الرِّيَاءِ فِي الْعِلْمِ فِي الْعَهْدِ الَّذِي عَقِبَهُ إِنْ شَاءَ اللهُ تَعَالَى، وَاللهُ تَعَالَى أَعْلَمُ.

The Prohibition of Answering Questions Pertaining to Sacred Knowledge Unless We Know That We and the Petitioner Are Sincere

A general covenant was taken from us by the Messenger of Allah ﷺ that we would not respond to any petitioner on any issue of knowledge unless we know ourselves and the petitioner to be sincere. If we do not know that, we should delay answering until we know that we are sincere – even if we were to wait a year or more – because investigating knowledge without sincerity is sinful. If we are sincere, yet the petitioner is not, we do not assist him in that issue.

If we know that we are prone to boasting our knowledge, our method is to then struggle to rid ourselves of conceit. We should also command our brethren to that and teach them the method of accomplishing it. When Sufyān al-Thawrī ﷺ was criticized for not sitting to teach people knowledge, he said, "By Allah! If we had known that they sought the Countenance of Allah the Exalted through knowledge, we would have gone to teach them in their houses. However, they seek knowledge to dispute with people and to practise it as a profession to obtain their livelihood."

Al-Fuḍayl ibn ʿIyāḍ ﷺ used to say, "If a person's intention is correct in seeking knowledge, he would only take from it that which he needs and can act upon. However, people have learned it for a reason apart from acting upon it."

It is related that Sufyān al-Thawrī entered upon al-Fuḍayl one day and said, "O Abū ʿAlī! Exhort us with a sermon."

Al-Fuḍayl responded:

> How can I exhort you, O gathering of scholars? You used to be lamps by which the lands were illuminated – then you became darkness. You were stars by which people were guided through the darkness of ignorance

أُخِذَ عَلَيْنَا الْعَهْدُ الْعَامُّ مِنْ رَسُولِ اللهِ ﷺ أَنْ لَا نُجِيبَ سَائِلًا سَأَلَنَا عَنْ مَسْأَلَةٍ فِي الْعِلْمِ إِلَّا إِنْ عَلِمْنَا مِنْ أَنْفُسِنَا وَمِنَ السَّائِلِ الْإِخْلَاصَ، فَإِنْ لَمْ نَعْلَمْ ذَلِكَ.. تَرَبَّصْنَا بِالْجَوَابِ، وَلَوْ مَكَثْنَا سَنَةً وَأَكْثَرَ.. حَتَّى نَجِدَ إِخْلَاصًا؛ لِأَنَّ الْخَوْضَ فِي الْعِلْمِ بِلَا إِخْلَاصٍ مَعْصِيَةٌ، وَبِتَقْدِيرِ إِخْلَاصِنَا فِي الْعِلْمِ دُونَ السَّائِلِ فَلَا نُسَاعِدُهُ عَلَيْهِ. وَطَرِيقُنَا إِذَا عَلِمْنَا مِنْ أَنْفُسِنَا الرِّيَاءَ فِي الْعِلْمِ أَنْ نُجَاهِدَ أَنْفُسَنَا عَلَى التَّخَلُّصِ مِنَ الرِّيَاءِ فِيهِ وَالْإِعْجَابِ بِهِ، وَنَأْمُرَ بِذَلِكَ إِخْوَانَنَا ثُمَّ نُعَلِّمَهُمْ بَعْدَ ذَلِكَ.

وَكَانَ سُفْيَانُ الثَّوْرِيُّ رَضِيَ اللهُ عَنْهُ إِذَا لَامُوهُ عَلَى عَدَمِ جُلُوسِهِ لِتَعْلِيمِ النَّاسِ الْعِلْمَ يَقُولُ: وَاللهِ؛ لَوْ عَلِمْنَا مِنْهُمْ أَنَّهُمْ يَطْلُبُونَ بِالْعِلْمِ وَجْهَ اللهِ الْعَظِيمِ.. لَأَتَيْنَاهُمْ فِي بُيُوتِهِمْ وَعَلَّمْنَاهُمْ، وَلَكِنَّهُمْ يَطْلُبُونَ الْعِلْمَ لِيُجَادِلُوا بِهِ النَّاسَ، وَيَحْتَرِفُوا بِهِ أَمْرَ مَعَاشِهِمْ.

وَكَانَ الْفُضَيْلُ بْنُ عِيَاضٍ رضى الله عنه يَقُولُ: لَوْ صَحَّتِ النِّيَّةُ فِي الْعِلْمِ.. لَمْ يَكُنْ عَمَلٌ يُقَدَّمُ عَلَيْهِ إِلَّا الْعَمَلَ وَمَا يُحْتَاجُ مِنْهُ، وَلَكِنْ تَعَلَّمُوهُ لِغَيْرِ الْعَمَلِ.

وَحُكِيَ أَنَّ سُفْيَانَ الثَّوْرِيَّ دَخَلَ عَلَى الْفُضَيْلِ يَوْمًا فَقَالَ: يَا أَبَا عَلِيٍّ؛ عِظْنَا بِمَوْعِظَةٍ، فَقَالَ الْفُضَيْلُ: وَمَاذَا أَعِظُكُمْ؟ كُنْتُمْ مَعَاشِرَ الْعُلَمَاءِ سُرُجًا يُسْتَضَاءُ بِكُمْ فِي الْبِلَادِ.. فَصِرْتُمْ ظُلْمَةً، وَكُنْتُمْ نُجُومًا يُهْتَدَى بِكُمْ فِي ظُلُمَاتِ الْجَهْلِ.. فَصِرْتُمْ حَيْرَةً، يَأْتِي أَحَدُكُمْ إِلَى هَؤُلَاءِ الْأُمَرَاءِ، فَيَجْلِسُ عَلَى فِرَاشِهِمْ وَيَأْكُلُ مِنْ طَعَامِهِمْ، ثُمَّ بَعْدَ ذَلِكَ يَدْخُلُ الْمَسْجِدَ، فَيَجْلِسُ يُدَرِّسُ الْعِلْمَ وَالْحَدِيثَ وَيَعِظُ النَّاسَ وَيَقُولُ: حَدَّثَنِي فُلَانٌ عَنْ فُلَانٍ عَنِ النَّبِيِّ ﷺ، وَاللهِ؛ مَا هَكَذَا كَانَ مَنْ يَحْمِلُ الْعِلْمَ، فَبَكَى سُفْيَانُ، ثُمَّ انْصَرَفَ.

> – then you became confused. One of you will go to one of these people of authority, sit on their couches, and eat their food. Afterwards, he goes to the mosque and teaches people knowledge and Hadith, exhorting and saying to them, "So-and-so narrated to me that the Prophet ﷺ ..." – by Allah, one does not bear knowledge in this way!

Sufyān then began to cry and went away.

Al-Fuḍayl ibn ʿIyāḍ also used to say, "If you see a scholar or a worshipper becoming happy at being attributed knowledge or piety in a gathering of rulers and people of authority, know that he is a show-off."

Sufyān ibn ʿUyaynah used to say:

> Among the signs of showing off in seeking knowledge is the student thinking that he is better than the masses due to knowledge. If anyone does that, his heart dies. Knowledge does not enliven the heart of its host unless he is sincere in it – if he becomes haughty with it, his face is turned towards the world, and his back turned away from the presence of Allah ﷻ.

You should know that the breeze of presence is that by which the heart comes alive. Hence, turning towards it gives life; turning away from it causes death, just as how the hearts of the disbelievers died when they turned away from Allah ﷻ.

Sufyān ibn ʿUyaynah also used to say, "If you see that a seeker of knowledge increases in disputation and avarice for this world with each increase in knowledge, do not teach him."

Kaʿb ibn al-Aḥbār used to say, "There will come a time where the ignorant among the people will possess knowledge. They will use it to vie with one another for nearness to the rulers, just as they vie with one another for women or as

وَكَانَ الْفُضَيْلُ بْنُ عِيَاضٍ رضى الله عنه يَقُولُ: إِذَا رَأَيْتُمُ الْعَالِمَ أَوِ الْعَابِدَ يَنْشَرِحُ لِذِكْرِهِ بِالْعِلْمِ وَالصَّلَاحِ فِي مَجَالِسِ الْأُمَرَاءِ وَالْأَكَابِرِ، فَاعْلَمُوا أَنَّهُ مُرَاءٍ.

وَكَانَ سُفْيَانُ بْنُ عُيَيْنَةَ رضى الله عنه يَقُولُ: مِنْ عَلَامَةِ الرِّيَاءِ فِي طَلَبِ الْعِلْمِ؛ أَنْ يَخْطِرَ فِي بَالِهِ أَنَّهُ خَيْرٌ مِنَ الْعَوَامِّ لِأَجْلِ الْعِلْمِ، وَمَنْ فَعَلَ ذَلِكَ.. مَاتَ قَلْبُهُ؛ فَإِنَّ الْعِلْمَ لَا يُحْيِي قَلْبَ صَاحِبِهِ إِلَّا إِنْ أَخْلَصَ فِيهِ، وَذَلِكَ أَنَّهُ إِذَا تَكَبَّرَ بِهِ.. صَارَ وَجْهُهُ لِلدُّنْيَا، وَظَهْرُهُ لِحَضْرَةِ اللهِ عَزَّوَجَلَّ.

وَاعْلَمْ أَنَّ رَائِحَةَ الْحَضْرَةِ هِيَ الَّتِي بِهَا حَيَاةُ الْقُلُوبِ، فَالْإِقْبَالُ عَلَيْهَا يُحْيِي وَالْإِدْبَارُ عَنْهَا يُمِيتُ، كَمَا مَاتَ قَلْبُ الْكُفَّارِ حِينَ أَعْرَضُوا عَنِ اللهِ عز وجل. وَكَانَ يَقُولُ أَيْضًا: إِذَا رَأَيْتُمْ طَالِبَ الْعِلْمِ.. كُلَّمَا ازْدَادَ عِلْمًا ازْدَادَ جِدَالًا وَرَغْبَةً فِي الدُّنْيَا، فَلَا تُعَلِّمُوهُ.

وَكَانَ كَعْبُ الْأَحْبَارِ رضى الله عنه يَقُولُ: سَيَأْتِي عَلَى النَّاسِ زَمَانٌ.. يَتَعَلَّمُ جُهَّالُهُمُ الْعِلْمَ، وَيَتَغَايَرُونَ بِهِ عَلَى الْقُرْبِ مِنَ الْأُمَرَاءِ، كَمَا يَتَغَايَرُونَ عَلَى النِّسَاءِ، أَوْ كَمَا يَتَغَايَرُ النِّسَاءُ عَلَى الرِّجَالِ، فَذَلِكَ حَظُّهُمْ مِنْ عِلْمِهِمْ.

women vie with one another over men. That will be the reward for their knowledge."

Ṣāliḥ al-Mārī ﷺ used to say, "From the signs of sincerity in seeking knowledge is that a person is delighted whenever described as ignorant or showing off. Similarly, from the signs of showing off is that one is angered by that." He also used to say, "It is possible that a person's knowledge is provision for his journey to the Fire. Therefore it does not befit anyone to be happy over his knowledge until he passes over the Ṣirāṭ. At that point, he will know the reality of whether his knowledge is a proof for or against him."

Ibrāhīm ibn Adham ﷺ used to say, "Knowledge calls for action. If responded to, it stays – if not, it leaves." He also used to say, "I passed by a stone on which was written, 'Turn me over and you will learn something.' So, I turned it over, and there was written on it: 'You do not act upon what you know, so how can you seek knowledge of that which you do not know?'" He also used to say, "Seek knowledge in order to act upon it. Many people were beguiled in their seeking until their knowledge became like mountains, yet their actions like specks of dust."

Dhū al-Nūn al-Miṣrī ﷺ used to say, "We met some people who were increased in abstinence from this world and decreased in its enjoyment with each increase in knowledge." He also used to say, "How can a student of knowledge act upon his knowledge without performing *tahajjud* in any part of the night, and instead sleeps during it – the time of the distribution of spoils, of the opening of the treasuries, and of the distribution of knowledge and gifts?"

ʿUmar ibn ʿAbd al-ʿAzīz ﷺ used to say, "How can you teach these people knowledge when they consume the unlawful and the doubtful? By Allah! They are like dead people being consumed by fire. Were they alive, they would have felt in their bellies the pain of the fire of this abode."

وَكَانَ صَالِحٌ الْمُرِّيُّ رضى الله عنه يَقُولُ: مِنْ عَلَامَةِ إِخْلَاصِ طَالِبِ الْعِلْمِ أَنْ يَنْشَرِحَ صَدْرُهُ كُلَّمَا وَصَفَهُ النَّاسُ بِالْجَهْلِ وَالرِّيَاءِ وَالسُّمْعَةِ، كَمَا أَنَّ مِنْ عَلَامَةِ رِيَائِهِ انْقِبَاضَ قَلْبِهِ مِنْ ذَلِكَ. وَكَانَ يَقُولُ: احْذَرُوا عَالِمَ الدُّنْيَا أَنْ تُجَالِسُوهُ.. خَوْفًا أَنْ يَفْتِنَكُمْ بِزَخْرَفَةِ لِسَانِهِ وَمَدْحِهِ لِلْعِلْمِ وَأَهْلِهِ مِنْ غَيْرِ عَمَلٍ بِهِ. وَكَانَ يَقُولُ: رُبَّمَا كَانَ عِلْمُ الْعَالِمِ زَادَهُ إِلَى النَّارِ، فَلَا يَنْبَغِي لِأَحَدٍ أَنْ يَفْرَحَ بِعِلْمِهِ إِلَّا بَعْدَ مُجَاوَزَةِ الصِّرَاطِ، وَهُنَاكَ يَعْلَمُ حَقِيقَةَ عِلْمِهِ.. هَلْ هُوَ حُجَّةٌ لَهُ أَوْ عَلَيْهِ.

وَكَانَ إِبْرَاهِيمُ بْنُ أَدْهَمَ رضى الله عنه يَقُولُ: يَهْتِفُ الْعِلْمُ بِالْعَمَلِ.. فَإِنْ أَجَابَهُ، وَإِلَّا ارْتَحَلَ. وَكَانَ يَقُولُ: مَرَرْتُ بِحَجَرٍ مَكْتُوبٍ عَلَيْهِ: (قَلِّبْنِي تَعْتَبِرْ).. فَقَلَّبْتُهُ، فَإِذَا عَلَيْهِ مَكْتُوبٌ: (أَنْتَ بِمَا تَعْلَمُ لَا تَعْمَلُ، فَكَيْفَ تَطْلُبُ عِلْمَ مَا لَا تَعْلَمُ)؟ وَكَانَ يَقُولُ: اطْلُبُوا الْعِلْمَ لِلْعَمَلِ؛ فَإِنَّ أَكْثَرَ النَّاسِ قَدْ غَلِطُوا فِي ذَلِكَ، فَصَارَ عِلْمُهُمْ كَالْجِبَالِ، وَعَمَلُهُمْ كَالْهَبَاءِ.

وَكَانَ ذُو النُّونِ الْمِصْرِيُّ رضى الله عنه يَقُولُ: أَدْرَكْنَا النَّاسَ وَأَحَدُهُمْ كُلَّمَا ازْدَادَ عِلْمًا ازْدَادَ فِي الدُّنْيَا زُهْدًا وَتَقَلُّلًا مِنْ أَمْتِعَتِهَا، وَنَرَاهُمُ الْيَوْمَ كُلَّمَا ازْدَادَ أَحَدُهُمْ عِلْمًا ازْدَادَ فِي الدُّنْيَا رَغْبَةً وَتَكْثِيرًا لِأَمْتِعَتِهَا. وَكَانَ يَقُولُ: كَيْفَ يَكُونُ طَالِبُ الْعِلْمِ عَامِلًا بِهِ وَهُوَ يَنَامُ وَقْتَ الْغَنَائِمِ، وَوَقْتَ فَتْحِ الْخَزَائِنِ، وَوَقْتَ نَشْرِ الْعُلُومِ وَالْمَوَاهِبِ فِي الْأَسْحَارِ، لَا يَتَهَجَّدُ مِنَ اللَّيْلِ سَاعَةً. وَكَانَ عُمَرُ بْنُ عَبْدِ الْعَزِيزِ رضى الله عنه يَقُولُ: كَيْفَ تُعَلِّمُونَ هَؤُلَاءِ الْعِلْمَ.. وَهُمْ يَأْكُلُونَ مِنَ الْحَرَامِ وَالشُّبُهَاتِ؟ وَاللهِ؛ إِنَّهُمْ كَالْأَمْوَاتِ الَّذِينَ يَرْتَعُونَ فِي النَّارِ، وَلَوْ أَنَّهُمْ كَانُوا أَحْيَاءً.. لَوَجَدُوا أَلَمَ النَّارِ فِي بُطُونِهِمْ مِنْ هَذِهِ الدَّارِ.

Manṣūr ibn al-Muʿtamir ﵀ used to say to the scholars of his time, "You are not scholars, you are only followers with knowledge: one of you hears an issue and only relates it. Were you to act upon your knowledge, you would repress your hunger, for all knowledge urges you to be cautious in your food and clothes to such an extent that none of you would find a loaf of bread to eat or a cloth to cover his private parts. By Allah, I wore a straw mat as a garment until I found a robe that was lawful!"

Rābiʿ ibn Khuthaym used to say, "How can a scholar show off his knowledge while he knows that any part of it wherein the Countenance of Allah isn't sought will be effaced?" Any time an *amīr* caught him by surprise and entered upon him during his lesson, he would become depressed because of it. Furthermore, if it reached him that one of the *umarā'* intended to visit him, he would not teach that day, fearing that the *amīr* would see him in the large gathering of his lesson. He also used to say, "From the signs of someone sincere in his knowledge is dejection within himself whenever someone of the ruling class praises him, [and he is as] agitated as he would feel with someone who discovered him committing adultery."

Al-Ḥasan al-Baṣrī used to say, "It is horrid enough that the seekers of knowledge in this age eat to their fill of what is lawful – how would it be, then, with the unlawful? By Allah, I would love for my food to become like a baked brick in my stomach, sufficing me until I died. For it has reached us that, when submerged in water, it (the baked brick) remains for three hundred or more years." He also used to say, "The caution of the scholars should be in doubtful things. However, their caution these days is only from apparent sin." He also used to say, "It has reached us that in the final age, there will be men who will learn knowledge for other than the sake of Allah, only so that it will not be lost. Its weight will burden them on the Day of Judgement; so let each person beware of (the evil of) his own ego."

وَكَانَ مَنْصُورُ بْنُ الْمُعْتَمِرِ رضي الله عنه يَقُولُ لِعُلَمَاءِ زَمَانِهِ: لَسْتُمْ عُلَمَاءَ، وَإِنَّمَا أَنْتُمْ مُقَلِّدُونَ بِالْعِلْمِ.. يَسْمَعُ أَحَدُكُمُ الْمَسْأَلَةَ وَيَحْكِيهَا فَقَطْ، وَلَوْ أَنَّكُمْ كُنْتُمْ تَعْمَلُونَ بِعِلْمِكُمْ.. لَتَجَرَّعْتُمُ الْغُصَصَ؛ فَإِنَّ الْعِلْمَ كُلَّهُ مُحَثُّكُمْ عَلَى التَّوَرُّعِ فِي الْمَأْكَلِ وَالْمَلْبَسِ، حَتَّى لَا يَجِدَ أَحَدُكُمْ رَغِيفًا يَأْكُلُهُ، وَلَا خِرْقَةً يُوَارِي بِهَا عَوْرَتَهُ، وَاللهِ؛ لَقَدْ لَبِسْتُ الْحَصِيرَ كَذَا كَذَا شَهْرًا.. حَتَّى وَجَدْتُ ثَوْبًا مِنْ حَلَالٍ.

وَكَانَ الرَّبِيعُ بْنُ خُثَيْمٍ يَقُولُ: كَيْفَ يُرَائِي الْعَالِمُ بِمَا يَعْلَمُ.. مَعَ عِلْمِهِ بِأَنَّ كُلَّ مَا لَا يُبْتَغَى بِهِ وَجْهُ اللهِ يَضْمَحِلُّ؟ وَكَانَ إِذَا دَخَلَ عَلَيْهِ أَمِيرٌ عَلَى غَفْلَةٍ.. وَهُوَ يُدَرِّسُ الْعِلْمَ يَغْتَمُّ لِذَلِكَ. وَكَانَ إِذَا بَلَغَهُ أَنَّ أَحَدًا مِنَ الْأُمَرَاءِ عَازِمٌ عَلَى زِيَارَتِهِ.. لَا يُدَرِّسُ عِلْمًا ذَلِكَ الْيَوْمَ خَوْفًا أَنْ يَرَاهُ ذَلِكَ الْأَمِيرُ وَهُوَ فِي مَحْفِلِ دَرْسِهِ الْعَظِيمِ. وَكَانَ يَقُولُ: مِنْ عَلَامَةِ الْمُخْلِصِ فِي عِلْمِهِ؛ أَنْ يَنْقَبِضَ فِي نَفْسِهِ إِذَا مَدَحَهُ الْأَكَابِرُ، وَيَتَأَثَّرَ كَمَا يَتَأَثَّرُ مِمَّنِ اطَّلَعَ عَلَيْهِ وَهُوَ يَزْنِي.

وَكَانَ الْحَسَنُ الْبَصْرِيُّ يَقُولُ: يَقْبُحُ عَلَى طَالِبِ الْعِلْمِ أَنْ يَشْبَعَ مِنَ الْحَلَالِ فِي هَذَا الزَّمَانِ، فَكَيْفَ بِمَنْ يَشْبَعُ مِنَ الْحَرَامِ؟ وَاللهِ؛ إِنِّي أَوَدُّ أَنَّ الْأَكْلَةَ تَصِيرُ فِي بَطْنِي كَالْآجُرَّةِ فَتَكْفِينِي حَتَّى أَمُوتَ؛ فَإِنَّهُ بَلَغَنَا أَنَّهَا تَمْكُثُ فِي الْمَاءِ ثَلَاثَمِائَةِ عَامٍ وَأَكْثَرَ. وَكَانَ يَقُولُ: وَرَعُ الْعُلَمَاءِ إِنَّمَا يَكُونُ فِي الشُّبُهَاتِ، وَإِنَّمَا وَرَعُهُمُ الْيَوْمَ عَنِ الْمَعَاصِي الظَّاهِرَةِ. وَكَانَ يَقُولُ: بَلَغَنَا أَنَّهُ يَأْتِي آخِرَ الزَّمَانِ رِجَالٌ يَتَعَلَّمُونَ الْعِلْمَ لِغَيْرِ اللهِ كَيْ لَا يَضِيعَ، ثُمَّ يَكُونُ عَلَيْهِمْ تَبِعَتُهُ يَوْمَ الْقِيَامَةِ، فَلْيُفَتِّشِ الْإِنْسَانُ نَفْسَهُ.

وَكَانَ بَكْرُ بْنُ عَبْدِ اللهِ الْمُزَنِيُّ رضي الله عنه يَقُولُ: عَلَامَةُ الْمُرَائِي

Bakr ibn ʿAbdullāh al-Muzanī ﵀ used to say, "The sign of someone boasting his knowledge is that he encourages people to learn so that they may learn from him – but would not do the same if said learning was sought from someone else."

ʿAbdullāh ibn al-Mubārak ﵀ used to say, "In this age, the reciters have been overcome by consumption of the unlawful and the doubtful until they are immersed in the desires of their bellies and private parts. Beware of sitting with them – they who trap the world with their knowledge as a net." He also used to say, "If it were not for a deficiency that had affected the people of Hadith and *fiqh*, they would have been the best of people. However, they began to take knowledge as a profession to obtain the world. Thusly were they humiliated in the Heavens and the Earth." He also used to say, "It is from a man's intelligence that he only seeks to increase his knowledge after he has acted upon what he knows, for knowledge is only sought for action."

Al-Shāfiʿī ﵀ used to say, "Seek knowledge while you are crying; by its increase, you only gain more proof against yourself on the Day of Judgement."

When Bishr al-Ḥāfī abandoned gathering in order to narrate Hadith, some people said to him, "What will you say to your Lord when He asks you on the Day of Judgement, 'Why did you not teach My servants?'" He said to them: "I will say, 'My Lord! You commanded me to be sincere in that, and I did not find myself to be sincere.'"

Sufyān al-Thawrī used to say, "If you see a seeker of knowledge eating a variety of foods and eating whatever he finds, do not teach him anything. For the one who does not act upon his knowledge is similar to the bitter apple tree (*ḥanẓal*): it increases in bitterness whenever increased in its nourishment with water." He also used to say, "If a slave were to learn all knowledge and then worship Allah (Exalted is He) until he became like a stiff post or a worn-out water skin, yet did not

بِعِلْمِهِ؛ أَنْ يُرَغِّبَ النَّاسَ فِي الْعِلْمِ لِيَقْرَؤُوا عَلَيْهِ، ثُمَّ إِنَّهُ إِذَا شَاوَرَهُ أَحَدٌ فِي الْقِرَاءَةِ عَلَى غَيْرِهِ.. لَا يُرَغِّبُهُ كُلَّ ذَلِكَ التَّرْغِيبِ.

وَكَانَ عَبْدُ اللهِ بْنُ الْمُبَارَكِ رضى الله عنه يَقُولُ: قَدْ غَلَبَ عَلَى الْقُرَّاءِ فِي هَذَا الزَّمَانِ أَكْلُ الْحَرَامِ وَالشُّبُهَاتِ، حَتَّى أَنَّهُمْ غَرِقُوا فِي شَهْوَةِ بُطُونِهِمْ وَفُرُوجِهِمْ، وَاتَّخَذُوا عِلْمَهُمْ شَبَكَةً يَصْطَادُونَ بِهَا الدُّنْيَا، فَإِيَّاكُمْ وَمُجَالَسَتَهُمْ. وَكَانَ يَقُولُ: لَوْلَا نَقْصٌ دَخَلَ عَلَى أَهْلِ الْحَدِيثِ وَالْفِقْهِ.. لَكَانُوا أَفْضَلَ النَّاسِ، وَلَكِنَّهُمْ صَارُوا يَحْتَرِفُونَ بِعِلْمِهِمْ وَيَصْطَادُونَ بِهِ الدُّنْيَا.. فَهَانُوا فِي مَلَكُوتِ السَّمَاوَاتِ وَالْأَرْضِ. وَكَانَ يَقُولُ: مِنْ عَقْلِ الرَّجُلِ أَنْ لَا يَطْلُبَ الزِّيَادَةَ مِنَ الْعِلْمِ إِلَّا إِذَا عَمِلَ بِمَا عَلِمَ، فَيَتَعَلَّمُ الْعِلْمَ كَيْ يَعْمَلَ بِهِ؛ إِذِ الْعِلْمُ إِنَّمَا يُطْلَبُ لِلْعَمَلِ.

وَكَانَ الشَّعْبِيُّ رضى الله عنه يَقُولُ: اطْلُبُوا الْعِلْمَ وَأَنْتُمْ تَبْكُونَ، فَإِنَّ أَحَدَكُمْ إِنَّمَا يُرِيدُ بِهِ زِيَادَةَ إِقَامَةِ الْحُجَّةِ عَلَى نَفْسِهِ يَوْمَ الْقِيَامَةِ.

وَلَمَّا تَرَكَ بِشْرٌ الْحَافِيُّ الْجُلُوسَ لِإِمْلَاءِ الْحَدِيثِ قَالُوا لَهُ: مَاذَا تَقُولُ لِرَبِّكَ إِذَا قَالَ لَكَ يَوْمَ الْقِيَامَةِ لِمَ لَا تُعَلِّمُ عِبَادِي الْعِلْمَ؟ فَقَالَ: أَقُولُ لَهُ يَا رَبِّ؛ قَدْ أَمَرْتَنِي فِيهِ بِالْإِخْلَاصِ، وَلَمْ أَجِدْ فِي نَفْسِي إِخْلَاصًا.

وَكَانَ سُفْيَانُ الثَّوْرِيُّ يَقُولُ: إِذَا رَأَيْتُمْ طَالِبَ الْعِلْمِ يَخْلِطُ فِي مَطْعَمِهِ، وَيَأْكُلُ كُلَّ مَا وَجَدَ.. فَلَا تُعَلِّمُوهُ الْعِلْمَ؛ فَإِنَّ مَنْ لَا يَعْمَلُ بِعِلْمِهِ شَبِيهٌ بِشَجَرِ الْحَنْظَلِ، كُلَّمَا ازْدَادَ رِيًّا بِالْمَاءِ.. ازْدَادَ مَرَارَةً. وَكَانَ يَقُولُ: لَوْ أَنَّ عَبْدًا تَعَلَّمَ الْعِلْمَ كُلَّهُ، ثُمَّ عَبَدَ اللهَ تَعَالَى حَتَّى يَصِيرَ كَالسَّارِيَةِ أَوِ الشَّنِّ الْبَالِي، ثُمَّ لَمْ يُفَتِّشْ عَلَى مَا يَدْخُلُ جَوْفَهُ أَحَلَالٌ هُوَ أَمْ حَرَامٌ.. مَا تَقَبَّلَ اللهُ مِنْهُ. وَكَانَ يَقُولُ: وَاللهِ؛ لَقَدْ أَدْرَكْنَا أَقْوَامًا يَرُوضُونَ الطَّالِبَ سِنِينَ كَثِيرَةً، وَلَا

discern with it the lawful or unlawful from what he eats, it will not be accepted by Allah." He also used to say, "By Allah! We met some people who would discipline the seeker of knowledge for many years without teaching him anything, until it became apparent to them that he had pious intentions in seeking knowledge."

ʿAbd al-Raḥmān ibn al-Qāsim used to say, "I served Imam Mālik ﷺ for twenty years: two years were spent learning knowledge, and the other eighteen on *adab*. I wish that I had spent the entirety of that time learning *adab*."

Imam al-Shāfiʿī ﷺ used to say, "Mālik ﷺ used to say, "O Muhammad, make your knowledge the salt to the flour that is your *adab*!"

Abū al-ʿIsmah said, "I spent the night with Imam Aḥmad, seeking (that he narrate to me) Hadith. He placed a container of water beside me for *tahajjud*. Coming for the dawn prayer, he found the container exactly how he had left it. He then asked me, 'Why have you come?' I said, 'I have come to seek Hadith.' He said, 'How can I teach you Hadith when you do not pray *tahajjud* at night?' Leave as you are.'"

ʿAbdullāh ibn al-Mubārak ﷺ used to say, "If someone bears the Qurʾan (in memory) and then inclines with his heart towards the world, he will have taken the signs of Allah in jest." He also used to say, "When a bearer of the Qurʾan disobeys his Lord, the Qurʾan calls out to him from his chest, 'I am not born for this reason. Where are my exhortations? Where are my prohibitions? Every letter of me says to you: Do not disobey your Lord.'"

Al-Nawawī ﷺ used to say, "You must be sincere in your knowledge so that Allah (Exalted is He) will benefit the servants by it." He also said, "It has never reached us about any scholar who did not act upon his knowledge and was seen after his death saying that Allah had forgiven him because of his knowledge." He also said, "One of the clearest proofs of boast-

يُعَلِّمُونَهُ شَيْئًا مِنَ الْعِلْمِ، حَتَّى يَظْهَرَ لَهُمْ صَلَاحُ نِيَّتِهِ فِي الْعِلْمِ. وَكَانَ عَبْدُ الرَّحْمَنِ بْنُ الْقَاسِمِ يَقُولُ: خَدَمْتُ الْإِمَامَ مَالِكًا رحمه الله تعالى عِشْرِينَ سَنَةً، فَكَانَ مِنْهَا سَنَتَانِ فِي الْعِلْمِ، وَثَمَانِيَةَ عَشَرَ سَنَةً فِي تَعْلِيمِ الْأَدَبِ، فَيَا لَيْتَنِي جَعَلْتُ الْمُدَّةَ كُلَّهَا أَدَبًا.

وَكَانَ الْإِمَامُ الشَّافِعِيُّ رَحِمَهُ اللَّهُ يَقُولُ: قَالَ لِي مَالِكٌ رَحِمَهُ اللَّهُ: يَا مُحَمَّدُ؛ اجْعَلْ عِلْمَكَ مِلْحًا، وَأَدَبَكَ دَقِيقًا.

وَقَالَ أَبُو عِصْمَةَ: بِتُّ لَيْلَةً عِنْدَ الْإِمَامِ أَحْمَدَ أَطْلُبُ الْحَدِيثَ، فَوَضَعَ لِي إِنَاءً فِيهِ مَاءٌ لِلتَّهَجُّدِ، فَجَاءَ إِلَى صَلَاةِ الصُّبْحِ فَوَجَدَ الْإِنَاءَ بِحَالِهِ، فَقَالَ لِي: لِمَاذَا جِئْتَ؟ فَقُلْتُ: جِئْتُ أَطْلُبُ الْحَدِيثَ، فَقَالَ: كَيْفَ أُعَلِّمُكَ الْحَدِيثَ وَلَيْسَ لَكَ تَهَجُّدٌ فِي اللَّيْلِ؟ اذْهَبْ لِحَالِ سَبِيلِكَ.

وَكَانَ عَبْدُ اللهِ بْنُ الْمُبَارَكِ رضى الله عنه يَقُولُ: مَنْ حَمَلَ الْقُرْآنَ ثُمَّ مَالَ بِقَلْبِهِ إِلَى الدُّنْيَا.. فَقَدِ اتَّخَذَ آيَاتِ اللهِ هُزُوًا وَلَعِبًا. وَكَانَ يَقُولُ: إِذَا عَصَى حَامِلُ الْقُرْآنِ رَبَّهُ.. نَادَاهُ الْقُرْآنُ مِنْ جَوْفِهِ: وَاللهِ؛ مَا لِهَذَا أُحْمَلُ، أَيْنَ مَوَاعِظِي وَزَوَاجِرِي؟ وَكُلُّ حَرْفٍ مِنِّي يَقُولُ لَكَ: لَا تَعْصِ رَبَّكَ.

وَكَانَ النَّوَوِيُّ رَحِمَهُ اللَّهُ يَقُولُ: عَلَيْكُمْ بِالْإِخْلَاصِ فِي الْعِلْمِ لِيَنْفَعَ اللَّهُ تَعَالَى بِهِ الْعِبَادَ، قَالَ: وَلَمْ يَبْلُغْنَا عَنْ أَحَدٍ مِنَ الْعُلَمَاءِ غَيْرِ الْعَامِلِينَ أَنَّهُ رُؤِيَ بَعْدَ مَوْتِهِ.. فَقَالَ: غَفَرَ اللَّهُ لِي بِعِلْمِي أَبَدًا. قَالَ: وَمِنَ الدَّلَائِلِ الصَّرِيحَةِ عَلَى رِيَاءِ الْعَالِمِ أَنْ يَتَأَذَّى مِمَّنْ يَقْرَأُ عَلَيْهِ إِذَا قَرَأَ عَلَى غَيْرِهِ.

ing one's knowledge is that one is offended if someone learns from him and then goes to learn from someone else."

Al-Shāfiʿī ﷺ used to say, "It is imperative that a scholar has a hidden portion of pious acts that are solely between him and Allah ﷻ. He should not depend solely upon knowledge – it is of little advantage in the Hereafter."

The statements of the scholars on sincerity in knowledge are many.

Whenever our Shaykh Shams al-Dīn al-Samanūdī ﷺ would perceive that a seeker of knowledge intends to obtain the world by way of being appointed a judge or accepting bribes, he would not teach him a single issue. He would say to him, "Purify your heart from love of the world so that you will be worthy of knowledge. Then come, and I will teach you knowledge." He also said, "Our Shaykh, the Knower of Allah (Exalted is He), Sīdī ʿAlī al-Nabatītī, would not teach anyone until he had asked him, 'O my son, what do you seek by the knowledge that you are asking me to teach you?' If he deemed his intention good, he would teach him; if not, he would teach him the proper intention, and then teach him." May Allah be pleased with him.

Al-Nasāʾī, al-Tirmidhī and others narrated the Prophetic Hadith:

> *The first person to be judged on the Day of Judgement will be a man who sought martyrdom and was given it. He (Allah) will recount to him his blessing, which he will recognize. He will say, 'What did you do with it?' He will say, 'I fought for Your sake until I was martyred.' He will say, 'You lie. Rather, you fought so that it would be said that 'So-and-so is brave,' and it was said.' Then it will be ordered and he will be dragged upon his face until he is thrown into the Fire.*

وَكَانَ الشَّافِعِيُّ رضي الله عنه يَقُولُ: يَنْبَغِي لِلْعَالِمِ أَنْ يَكُونَ لَهُ خَبِيئَةٌ مِنَ الْعَمَلِ الصَّالِحِ فِيمَا بَيْنَهُ وَبَيْنَ اللهِ عَزَّوَجَلَّ، وَلَا يَعْتَمِدُ عَلَى الْعِلْمِ فَقَطْ؛ فَإِنَّهُ قَلِيلُ الْجَدْوَى فِي الْآخِرَةِ اهـ.

وَأَقَاوِيلُ الْعُلَمَاءِ فِي الْإِخْلَاصِ فِي الْعِلْمِ كَثِيرَةٌ مَشْهُورَةٌ.

وَكَانَ شَيْخُنَا الشَّيْخُ شَمْسُ الدِّينِ السَّمَانُودِيُّ رحمه الله تعالى إِذَا تَفَرَّسَ فِيمَنْ يَطْلُبُ الْعِلْمَ أَنَّهُ يُرِيدُ يَصْطَادُ بِهِ الدُّنْيَا بِطَرِيقِ وِلَايَةِ الْقَضَاءِ وَقَبُولِ الرِّشَا.. لَا يُعَلِّمُهُ مَسْأَلَةً وَاحِدَةً، وَيَقُولُ لَهُ: طَهِّرْ قَلْبَكَ مِنْ مَحَبَّةِ الدُّنْيَا حَتَّى تَصْلُحَ لِلْعِلْمِ، ثُمَّ تَعَالَ؛ أُعَلِّمْكَ الْعِلْمَ. ثُمَّ قَالَ: وَكَانَ شَيْخُنَا الْعَارِفُ بِاللهِ تَعَالَى سَيِّدِي عَلِيٌّ النَّبْتِيتِيُّ لَا يُعَلِّمُ أَحَدًا حَتَّى يَقُولَ لَهُ: يَا وَلَدِي؛ مَا نَوَيْتَ بِهَذَا الْعِلْمِ الَّذِي تَطْلُبُ مِنِّي أَنْ أُعَلِّمَكَ؟ فَإِنْ رَأَى نِيَّتَهُ صَالِحَةً.. عَلَّمَهُ، وَإِلَّا عَلَّمَهُ النِّيَّةَ، ثُمَّ عَلَّمَهُ - رَضِيَ اللَّهُ عَنْهُ - وَاللهُ أَعْلَمُ.

وَرَوَى النَّسَائِيُّ وَالتِّرْمِذِيُّ وَغَيْرُهُمَا مَرْفُوعًا: «أَوَّلُ النَّاسِ يُقْضَى عَلَيْهِ يَوْمَ الْقِيَامَةِ رَجُلٌ اسْتُشْهِدَ، فَأُتِيَ بِهِ فَعَرَّفَهُ نِعَمَهُ فَعَرَفَهَا، فَقَالَ: فَمَا عَمِلْتَ فِيهَا؟ قَالَ: قَاتَلْتُ فِيكَ حَتَّى اسْتُشْهِدْتُ، فَقَالَ: كَذَبْتَ، وَلَكِنَّكَ قَاتَلْتَ لِأَنْ يُقَالَ: فُلَانٌ جَرِيءٌ، فَقَدْ قِيلَ، ثُمَّ أُمِرَ بِهِ فَسُحِبَ عَلَى وَجْهِهِ حَتَّى أُلْقِيَ فِي النَّارِ، وَرَجُلٌ تَعَلَّمَ الْعِلْمَ وَعَلَّمَهُ وَقَرَأَ الْقُرْآنَ، فَأُتِيَ بِهِ فَعَرَّفَهُ نِعَمَهُ فَعَرَفَهَا، فَقَالَ: فَمَا عَمِلْتَ فِيهَا؟ قَالَ: تَعَلَّمْتُ الْعِلْمَ وَعَلَّمْتُهُ وَقَرَأْتُ فِيكَ الْقُرْآنَ، قَالَ: كَذَبْتَ، وَلَكِنَّكَ تَعَلَّمْتَ لِيُقَالَ: فُلَانٌ عَالِمٌ، وَقَرَأْتَ الْقُرْآنَ لِيُقَالَ: هُوَ قَارِئٌ، فَقَدْ قِيلَ، ثُمَّ سُحِبَ عَلَى وَجْهِهِ حَتَّى أُلْقِيَ فِي النَّارِ، وَرَجُلٌ وَسَّعَ اللهُ عَلَيْهِ وَأَعْطَاهُ مِنْ أَصْنَافِ الْمَالِ، فَأُتِيَ بِهِ فَعَرَّفَهُ نِعَمَهُ فَعَرَفَهَا، قَالَ: فَمَا عَمِلْتَ فِيهَا؟ قَالَ: مَا تَرَكْتُ مِنْ سَبِيلٍ تُحِبُّ أَنْ

A man who learned religious knowledge taught it and recited the Qurʾan. He will be brought and Allah will recount his favour upon him, which he will recognize. He will then say to him, 'What did you do with it?' He will say, 'I learned religious knowledge, taught it, and recited the Qurʾan for Your sake.' He will respond, 'You lie. Rather, you learned knowledge so that it would be said that 'So-and-so is a scholar.' And you recited Qurʾan so that it would be said that he is a reciter, and it was said.' Then he will be dragged upon his face until he is thrown into the Fire.

A man whom Allah granted much and gave him all kinds of wealth will be brought and Allah will recount to him His favours, which he will recognize. He will say to him, 'What did you do with it?' He will say, 'I did not leave anything on which You love people to spend, except that I spent on it for Your sake.' He will reply, 'You lie. You did it so that it would be said that 'So-and-so is generous', and it was said.' Then it will be commanded and he will be dragged upon his face until he is thrown into the Fire.

Al-Tirmidhī and others narrated the Prophetic Hadith: "*If someone seeks knowledge in order to vie with the scholars through it, to show off in front of the ignorant, or to turn people's faces towards him, Allah will cause him to enter the Fire.*"

Ibn Mājah narrated the Prophetic Hadith: "*Some people from my nation will learn fiqh of the religion and the recitation of the Qurʾan. They will then say, 'We will go to the leaders and seek a portion of their worldly possessions and avoid their evil with our religion.' However, it will not happen like that; just as you can only harvest splinters from shoots of palm trees, you can only obtain sinfulness and disobedience through proximity to them.*"

ʿAbd al-Razzāq and others narrated that Ibn Masʿūd ﵁ said, "How will you be when you are surrounded by a strife

يُنفَقَ فِيهَا إِلَّا أَنْفَقْتُ فِيهَا لَكَ، قَالَ: كَذَبْتَ، وَلَكِنَّكَ فَعَلْتَ لِيُقَالَ: هُوَ جَوَّادٌ، وَقَدْ قِيلَ، ثُمَّ أُمِرَ بِهِ فَسُحِبَ عَلَى وَجْهِهِ حَتَّى أُلْقِيَ فِي النَّارِ».

وَقَوْلُهُ «جَرِيءٌ» بِالْمَدِّ: أَيْ شُجَاعٌ.

وَرَوَى التِّرْمِذِيُّ وَغَيْرُهُ مَرْفُوعًا: «مَنْ طَلَبَ الْعِلْمَ لِيُجَارِيَ بِهِ الْعُلَمَاءَ أَوْ يُمَارِيَ بِهِ السُّفَهَاءَ أَوْ لِيَصْرِفَ بِهِ وُجُوهَ النَّاسِ إِلَيْهِ.. أَدْخَلَهُ اللهُ النَّارَ».

وَرَوَى ابْنُ مَاجَهْ مَرْفُوعًا: «سَيَتَفَقَّهُ نَاسٌ مِنْ أُمَّتِي فِي الدِّينِ، يَقْرَؤُونَ الْقُرْآنَ يَقُولُونَ: نَأْتِي الْأُمَرَاءَ نُصِيبُ مِنْ دُنْيَاهُمْ وَنَعْتَزِلُهُمْ بِدِينِنَا، وَلَا يَكُونُ ذَلِكَ، كَمَا لَا يُجْتَنَى مِنَ الْقَتَاءِ إِلَّا الشَّوْكُ، وَكَذَلِكَ لَا يُجْتَنَى مِنْ قُرْبِهِمْ إِلَّا الْخَطَايَا وَالْآثَامُ».

وَرَوَى عَبْدُ الرَّزَّاقِ وَغَيْرُهُ عَنِ ابْنِ مَسْعُودٍ رضى الله عنه أَنَّهُ قَالَ: كَيْفَ بِكُمْ إِذَا لَابَسَتْكُمْ فِتْنَةٌ.. يَرْبُو فِيهَا الصَّغِيرُ، وَيَهْرَمُ مِنْهَا الْكَبِيرُ، وَتُتَّخَذُ سَيِّئَةً، فَإِذَا تُرِكَتْ، يُقَالُ: تُرِكَتِ السُّنَّةُ، فَقِيلَ لَهُ: وَمَتَى ذَلِكَ؟ فَقَالَ: إِذَا قَلَّتْ أُمَنَاؤُكُمْ وَكَثُرَتْ أُمَرَاؤُكُمْ، وَقَلَّتْ فُقَهَاؤُكُمْ وَكَثُرَتْ خَطَايَاكُمْ، وَتَفَقَّهَ النَّاسُ لِغَيْرِ الدِّينِ، وَالْتُمِسَتِ الدُّنْيَا بِعَمَلِ الْآخِرَةِ. وَفِي رِوَايَةٍ: وَتُعُلِّمَ الْعِلْمُ لِغَيْرِ الْعَمَلِ».

where evil will be adopted, in which the young will be raised and the elderly will grow old, such that if you abandon it, it will be said to you, 'You have abandoned the Sunnah'?" He was asked, "When will that occur?" He responded, "When there are few trustworthy people among you and you have many leaders, when few people among you have deep understanding, sins are multiplied, people learn *fiqh* for other than the sake of religion and seek the world through the acts of the Hereafter."[44]

Imam Aḥmad, Ibn Ḥibbān, al-Bayhaqī and al-Ḥākim[45] all narrated the Prophetic Hadith: "*Give glad tidings to this nation of praise, firmness, elevation, and establishment in the Earth. However, if any of them does the acts of the Hereafter for the sake of this world, he will have no portion of the Hereafter.*"

Al-Ṭabarānī and al-Bayhaqī narrated the Prophetic Hadith: "*If someone boasts his knowledge and actions to people, Allah will show people his reality, belittle him, and humiliate him.*"[46]

Al-Bayhaqī narrated the Prophetic Hadith: "*Maintaining an act is more difficult than the act itself. Indeed, a man will perform an action for which the performance of a good deed in secret will be recorded for him – thus, his reward will be multiplied seventy times over. However, Shaytan will stick to him until he mentions it to someone and speaks about it openly – thus, it will be written as a good deed that is performed openly, so the multiplication of the reward of that act will be erased. Then, that Shaytan will stick to him until he likes that his act is being mentioned, such that it is then recorded as boasting.*"

---

(44) In another narration, he said, "… and knowledge is sought for reasons other than acting upon it."

(45) He said the narrated Hadith is authentic.

(46) The meaning of his words is that for each instant that he manifests his knowledge to people out of boastfulness, Allah (Exalted is He) will expose his corrupt intention in his knowledge on the Day of Judgement. So, He will expose him in front of all those to whom he had showed off in this world.

وَرَوَى الْإِمَامُ أَحْمَدُ وَابْنُ حِبَّانَ فِي «صَحِيحِهِ» وَالْبَيْهَقِيُّ وَالْحَاكِمُ وَقَالَ: صَحِيحُ الْإِسْنَادِ مَرْفُوعًا: «بَشِّرْ هَذِهِ الْأُمَّةَ بِالثَّنَاءِ وَالدِّينِ وَالرِّفْعَةِ وَالتَّمْكِينِ فِي الْأَرْضِ، فَمَنْ عَمِلَ مِنْهُمْ عَمَلَ الْآخِرَةِ لِلدُّنْيَا.. لَمْ يَكُنْ لَهُ فِي الْآخِرَةِ مِنْ نَصِيبٍ».

وَرَوَى الطَّبَرَانِيُّ وَالْبَيْهَقِيُّ مَرْفُوعًا: «مَنْ سَمَّعَ النَّاسَ بِعِلْمِهِ وَعَمَلِهِ، سَمَّعَ اللهُ بِهِ سَامِعَ خَلْقِهِ وَصَغَّرَهُ وَحَقَّرَهُ».

وَقَوْلُهُ: «سَمَّعَ» بِتَشْدِيدِ الْمِيمِ، وَمَعْنَاهُ: أَنَّ كُلَّ مَنْ أَظْهَرَ عِلْمَهُ لِلنَّاسِ رِيَاءً، أَظْهَرَ اللهُ تَعَالَى نِيَّتَهُ الْفَاسِدَةَ فِي عَمَلِهِ يَوْمَ الْقِيَامَةِ، وَفَضَحَهُ عَلَى رُؤُوسِ الْأَشْهَادِ الَّذِينَ رَاءَاهُمْ فِي دَارِ الدُّنْيَا.

وَرَوَى الْبَيْهَقِيُّ مَرْفُوعًا: «إِنَّ الْإِبْقَاءَ عَلَى الْعَمَلِ أَشَدُّ مِنَ الْعَمَلِ، وَإِنَّ الرَّجُلَ لَيَعْمَلُ الْعَمَلَ فَيُكْتَبُ لَهُ عَمَلٌ صَالِحٌ مَعْمُولٌ بِهِ فِي السِّرِّ، فَيَضْعَفُ أَجْرُهُ سَبْعِينَ ضِعْفًا، فَلَا يَزَالُ بِهِ الشَّيْطَانُ حَتَّى يَذْكُرَهُ وَيُعْلِنَهُ، فَيُكْتَبُ عَلَانِيَةً وَيُمْحَى تَضْعِيفُ أَجْرِهِ كُلِّهِ، ثُمَّ لَا يَزَالُ بِهِ حَتَّى يُحِبَّ أَنْ يُذْكَرَ بِهِ وَيُكْتَبَ رِيَاءً».

Al-Ṭabarānī narrated the Prophetic Hadith: "*Indeed, Allah (Exalted is He) will say to someone who worshipped Him to show off and to be known, 'By My Might and Majesty, why did you worship Me?' He will say, 'By Your Might and Majesty, I worshipped you to show off to people.' He will say, 'None of it was lifted up to Me – take him to the Fire.'*"

Al-Ṭabarānī and al-Bayhaqī narrated the Prophetic Hadith: "*On the Day of Judgement, some rolled-up scrolls will be brought and unfurled before Allah ﷻ. Allah (Exalted is He) will say, 'Throw out this and accept this.' The Angels will say, 'By Your Might and Majesty, we only saw good.' Allah ﷻ will say, 'That was for other than My sake; I only accept that which is done for My sake.'*"[47]

Al-Bayhaqī narrated that Ibn ʿAbbās said, "If someone shows off any act of his in this world, Allah will entrust him to his action on the Day of Judgement. He will say to him, 'Investigate – does it avail you of anything?'"

Al-Ṭabarānī narrated the Prophetic Hadith: "*Indeed, there is a valley in Hell called Habhab; Allah has prepared it for the reciters who show off with their acts.*" In another Hadith he said, "*In Hell there is a valley from which Hell itself seeks refuge four hundred times each day. Allah has prepared it for the reciters who show off their works in this world.*"

Abū Yaʿlā and others narrated the Prophetic Hadith: "*Whoever performs his prayer excellently when people can see him and performs it in a lazy manner when he is alone, that is a disparage-*

---

(47) I (al-Shaʿrānī) say: The meaning of "for the sake of Allah (Exalted is He)", and Allah knows best, is from the standpoint of its being legislated by its performance to obey His command – that is, "for the sake of Allah (Exalted is He)". This is further clarified by the fact that each act can face one of two directions: one facing the creation and the other facing the Truth. That which corresponds to the Sacred Law will be facing the Truth; that which is at odds with it (the Sacred Law) will be facing the creation. So, understand – and Allah knows best.

وَرَوَى الطَّبَرَانِيُّ مَرْفُوعًا: «إِنَّ اللهَ تَعَالَى يَقُولُ لِمَنْ عَبَدَهُ رِيَاءً وَسُمْعَةً: بِعِزَّتِي وَجَلَالِي؛ مَا أَرَدْتَ بِعِبَادَتِي؟ قَالَ: بِعِزَّتِكَ وَجَلَالِكَ؛ رِيَاءَ النَّاسِ، قَالَ: لَمْ يَصْعَدْ إِلَيَّ مِنْهُ شَيْءٌ.. انْطَلِقُوا بِهِ إِلَى النَّارِ».

وَرَوَى الطَّبَرَانِيُّ وَالْبَيْهَقِيُّ مَرْفُوعًا: «يُؤْتَى يَوْمَ الْقِيَامَةِ بِصُحُفٍ مُخْتَتَمَةٍ وَتُفْتَحُ بَيْنَ يَدَيِ اللهِ عَزَّ وَجَلَّ، فَيَقُولُ اللهُ تَعَالَى: أَلْقُوا هَذِهِ وَاقْبَلُوا هَذِهِ، فَتَقُولُ الْمَلَائِكَةُ: وَعِزَّتِكَ وَجَلَالِكَ؛ مَا رَأَيْنَا إِلَّا خَيْرًا، فَيَقُولُ اللهُ عَزَّ وَجَلَّ: إِنَّ هَذَا كَانَ لِغَيْرِ وَجْهِي، وَإِنِّي لَا أَقْبَلُ إِلَّا مَا ابْتُغِيَ بِهِ وَجْهِي».

قُلْتُ: وَالْمُرَادُ - وَاللهُ أَعْلَمُ - بِوَجْهِ اللهِ تَعَالَى هُوَ وَجْهُ التَّشْرِيعِ بِأَنْ يُفْعَلَ ذَلِكَ امْتِثَالًا لِأَمْرِهِ، فَهَذَا هُوَ وَجْهُهُ تَعَالَى.

وَإِيضَاحُ ذَلِكَ أَنَّ كُلَّ عَمَلٍ لَهُ وَجْهَانِ؛ وَجْهٌ إِلَى الْكَوْنِ وَوَجْهٌ إِلَى الْحَقِّ، فَمَا وَافَقَ الشَّرْعَ كَانَ وَجْهًا لِلْحَقِّ، وَمَا خَالَفَهُ كَانَ لِغَيْرِ الْحَقِّ تَعَالَى، فَافْهَمْ وَاللهُ أَعْلَمُ.

وَرَوَى الْبَيْهَقِيُّ عَنِ ابْنِ عَبَّاسٍ أَنَّهُ قَالَ: «مَنْ رَاءَى بِشَيْءٍ فِي الدُّنْيَا بِعَمَلِهِ، وَكَّلَهُ اللهُ يَوْمَ الْقِيَامَةِ إِلَى عَمَلِهِ، وَقَالَ لَهُ: انْظُرْ هَلْ يُغْنِي عَنْكَ شَيْئًا». قَوْلُهُ «بِعَمَلِهِ»: أَيْ مِنْ عَمَلِهِ.

وَرَوَى الطَّبَرَانِيُّ مَرْفُوعًا: «إِنَّ فِي جَهَنَّمَ وَادِيًا يُقَالُ لَهُ هَبْهَبُ، أَعَدَّهُ اللهُ لِلْقُرَّاءِ الْمُرَائِينَ بِعَمَلِهِمْ». وَفِي رِوَايَةٍ: «إِنَّ فِي جَهَنَّمَ وَادِيًا تَتَعَوَّذُ مِنْهُ جَهَنَّمُ كُلَّ يَوْمٍ أَرْبَعَمِائَةِ مَرَّةٍ، أَعَدَّهُ اللهُ لِلْقُرَّاءِ الْمُرَائِينَ بِأَعْمَالِهِمْ فِي الدُّنْيَا».

وَرَوَى أَبُو يَعْلَى وَغَيْرُهُ مَرْفُوعًا: «مَنْ أَحْسَنَ صَلَاتَهُ حَيْثُ يَرَاهُ النَّاسُ، وَأَسَاءَهَا حَيْثُ يَخْلُو، فَتِلْكَ اسْتِهَانَةٌ اسْتَهَانَ بِهَا رَبَّهُ تَبَارَكَ وَتَعَالَى».

ment with which he has disrespected his Lord (Blessed and Exalted is He)."

Al-Bayhaqī narrated the Prophetic Hadith: "*If someone fasts to be seen by people, he has associated partners with his Lord. If someone gives charity to be seen by people, he has associated partners with his Lord. And whoever prays to be seen by people has associated partners with his Lord.*"

Imam Aḥmad and others narrated the Prophetic Hadith: "*O people! Protect yourselves from this polytheism, for it is more hidden than the crawling of an ant.*" It was said, "How should we protect ourselves from it, when it is more hidden than the crawling of an ant, O Messenger of Allah?" He said, "*Say: O Allah, we seek refuge in You from associating anything with You while we know. And we seek Your forgiveness for that which we do not know.*"

Imam Aḥmad and al-Ṭabarānī narrated the following Prophetic Hadith with a good chain of transmission: "*The thing I fear most for you is the lesser polytheism.*" The people said, "What is the lesser polytheism, O Messenger of Allah?" He said, "*Showing off. When people are being rewarded for their works, Allah ﷻ will say, 'Go to those from whom you showed off in the world – see if you find any reward with them.'*"

Al-Tirmidhī, Ibn Mājah, Ibn Ḥibbān, and al-Bayhaqī all narrated the Prophetic Hadith: "*When Allah gathers the first and the last on the Day of Judgement, a day which will undoubtedly occur, a caller will call out, 'Whoever has associated partners with Allah in his acts, then let him seek its reward with them (the partners). For Allah is more free of the need of partnership than any of those partners (you've associated).'*"[48]

---

(48) In a separate Hadith, it is narrated with the following words: "*And if someone has performed any work in which he associated others with Me, it (the act) belongs to the partner – and I am free of it.*"

وَرَوَى الْبَيْهَقِيُّ مَرْفُوعًا: «مَنْ صَامَ يُرَائِي النَّاسَ فَقَدْ أَشْرَكَ، وَمَنْ تَصَدَّقَ يُرَائِي فَقَدْ أَشْرَكَ، وَمَنْ صَلَّى يُرَائِي فَقَدْ أَشْرَكَ».

وَرَوَى الْإِمَامُ أَحْمَدُ وَغَيْرُهُ مَرْفُوعًا: «يَا أَيُّهَا النَّاسُ؛ اتَّقُوا هَذَا الشِّرْكَ فَإِنَّهُ أَخْفَى مِنْ دَبِيبِ النَّمْلِ»، فَقِيلَ: فَكَيْفَ نَتَّقِيهِ وَهُوَ أَخْفَى مِنْ دَبِيبِ النَّمْلِ يَا رَسُولَ اللهِ؟ فَقَالَ: «قُولُوا: اللَّهُمَّ؛ إِنَّا نَعُوذُ بِكَ أَنْ نُشْرِكَ بِكَ شَيْئًا نَعْلَمُهُ، وَنَسْتَغْفِرُكَ لِمَا لَا نَعْلَمُهُ».

وَرَوَى الْإِمَامُ أَحْمَدُ وَالطَّبَرَانِيُّ بِإِسْنَادٍ جَيِّدٍ مَرْفُوعًا: «إِنَّ أَخْوَفَ مَا أَخَافُ عَلَيْكُمُ الشِّرْكُ الْأَصْغَرُ»، قَالُوا: وَمَا الشِّرْكُ الْأَصْغَرُ يَا رَسُولَ اللهِ؟ قَالَ: «الرِّيَاءُ، يَقُولُ اللهُ عَزَّ وَجَلَّ إِذَا جُوزِيَ النَّاسُ بِأَعْمَالِهِمْ: اذْهَبُوا إِلَى الَّذِينَ كُنْتُمْ تُرَاؤُونَ فِي الدُّنْيَا، فَانْظُرُوا هَلْ تَجِدُونَ عِنْدَهُمْ جَزَاءً».

وَرَوَى التِّرْمِذِيُّ وَابْنُ مَاجَهْ وَابْنُ حِبَّانَ فِي «صَحِيحِهِ» وَالْبَيْهَقِيُّ مَرْفُوعًا: «إِذَا جَمَعَ اللهُ الْأَوَّلِينَ وَالْآخِرِينَ يَوْمَ الْقِيَامَةِ لِيَوْمٍ لَا رَيْبَ فِيهِ، نَادَى مُنَادٍ: مَنْ كَانَ أَشْرَكَ فِي عَمَلِهِ لِلَّهِ أَحَدًا.. فَلْيَطْلُبْ ثَوَابَهُ مِنْ عِنْدِهِ؛ فَإِنَّ اللهَ أَغْنَى الشُّرَكَاءِ عَنِ الشِّرْكِ».

زَادَ فِي رِوَايَةٍ: «فَمَنْ عَمِلَ عَمَلًا أَشْرَكَ فِيهِ غَيْرِي، فَهُوَ لِلَّذِي أَشْرَكَ، وَأَنَا مِنْهُ بَرِيءٌ».

Imam Aḥmad narrated that ʿUbādah ibn Ṣāmit said, "Some people will recite the Qur'an upon the tongue of the Messenger Muhammad ﷺ, considering licit what he allowed, prohibiting what he prohibited, and observing all of what he observes. However, they will not obtain a thing from it, except the way a dead person obtains the head of a donkey."[49]

(49) [We have omitted the final Hadith from this section as it has been declared fabricated (*mawḍūʿ*) by the Hadith scholars, chief among them al-Ḥāfiẓ al-Mundhirī, who said, "The signs of fabrication are evident in this Hadith: in all of its chains of narration, and all of its statements." Despite this, Imam al-Shaʿrānī said about it: "It is possible that the Hadith has an authentic, sound, or weak source, but its wording was forgotten. So, the narrator explained it in his own words." While this may be true, the Hadith in question did not add anything to the discussion that had already taken place, so leaving it out is not an issue.]

وَرَوَى الْإِمَامُ أَحْمَدُ عَنْ عُبَادَةَ بْنِ الصَّامِتِ قَالَ: «سَيَقْرَأُ نَاسٌ الْقُرْآنَ عَلَى لِسَانِ مُحَمَّدٍ ﷺ، فَيُحِلُّونَ حَلَالَهُ وَيُحَرِّمُونَ حَرَامَهُ، وَيَنْزِلُونَ عِنْدَ مَنَازِلِهِ لَا يَحُوزُونَ مِنْهُ شَيْئًا إِلَّا كَمَا يَحُوزُ رَأْسُ الْحِمَارِ الْمَيِّتِ».

The Prohibition of Boasting One's Knowledge

A general covenant was taken from us by the Messenger of Allah ﷺ that we would neither boast any knowledge at all nor conceal it from someone whom we know to be sincere in it, even if he were to reject us as a consequence of our teaching it to him.

I heard Sīdī ʿAlī al-Khawwāṣ ؓ saying, "From the signs of the teacher's sincerity in his knowledge is that he pays attention neither to people's recognition of his teachings nor their rejection of him. Anyone who is offended by his students leaving him and learning from someone else has not smelled the aroma of sincerity. Rather, he is showing off with his knowledge."

In his book *al-Tibyān*[50] and in the introduction to *Sharḥ al-Muhadhdhab*, Imam al-Nawawī expressed it in the following way: "You should know that among the most important matters to which the teacher has been ordered is that he is unbothered by someone learning from him and then going to learn from someone else. This is a misfortune that afflicts the ignorant teachers because of their foolishness and corrupt intentions. It is a clear evidence of their not intending by their teaching the noble Countenance of Allah."

I heard our Shaykh, the Shaykh al-Islām Zakariyyā ؓ, saying, "Beware of concealing knowledge from your enemy. For the Sacred Legislation, in reality, only belongs to Allah and His Messenger. And from the indispensable conditions of being a lover of Allah and His Messenger ﷺ is that one desires the dissemination of everything that Allah and His Messenger ﷺ have legislated to all people, whether friend or foe."

(50) [*Al-Tibyān fī Ādāb Ḥamalat al-Qurʾān*, translated into English by Shaykh Musa Furber as *Etiquette with the Quran*.]

أُخِذَ عَلَيْنَا الْعَهْدُ الْعَامُّ مِنْ رَسُولِ اللهِ ﷺ أَنْ لَا نُمَارِيَ بِالْعِلْمِ قَطُّ وَلَا نَكْتُمَهُ عَنْ أَحَدٍ عَلِمْنَا مِنْهُ الْإِخْلَاصَ فِيهِ، وَلَوْ كَفَرَ هُوَ بِتَعْلِيمِنَا لَهُ، كَمَا أَنَّ الْإِخْلَاصَ مِنْ شَرْطِ الْمُعَلِّمِ أَيْضًا.

وَسَمِعْتُ سَيِّدِي عَلِيًّا الْخَوَّاصَ رَحِمَهُ اللهُ يَقُولُ: مِنْ عَلَامَةِ إِخْلَاصِ الْمُعَلِّمِ أَنْ لَا يَلْتَفِتَ إِلَى اعْتِرَافِ النَّاسِ بِتَعْلِيمِهِ أَوْ كُفْرَانِهِمْ بِهِ، وَكُلُّ مَنْ تَكَدَّرَ مِمَّنْ تَرَكَهُ مِنْ طَلَبَتِهِ وَقَرَأَ عَلَى غَيْرِهِ فَمَا شَمَّ لِلْإِخْلَاصِ رَائِحَةً وَهُوَ مُرَاءٍ بِعِلْمِهِ اهـ.

وَعِبَارَةُ الْإِمَامِ النَّوَوِيِّ فِي كِتَابِ التِّبْيَانِ وَفِي مُقَدِّمَةِ شَرْحِ الْمُهَذَّبِ.

اعْلَمْ أَنَّ مِنْ أَهَمِّ مَا يُؤْمَرُ بِهِ الْمُعَلِّمُ أَنْ لَا يَتَأَذَّى مِمَّنْ يَقْرَأُ عَلَى غَيْرِهِ، قَالَ: وَهَذِهِ مُصِيبَةٌ يُبْتَلَى بِهَا جَهَلَةُ الْمُعَلِّمِينَ لِغَبَاوَتِهِمْ وَفَسَادِ نِيَّتِهِمْ، وَهُوَ مِنَ الدَّلَائِلِ الصَّرِيحَةِ عَلَى عَدَمِ إِرَادَتِهِمْ بِالتَّعْلِيمِ وَجْهَ اللهِ الْكَرِيمِ اهـ.

وَسَمِعْتُ شَيْخَنَا شَيْخَ الْإِسْلَامِ زَكَرِيَّا رَحِمَهُ اللهُ يَقُولُ: إِيَّاكَ أَنْ تَكْتُمَ الْعِلْمَ عَنْ عَدُوِّكَ؛ فَإِنَّ الشَّرْعَ حَقِيقَةً إِنَّمَا هُوَ لِلَّهِ وَلِرَسُولِهِ، وَمِنْ شَرْطِ كُلِّ مُحِبٍّ لِلَّهِ وَلِرَسُولِهِ أَنْ يُحِبَّ نَشْرَ مَا شَرَعَهُ اللهُ وَرَسُولُهُ فِي جَمِيعِ الْخَلْقِ سَوَاءٌ كَانُوا أَصْدِقَاءَ أَوْ أَعْدَاءَ.

An immense warning has also been issued regarding one who hides knowledge from its people, as will come in some *aḥādīth*. Imam al-Shāfiʿī ﵀ used to recite:

> Should I spread knowledge among the shepherds of sheep,
> Or spread well-arranged verses among those lavishing in comfort?

Until he said:

> So, Allah, the Most Generous, facilitates by His Grace,
> And I meet someone worthy of knowledge and wisdom,
> I will spread benefit and benefit by their love,
> If not, it will be locked up and concealed with me,
> If someone blesses an ignorant with knowledge, he has wasted it,
> While whoever withholds it from those worthy has oppressed them.

I heard my brother, Afḍal al-Dīn ﵀, say:

> The Lawgiver ﷺ only threatened the pious predecessors for their concealing knowledge in order to give them courage so that they would speak, in spite of their fear of fame. As for people today, if the warning were given against speaking (on knowledge), they would speak and never shut up. For each of the pious predecessors would, out of their abundant sincerity, love that their brother be made famous for knowledge. So, they would display to people the strength of the light of their brethren and the weakness of their own

وَقَدْ جَاءَ التَّحْذِيرُ الْعَظِيمُ فِي حَقِّ مَنْ كَتَمَ الْعِلْمَ عَنْ أَهْلِهِ كَمَا سَيَأْتِي فِي الْأَحَادِيثِ، وَكَانَ الْإِمَامُ الشَّافِعِيُّ رَضِيَ اللهُ عَنْهُ يُنْشِدُ:

أَأَنْثُرُ عِلْمًا بَيْنَ رَاعِيَةِ الْغَنَمْ   وَأَنْثُرُ مَنْظُومًا لِسَارِحَةِ النَّعَمْ

إِلَى أَنْ قَالَ:

فَإِنْ يَسَّرَ اللهُ الْكَرِيمُ بِفَضْلِهِ   وَأَدْرَكْتُ أَهْلًا لِلْعُلُومِ وَلِلْحِكَمْ
بَثَثْتُ مُفِيدًا وَاسْتَفَدْتُ وِدَادَهُمْ   وَإِلَّا فَمَخْزُونٌ لَدَيَّ وَمُكْتَتَمْ
وَمَنْ مَنَحَ الْجُهَّالَ عِلْمًا أَضَاعَهُ   وَمَنْ مَنَعَ الْمُسْتَوْجِبِينَ فَقَدْ ظَلَمْ

وَسَمِعْتُ أَخِي أَفْضَلَ الدِّينِ رَحِمَهُ اللهُ يَقُولُ: إِنَّمَا تَوَعَّدَ الشَّارِعُ ﷺ السَّلَفَ الصَّالِحَ إِذَا كَتَمُوا الْعِلْمَ تَشْجِيعًا لَهُمْ حَتَّى يَتَكَلَّمُوا بِهِ لِخَوْفِهِمْ مِنَ الشُّهْرَةِ، وَأَمَّا النَّاسُ الْيَوْمَ فَلَوْ كَانَ التَّحْذِيرُ فِي الْكَلَامِ لَتَكَلَّمُوا وَلَمْ يَسْكُتُوا، فَكَانَ السَّلَفُ الصَّالِحُ لِكَثْرَةِ إِخْلَاصِهِمْ يَوَدُّ كُلُّ وَاحِدٍ مِنْهُمْ أَنْ لَوْ كَانَتِ الشُّهْرَةُ بِالْعِلْمِ لِأَخِيهِ فَكَانُوا يُقَوُّونَ نُورَ إِخْوَانِهِمْ وَيُضْعِفُونَ نُورَهُمْ عِنْدَ النَّاسِ، وَرُبَّمَا عُرِضَتِ الْمَسْأَلَةُ الْوَاحِدَةُ عَلَى ثَلَاثِينَ نَفْسًا وَكُلٌّ مِنْهُمْ يَرُدُّهَا حَتَّى تَجِيءَ إِلَى الْأَوَّلِ خَوْفًا مِنَ الْقَوْلِ فِي دِينِ اللهِ بِالرَّأْيِ اهـ .

light. Perhaps a single issue would be presented to thirty people among them, and each of them would refuse to answer until it returns to the first person. That was due to their fear of speaking on the religion of Allah according to opinion.

You should know, O brother, that the prohibition of quarrelling over knowledge is due to the contempt that occurs thereby. For example, two [of the] *fuqahā'* may sit and speak about knowledge, not intending to act upon it, while their hearts are completely negligent of action. Thus, one of them will cause the other to doubt something that he had understood. He will cause him to doubt without teaching him its solution. However, if he then obliges him by teaching him the solution to that doubt, it would not be prohibited. Rather, it is desirable, because it is a way to test one's student and show him where his knowledge and ignorance lie. Many times, a student of knowledge will be convinced of the correctness of his understanding of a verse or a Hadith, then sit with one of the people of disputation who will toy with him with some matter, causing him to doubt. So, that student will begin to doubt what he had been certain of. However, that is not the affair of the people of sincere faith.

This is the meaning that I understood from the wisdom of the prohibition of quarrelling over knowledge. I extracted it from the Hadith that Muslim and others narrated regarding the vision of the Creator ﷻ on the Day of Judgement: "*Do you dispute about seeing the Sun or the Moon which are not covered by clouds?*"[51]

---

(51) The *mufassirīn* explained the word "dispute" to mean "do you doubt" – that would thus be the meaning. And if someone should come upon something narrated to that effect, he should add it here in this book. And Allah knows best.

وَاعْلَمْ يَا أَخِي أَنَّ حِكْمَةَ النَّهْيِ عَنِ الْمُمَارَاةِ فِي الْعِلْمِ هُوَ لِلِاسْتِهَانَةِ بِهِ، فَيَجْلِسُ الْفَقِيهَانِ يَتَكَلَّمَانِ بِالْعِلْمِ وَلَا يَقْصِدَانِ الْعَمَلَ وَقُلُوبُهُمْ غَافِلَةٌ عَنِ الْعَمَلِ بِالْكُلِّيَّةِ، وَيُشَكِّكُ كُلُّ وَاحِدٍ مِنْهُمَا الْآخَرَ فِيمَا يَفْهَمُهُ، وَيُدْخِلُ عَلَيْهِ الشُّبْهَةَ وَلَا يُعَلِّمُهُ بِالْجَوَابِ، وَإِلَّا فَلَوْ شَكَّكَهُ ثُمَّ أَجَابَهُ وَعَلَّمَهُ الْجَوَابَ.. لَمَا نُهِيَ عَنْهُ بَلْ هُوَ مَطْلُوبٌ؛ لِأَنَّ فِيهِ امْتِحَانًا لِلطَّالِبِ لِيُخْتَبَرَ بِهِ عِلْمُهُ وَجَهْلُهُ، وَكَثِيرًا مَا يَكُونُ طَالِبُ الْعِلْمِ جَازِمًا بِحُكْمِ فَهْمِهِ مِنَ الْآيَةِ أَوِ الْحَدِيثِ فَيَجْلِسُ مَعَ بَعْضِ الْمُجَادِلِينَ فَيُدْخِلُ عَلَيْهِ التَّشْكِيكَ، ثُمَّ يَلْتَهِي عَنْهُ بِأَمْرٍ فَيَصِيرُ ذَلِكَ الطَّالِبُ مُتَرَدِّدًا فِيمَا كَانَ جَازِمًا بِهِ، وَلَيْسَ ذَلِكَ مِنْ شَأْنِ أَهْلِ الْإِيمَانِ الصَّادِقِ، وَهَذَا الْمَعْنَى الَّذِي فَهِمْتُهُ مِنْ حِكْمَةِ النَّهْيِ عَنِ الْمُمَارَاةِ، اقْتَبَسْتُهُ مِنْ حَدِيثِ مُسْلِمٍ وَغَيْرِهِ فِي شَأْنِ رُؤْيَةِ الْبَارِي جَلَّ وَعَلَا فِي الْقِيَامَةِ: «هَلْ تُمَارُونَ فِي رُؤْيَةِ الشَّمْسِ وَالْقَمَرِ لَيْسَ دُونَهُمَا سَحَابٌ» الْحَدِيثَ.

فَفَسَّرَ الشَّارِحُونَ هُنَاكَ قَوْلَهُ «تُمَارُونَ» أَيْ: تَشُكُّونَ، فَكَذَلِكَ يَكُونُ الْمَعْنَى هُنَا، وَمَنْ ظَفِرَ بِنَقْلٍ فِي ذَلِكَ فَلْيُلْحِقْهُ بِهَذَا الْمَوْضِعِ مِنْ هَذَا الْكِتَابِ. وَاللهُ أَعْلَمُ.

Al-Tirmidhī and others narrated the Prophetic Hadith: "*If someone learns knowledge in order to argue with the scholars or boast to the ignorant, let him prepare his seat in the Fire.*"

Abū Dāwūd, al-Tirmidhī, and others narrated the Prophetic Hadith: "*If Allah gives someone knowledge and he withholds it from Allah's servants, taking a payment for it and selling it for a price, he will be struck with a whip of fire, and a caller will call out, 'This is the one to whom Allah has given knowledge, yet he withheld it from Allah's servants, taking a payment for it and selling it for a price.' He will continue in that state until the judgement concludes.*"

وَرَوَى التِّرْمِذِيُّ وَغَيْرُهُ مَرْفُوعًا: «مَنْ تَعَلَّمَ الْعِلْمَ لِيُجَادِلَ بِهِ الْعُلَمَاءَ أَوْ لِيُمَارِيَ بِهِ السُّفَهَاءَ فَلْيَتَبَوَّأْ مَقْعَدَهُ مِنَ النَّارِ».

وَرَوَى أَبُو دَاوُدَ وَالتِّرْمِذِيُّ وَغَيْرُهُمَا مَرْفُوعًا: «مَنْ آتَاهُ اللهُ عِلْمًا فَبَخِلَ بِهِ عَنْ عِبَادِ اللهِ وَأَخَذَ عَلَيْهِ طَمَعًا وَشَرَى بِهِ ثَمَنًا، وَكَذَا وَكَذَا حَتَّى يَفْرُغَ الْحِسَابُ». وَاللهُ تَعَالَى أَعْلَمُ.

The Prohibition of Being Careless in the Narration of Hadith

A general covenant was taken from us by the Messenger of Allah ﷺ that we would not be careless in narrating *aḥādīth*. Rather, we should confirm any Hadith that we relate from the Messenger of Allah ﷺ, not narrating anything until we have with us its authenticity.

Sīdī ʿAlī al-Khawwāṣ used to say:

> It is imperative that a *faqīh* not relate any Hadith unless he has a sign by which he knows that it is from the Messenger of Allah ﷺ. That sign is either by way of transmission or by way of asking the Prophet ﷺ directly, in a waking vision, about the Hadith and his response of "It is something I said." This only applies to that which is considered weak by way of transmission; as for what is authenticated or considered sound by way of the *muḥaddithīn*, there is no need to ask him ﷺ.
>
> Thereafter, you should know, O brother, that the people that have most exposed this affair of *taṣawwuf* to criticism are those who have no foothold in the path. For they may relate something about the Messenger of Allah ﷺ that is not from his speech, due to their lack of spiritual experience and inability to distinguish between Prophetic speech and non-Prophetic speech. If they had been among the *ʿārifīn*, they would have recognized Prophetic speech and distinguished it from other speech. Indeed, the bright light of Prophecy is not hidden from he in whose heart is light.
>
> I heard one of them relate the statement of Abū Muhammad al-Kettānī: "I saw the Prophet ﷺ and said to him, 'O Messenger of Allah! Supplicate to Allah for me that my heart will never die.' He said to me, 'Recite

أُخِذَ عَلَيْنَا الْعَهْدُ الْعَامُّ مِنْ رَسُولِ اللهِ ﷺ أَنْ لَا نَتَهَوَّرَ فِي رِوَايَةِ الْحَدِيثِ بَلْ نَتَثَبَّتُ فِي كُلِّ حَدِيثٍ نَرْوِيهِ عَنْ رَسُولِ اللهِ ﷺ، وَلَا نَرْوِيهِ عَنْهُ إِلَّا إِنْ كَانَ لَنَا بِهِ رِوَايَةٌ صَحِيحَةٌ.

وَكَانَ سَيِّدِي عَلِيٌّ الْخَوَّاصُ رحمه الله تعالى يَقُولُ: لَا يَنْبَغِي لِفَقِيهٍ أَنْ يَرْوِيَ عَنْ رَسُولِ اللهِ ﷺ حَدِيثًا إِلَّا إِنْ كَانَ لَهُ بِهِ عَلَامَةٌ يَعْرِفُ بِهَا أَنَّ ذَلِكَ مِنْ كَلَامِ رَسُولِ اللهِ ﷺ، إِمَّا مِنْ طَرِيقِ النَّقْلِ وَإِمَّا مِنْ طَرِيقِ سُؤَالِهِ لِلنَّبِيِّ ﷺ عَنْ ذَلِكَ الْحَدِيثِ. وَقَوْلُهُ: هُوَ مِنْ كَلَامِي يَقَظَةً وَمُشَافَهَةً، هَذَا كُلُّهُ فِيمَا كَانَ ضَعِيفًا مِنْ طَرِيقِ النَّقْلِ، أَمَّا مَا صَحَّ مِنْ طَرِيقِ الْمُحَدِّثِينَ وَاسْتُحْسِنَ.. فَلَا يَحْتَاجُ إِلَى سُؤَالِهِ ﷺ فِيهِ.

فَاعْلَمْ يَا أَخِي أَنَّ أَكْثَرَ مَنْ يَقَعُ فِي خِيَانَةِ هَذَا الْعَهْدِ الْمُتَصَوِّفَةُ الَّذِينَ لَا قَدَمَ لَهُمْ فِي الطَّرِيقِ، فَرُبَّمَا رَوَوْا عَنْ رَسُولِ اللهِ ﷺ مَا لَيْسَ مِنْ كَلَامِهِ لِعَدَمِ ذَوْقِهِمْ وَعَدَمِ فُرْقَانِهِمْ بَيْنَ كَلَامِ النُّبُوَّةِ وَكَلَامِ غَيْرِهَا، وَلَوْ أَنَّهُمْ كَانُوا مِنَ الْعَارِفِينَ لَعَرَفُوا كَلَامَ النُّبُوَّةِ وَمَيَّزُوهُ عَنْ غَيْرِهِ، فَإِنَّ لَامِعَةَ نُورِ النُّبُوَّةِ لَا تَخْفَى عَلَى مَنْ فِي قَلْبِهِ نُورٌ.

وَقَدْ سَمِعْتُ بَعْضَهُمْ يَحْكِي قَوْلَ أَبِي مُحَمَّدٍ الْكَتَّانِيِّ رَأَيْتُ النَّبِيَّ ﷺ، فَقُلْتُ لَهُ: يَا رَسُولَ اللهِ؛ ادْعُ اللهَ لِي أَنْ لَا يُمِيتَ قَلْبِي، فَقَالَ: قُلْ كُلَّ يَوْمٍ أَرْبَعِينَ مَرَّةً: يَا حَيُّ يَا قَيُّومُ؛ لَا إِلَهَ إِلَّا أَنْتَ، وَهِيَ رُؤْيَةُ مَنَامٍ. فَصَارَ هَذَا يَرْوِيهِ عَنْهُ عَلَى إِيهَامِ أَنَّهُ ﷺ قَالَهُ لِأَصْحَابِهِ، وَرَوَاهُ عَنْهُ الْأَئِمَّةُ الْحُفَّاظُ وَهُوَ وَهْمٌ فَاحِشٌ، فَلَوْلَا أَنَّنِي أَعْلَمْتُهُ بِذَلِكَ مَا عَلِمَهُ.

وَسَمِعْتُ شَيْخَنَا شَيْخَ الْإِسْلَامِ زَكَرِيَّا رَحِمَهُ اللهُ يَقُولُ: إِنَّمَا قَالَ بَعْضُ الْمُحَدِّثِينَ: أَكْذَبُ النَّاسِ الصَّالِحُونَ؛ لِغَلَبَةِ سَلَامَةِ بَوَاطِنِهِمْ، فَيَظُنُّونَ

every day: O Living, O Eternal! There is no god but You.'" That was in a dream; this person, however, began to narrate it as if he ﷺ had said it to his Companions, and some of the Imams of Hadith narrated from him – both he and they have transgressed. If I had not informed him of that, he would not have known.

Some of the *muḥaddithīn* only said that the people who lie the most are the pious because of the purity of their inner being. Thus, they think well of all people and believe that they would not lie on the Messenger of Allah ﷺ. Thus, what they mean by the pious are the worshippers who, having no portion of the knowledge of rhetoric, are unable to distinguish between the Prophetic words and others. That is the opposite of the *ʿārifīn*, to whom that is not hidden. In fact, one of them used to distinguish the noble voice from others from behind a veil because those words are from the fragrance of the Messenger of Allah ﷺ.

Allah (Exalted is He) has blessed me to be able to distinguish the Prophetic words from others by way of the sweetness of expert composition, for no one is more eloquent than the Messenger of Allah ﷺ. In fact, it is possible that a Companion heard something from the Messenger of Allah ﷺ and its meaning is maintained in his heart, but he forgot some of the words. He will then complete the Hadith with his own words – in that case, I recognize it by the weakening of the composition. Perhaps some of the *muḥaddithīn* would consider such a Hadith fabricated[52], while the reality is that the wording alone

---

(52) [This refers to a capacity that the *muḥaddithīn* develop where, through constant study of the *aḥādīth* of the Messenger of Allah ﷺ and reports about others, they develop a taste for the Prophetic words and utterances, being able to distinguish them

بِالنَّاسِ الْخَيْرَ وَأَنَّهُمْ لَا يَكْذِبُونَ عَلَى رَسُولِ اللهِ ﷺ، فَمُرَادُهُمْ بِالصَّالِحِينَ الْمُتَعَبِّدُونَ الَّذِينَ لَا غَوْصَ لَهُمْ فِي عِلْمِ الْبَلَاغَةِ فَلَا يُفَرِّقُونَ بَيْنَ كَلَامِ النُّبُوَّةِ وَغَيْرِهِ، بِخِلَافِ الْعَارِفِينَ فَإِنَّهُمْ لَا يَخْفَى عَلَيْهِمْ ذَلِكَ، حَتَّى أَنَّ بَعْضَهُمْ كَانَ يَعْرِفُ صَوْتَ الشَّرِيفِ مِنْ غَيْرِهِ مِنْ وَرَاءِ حِجَابٍ لِكَوْنِهِ مِنْ رَائِحَةِ رَسُولِ اللهِ ﷺ اهـ.

وَقَدْ مَنَّ اللهُ تَعَالَى عَلَيَّ بِتَمْيِيزِ كَلَامِ النُّبُوَّةِ مِنْ غَيْرِهِ مِنْ حَيْثُ حَلَاوَةُ التَّرْكِيبِ الْعِلْمِيِّ بِأَنَّهُ لَا أَحَدٌ يَقْدِرُ عَلَى فَصَاحَةِ رَسُولِ اللهِ ﷺ، فَرُبَّمَا سَمِعَ الصَّحَابِيُّ شَيْئًا مِنْ رَسُولِ اللهِ ﷺ، فَذَهَبَ عَنْهُ حِفْظُ بَعْضِ اللَّفْظِ وَالْمَعْنَى مَوْفُورٌ فِي قَلْبِهِ، فَيُكْمِلُ لَنَا الْحَدِيثَ بِلَفْظِهِ هُوَ، فَأَعْرِفُهُ بِرَكَاكَةِ تَرْكِيبِهِ، وَرُبَّمَا ظَنَّ بَعْضُ الْمُحَدِّثِينَ أَنَّ ذَلِكَ الْحَدِيثَ مَوْضُوعٌ، وَالْحَالُ أَنَّ الْوَضْعَ إِنَّمَا هُوَ فِي مِثْلِ لَفْظَةٍ وَنَحْوِهَا، وَأَصْلُ الْحَدِيثِ صَحِيحٌ عَنْ رَسُولِ اللهِ ﷺ.

was what was invented, while the original meaning of the Hadith is authentic from the Messenger of Allah ﷺ.

So, O brother, learn the science of Hadith, so that you may exclude yourself from lying upon the Messenger of Allah ﷺ, even unintentionally.[53]

And Allah is Most Forgiving, Most Merciful.[54]

---

from others through intuition. So, the author here intends that if a *muḥaddith* comes upon such a Hadith where the Companion has completed it with his own words, he would consider such a Hadith to be fabricated, though it is not.]

(53) Al-Bukhārī, Muslim, and others narrate the Prophetic Hadith: "*If someone intentionally lies upon me, let him prepare his seat in the Fire.*" Al-Ṭabarānī and others narrated the same Hadith, but without the word "intentionally".

(54) *Al-Baqarah*, 218.

فَتعَلَّمْ يَا أَخِي عِلْمَ الْحَدِيثَ لِتَخْرُجَ مِنَ الْوُقُوعِ فِي الْكَذِبِ عَلَى رَسُولِ اللهِ ﷺ وَلَوْ بِغَيْرِ قَصْدٍ. وَاللهُ تَعَالَى أَعْلَمُ.

وَرَوَى الشَّيْخَانِ وَغَيْرُهُمَا مَرْفُوعًا: «مَنْ كَذَبَ عَلَيَّ مُتَعَمِّدًا، فَلْيَتَبَوَّأْ مَقْعَدَهُ مِنَ النَّارِ». قَالَ الْجَلَالُ السُّيُوطِيُّ: إِنَّهُ مُتَوَاتِرٌ.

وَرَوَى الطَّبَرَانِيُّ مَرْفُوعًا: «مَنْ كَذَبَ عَلَيَّ، فَلْيَتَبَوَّأْ مَقْعَدَهُ مِنَ النَّارِ» بِإِسْقَاطِ قَوْلِهِ «مُتَعَمِّدًا». (وَاللهُ غَفُورٌ رَحِيمٌ).

The Prohibition of Being Deluded with the Memorization of Knowledge That Is Unaccompanied by Practice

A general covenant was taken from us by the Messenger of Allah ﷺ that we would not delude ourselves by not acting on the knowledge we acquire, as is the case with most people these days. The pious predecessors considered that to be a sin and would seek forgiveness for each issue that they learned but had not put into practice. And if that is someone's point of view, the delusion that accompanies knowledge departs from him. Next, you should know, O brother, that Allah (Exalted is He) has allotted among the people those who act upon their knowledge, those given knowledge but without action, and those for whom Allah has neither allotted knowledge nor action. For anyone that does not act upon his knowledge, it is imperative that they always seek forgiveness and repent, as well as to frequently teach people knowledge so that perhaps they may act upon it. It will be recorded as such in the register of the one who taught them since he had lacked acting upon his knowledge; however, he should also seek forgiveness for it. For it is possible that people's acting upon the scholar's knowledge will not repair the deficiency that is his abandoning of acting upon what he knows. Shaykh Ibn al-ʿArabī used to say:

> If someone inspects truly, he will not find any intelligent person save that he acts upon what he knows. It is impossible for him to abandon acting upon it ever, as long as he possesses intelligence. If he acts upon his knowledge in accordance with the pure Sacred Law – directly acting upon it with sincerity – he will have acted upon his knowledge. If he, on the other hand, falls into disobedience and then seeks forgiveness for it and repents, in that case, too, he will have acted upon what he knows. Had it not been for his knowledge, he would

أُخِذَ عَلَيْنَا الْعَهْدُ الْعَامُّ مِنْ رَسُولِ اللهِ ﷺ أَنْ لَا نَغْتَرَّ بِحِفْظِ الْعِلْمِ الَّذِي يُطْلَبُ مِنَّا الْعَمَلُ بِهِ مِنْ غَيْرِ عَمَلٍ كَمَا عَلَيْهِ غَالِبُ النَّاسِ الْيَوْمَ، وَمَا هَكَذَا كَانَ السَّلَفُ الصَّالِحُ رَضِيَ اللهُ عَنْهُمْ، فَقَدْ بَلَغَنَا أَنَّهُمْ كَانُوا يَسْتَغْفِرُونَ اللهَ مِنْ كُلِّ مَسْئَلَةٍ لَمْ يَعْمَلُوا بِهَا وَيَعُدُّونَ ذَلِكَ ذَنْبًا، وَمَنْ كَانَ هَذَا مَشْهَدُهُ ذَهَبَ عَنْهُ الِاغْتِرَارُ بِالْعِلْمِ.

ثُمَّ اعْلَمْ يَا أَخِي؛ أَنَّ مِنَ النَّاسِ مَنْ قَسَمَ اللهُ تَعَالَى لَهُ الْعَمَلَ بِمَا عَلِمَ، وَمِنْهُمْ مَنْ قَسَمَ اللهُ لَهُ الْعِلْمَ مِنْ غَيْرِ عَمَلٍ، وَمِنْهُمْ مَنْ قَسَمَ اللهُ لَهُ الْعَمَلَ بِغَيْرِ عِلْمٍ، وَمِنْهُمْ مَنْ لَمْ يُقْسَمْ لَهُ عِلْمٌ وَلَا عَمَلٌ، فَالْوَاجِبُ عَلَى كُلِّ مَنْ لَمْ يَعْمَلْ بِعِلْمِهِ كَثْرَةُ الِاسْتِغْفَارِ وَالتَّوْبَةِ وَالْإِكْثَارُ مِنْ تَعْلِيمِ الْعِلْمِ لِلنَّاسِ؛ لَعَلَّهُمْ يَعْمَلُونَ بِهِ فَيَكُونُ ذَلِكَ فِي صَحَائِفِ مَنْ عَلَّمَهُمْ، حَيْثُ فَاتَهُ الْعَمَلُ بِمَا عَلِمَ ثُمَّ يَسْتَغْفِرُ مِنْ ذَلِكَ، فَرُبَّمَا لَا يَكُونُ عَمَلُ النَّاسِ بِعِلْمِ الْعَالِمِ يُجْبِرُ خَلَلَ تَرْكِهِ هُوَ الْعَمَلَ بِمَا عَلِمَ.

وَكَانَ الشَّيْخُ مُحْيِي الدِّينِ بْنُ الْعَرَبِيِّ رَحِمَهُ اللهُ يَقُولُ: مَنْ حَقَّقَ النَّظَرَ لَمْ يَجِدْ عَاقِلًا إِلَّا وَهُوَ عَامِلٌ بِعِلْمِهِ لَا يُمْكِنُهُ أَنْ يَتْرُكَ الْعَمَلَ بِهِ أَبَدًا مَا دَامَ عَاقِلًا، وَذَلِكَ أَنَّهُ إِنْ عَمِلَ بِعِلْمِهِ عَلَى وَفْقِ الشَّرِيعَةِ الْمُطَهَّرَةِ بِأَنْ بَاشَرَ الْعَمَلَ عَلَى وَجْهِ الْإِخْلَاصِ فِيهِ فَهُوَ عَامِلٌ بِعِلْمِهِ، وَإِنْ وَقَعَ فِي مَعْصِيَةٍ.. فَاسْتَغْفَرَ مِنْهَا وَتَابَ فَقَدْ عَمِلَ أَيْضًا بِعِلْمِهِ، فَإِنَّهُ لَوْلَا عِلْمُهُ مَا اهْتَدَى لِكَوْنِ ذَلِكَ مَعْصِيَةً، فَمَا جَعَلَهُ يَتُوبُ مِنْهَا إِلَّا الْعِلْمُ، فَمِثْلُ هَذَا قَدْ يَنْفَعُهُ عِلْمُهُ عَلَى كُلِّ حَالٍ اهـ.

> not have realized that it was disobedience and sought forgiveness. It was only knowledge that caused him to repent. Someone in this situation will have benefitted from his knowledge in every situation.

If someone wants to act upon this covenant, he needs to travel upon the hand of a *shaykh* so that he may elevate him to the levels of vigilance of Allah (Exalted is He) and fear of His punishment, until he recognizes each issue that he has learned but has failed to act upon and seeks forgiveness for them. Thus, no issue in any of the sections of knowledge that he has not acted upon will be hidden from him. That was the situation of the scholars who acted upon their knowledge. I heard our Shaykh, the Shaykh al-Islām Zakariyyā al-Anṣārī ﷺ, say, "Any *faqīh* that does not meet with people (of the path) is like dry bread without any seasoning." I also heard Sīdī ʿAlī al-Khawwāṣ ﷺ say:

> The seeker of knowledge is not complete until he meets with one of the *shuyūkh* of the path so that he may save him from the heedlessness of the ego and the presence of deception. Whoever does not meet with the people of the path, in most cases he will inevitably fall into the deception of claiming to act upon his knowledge; if anyone accuses him of little action, he rejects him with proofs that are not accepted in the presence of Allah. If anyone doubts what I have said, let him put my words to the test.

So, O brother, travel by the hand of a *shaykh*. Stick to serving him and be patient with his harshness and his abstruse matters; he intends to show you a precious thing that cannot be purchased with worldly goods. For knowledge is an immense undertaking, and the ego spoils it in a way that may be hidden

وَيَحْتَاجُ مَنْ يُرِيدُ الْعَمَلَ بِهَذَا الْعَهْدِ إِلَى سُلُوكٍ عَلَى يَدِ شَيْخٍ لِيُرَقِّيَهُ إِلَى دَرَجَاتِ الْمُرَاقَبَةِ لِلَّهِ تَعَالَى وَالْخَوْفِ مِنْ عَذَابِهِ، حَتَّى يَعْرِفَ كُلَّ مَسْأَلَةٍ تَرَكَ الْعَمَلَ بِهَا وَيَسْتَغْفِرَ، فَلَا يَلْتَبِسُ عَلَيْهِ مَسْأَلَةٌ وَاحِدَةٌ مِنْ كُلِّ بَابٍ لَمْ يَعْمَلْ بِهَا، كَمَا كَانَ عَلَيْهِ الْعُلَمَاءُ الْعَامِلُونَ.

وَسَمِعْتُ شَيْخَنَا شَيْخَ الْإِسْلَامِ زَكَرِيَّا رحمه الله تعالى يَقُولُ: كُلُّ فَقِيهٍ لَا يَجْتَمِعُ بِالْقَوْمِ.. فَهُوَ كَالْخُبْزِ الْحَافِ بِلَا أُدْمٍ.

وَسَمِعْتُ سَيِّدِي عَلِيًّا الْخَوَّاصَ رَحِمَهُ اللهُ يَقُولُ: لَا يَكْمُلُ طَالِبُ الْعِلْمِ إِلَّا بِالِاجْتِمَاعِ عَلَى أَحَدٍ مِنْ أَشْيَاخِ الطَّرِيقِ؛ لِيُخْرِجَهُ مِنْ رُعُونَاتِ النُّفُوسِ وَمِنْ حَضَرَاتِ تَلْبِيسِ النَّفْسِ، وَمَنْ لَمْ يَجْتَمِعْ عَلَى أَهْلِ الطَّرِيقِ فَمِنْ لَازِمِهِ التَّلْبِيسُ غَالِبًا وَدَعْوَى الْعَمَلِ بِمَا عَلِمَ، وَكُلُّ مَنْ نَسَبَهُ إِلَى قِلَّةِ الْعَمَلِ أَقَامَ عَلَيْهِ الْأَدِلَّةَ الَّتِي لَا تَمْشِي عِنْدَ اللهِ، وَمَنْ شَكَّ فِي قَوْلِي هَذَا فَلْيُجَرِّبْ.

فَاسْلُكْ يَا أَخِي عَلَى يَدِ شَيْخٍ وَالْزَمْ خِدْمَتَهُ وَاصْبِرْ عَلَى جَفَائِهِ لَكَ وَتَغَرُّبَاتِهِ عَلَيْكَ؛ فَإِنَّ الَّذِي يُرِيدُ أَنْ يُطْلِعَكَ عَلَيْهِ أَمْرٌ نَفِيسٌ لَا يُقَابَلُ بِالْأَعْرَاضِ الدُّنْيَوِيَّةِ، فَإِنَّ لِلْعِلْمِ رِيَاسَةً عَظِيمَةً وَلِلنَّفْسِ فِيهِ دَسَائِسُ رُبَّمَا خَفِيَتْ عَلَى مَشَايِخِ الْعِلْمِ فَضْلًا عَنِ الطَّلَبَةِ: (وَاللَّهُ يَهْدِي مَنْ يَشَاءُ إِلَى صِرَاطٍ مُسْتَقِيمٍ).

to the scholars of exoteric knowledge, to say nothing of the students. *And Allah guides whomever He wills to a Straight Path.*[55]

Muslim and others narrated that the Messenger ﷺ used to make the following supplication: "*O Allah! I seek refuge in you from an insatiable soul and from knowledge that does not benefit.*" Al-Bukhārī, Muslim, and others narrated the Prophetic Hadith: "*A man will be brought on the Day of Judgement and cast into the Fire. His intestines will spill out, and he will go around them like a donkey around the millstone. The people of the Fire will gather around him and say, 'What is with you, O So-and-so? Did you not used to command us to good and forbid us evil?' He will respond, 'I used to command you to good but would not do it myself. And I used to forbid you evil but would commit it myself.'*" Al-Bazzār and others narrated the Prophetic Hadith: "*The similitude of those who teach people good but neglect themselves is like the wick that illuminates things for people while it burns itself out.*" Al-Ṭabarānī narrated the Prophetic Hadith: "*Every knowledge is a burden on its possessor unless he acts upon it.*" In another Prophetic Hadith, he narrated: "*The person who will receive the severest punishment on the Day of Judgement is a scholar by whose knowledge Allah did not benefit him.*" Aḥmad and al-Bayhaqī narrated that Manṣūr ibn Zadhan said, "It has been conveyed to us that the people of the Fire will bellow from the stench of the scholar who did not benefit from his knowledge. They will ask him, 'What did you used to do, O unclean one? You have harmed us with your putrid smell – are our suffering and harm not enough?' He will reply, 'I was a scholar, but I did not benefit by my knowledge.'" And Allah (Exalted is He) knows best.

(55) *Al-Nūr*, 46.

وَرَوَى مُسْلِمٌ وَغَيْرُهُ أَنَّ رَسُولَ اللهِ ﷺ كَانَ يَقُولُ فِي دُعَائِهِ: «اللَّهُمَّ؛ إِنِّي أَعُوذُ بِكَ مِنْ نَفْسٍ لَا تَشْبَعُ، وَمِنْ عِلْمٍ لَا يَنْفَعُ».

وَرَوَى الشَّيْخَانِ وَغَيْرُهُمَا مَرْفُوعًا: «يُجَاءُ بِالرَّجُلِ يَوْمَ الْقِيَامَةِ فَيُلْقَى فِي النَّارِ فَتَنْدَلِقُ أَقْتَابُهُ فَيَدُورُ بِهَا كَمَا يَدُورُ الْحِمَارُ فِي الرَّحَى، فَيَجْتَمِعُ إِلَيْهِ أَهْلُ النَّارِ فَيَقُولُونَ: يَا فُلَانُ؛ مَا شَأْنُكَ؟ أَلَيْسَ كُنْتَ تَأْمُرُنَا بِالْمَعْرُوفِ وَتَنْهَانَا عَنِ الْمُنْكَرِ؟ فَيَقُولُ: كُنْتُ آمُرُكُمْ بِالْخَيْرِ وَلَا آتِيهِ، وَأَنْهَاكُمْ عَنِ الشَّرِّ وَآتِيهِ».

وَرَوَى الْبَزَّارُ وَغَيْرُهُ مَرْفُوعًا: «مَثَلُ الَّذِي يُعَلِّمُ النَّاسَ الْخَيْرَ وَيَنْسَى نَفْسَهُ، كَمَثَلِ الْفَتِيلَةِ تُضِيءُ عَلَى النَّاسِ وَتَحْرِقُ هِيَ نَفْسَهَا».

وَرَوَى الطَّبَرَانِيُّ مَرْفُوعًا: «كُلُّ عِلْمٍ وَبَالُهُ عَلَى صَاحِبِهِ إِلَّا مَنْ عَمِلَ بِهِ».

وَفِي رِوَايَةٍ لَهُ مَرْفُوعًا: «أَشَدُّ النَّاسِ عَذَابًا يَوْمَ الْقِيَامَةِ عَالِمٌ لَمْ يَنْفَعْهُ اللهُ بِعِلْمِهِ».

وَرَوَى الْإِمَامُ أَحْمَدُ وَالْبَيْهَقِيُّ عَنْ مَنْصُورِ بْنِ زَاذَانَ قَالَ: بَلَغَنَا أَنَّ الْعَالِمَ إِذَا لَمْ يَنْتَفِعْ بِعِلْمِهِ تَصِيحُ أَهْلُ النَّارِ مِنْ نَتْنِ رِيحِهِ، وَيَقُولُونَ لَهُ: مَاذَا كُنْتَ تَفْعَلُ يَا خَبِيثُ؛ فَقَدْ آذَيْتَنَا بِنَتْنِ رِيحِكَ؟ أَمَا يَكْفِيكَ مَا نَحْنُ فِيهِ مِنَ الْأَذَى وَالشَّرِّ، فَيَقُولُ لَهُمْ: كُنْتُ عَالِمًا، فَلَمْ أَنْتَفِعْ بِعِلْمِي. وَاللهُ تَعَالَى أَعْلَمُ.

The Prohibition of Laying Claim to Knowledge Unless It Is for a Reason Sanctioned in the Sacred Law

A general covenant was taken from us by the Messenger of Allah ﷺ that we would not lay claim to knowledge unless it was for a reason sanctioned in the Sacred Law. Nor would we ever say that we are among the most knowledgeable of people – not with our tongue and not with our heart. How could we do that when we know that, in our own land, there are those more knowledgeable than us – to say nothing at all of the region in which we live? If we are indeed decreed to lay claim to knowledge, even in a moment of intense anger, it is imperative that we immediately repent and seek forgiveness for the outburst, out of fear that the anger of Allah ﷻ would descend upon us. However, never will such a misfortune ever befall anyone who is intelligent. For there is no knowledge that a slave may learn or encompass a portion of except that he was preceded to it – and it was codified – by scholars of whom he does not even deserve to be a student.

Once, a person laid claim to knowledge saying, "By Allah! I do not know anyone from Abū Bakr al-Ṣiddīq to our time who is more knowledgeable than me in any science." A young, beardless man stood up and said to him, "Are you more knowledgeable than Imam al-Shāfiʿī? Are you more knowledgeable than Sībawayh? Are you more knowledgeable than the scholars of the fundamentals? Are you more knowledgeable than the scholars of *maʿānī* and *bayān*? Are you more knowledgeable than the Imams of *tafsīr*? Are you—? Are you—?" He continued for some time. The claimant did not know what to say, and so was exposed in the gathering.

أُخِذَ عَلَيْنَا الْعَهْدُ الْعَامُّ مِنْ رَسُولِ اللهِ ﷺ أَنْ لَا نَدَّعِيَ الْعِلْمَ إِلَّا لِغَرَضٍ شَرْعِيٍّ، وَلَا نَقُولُ أَبَدًا نَحْنُ مِنْ أَعْلَمِ النَّاسِ، لَا بِلِسَانِنَا وَلَا بِقَلْبِنَا، وَمِنْ أَيْنَ لَنَا ذَلِكَ وَنَحْنُ نَعْلَمُ أَنَّ فِي بَلَدِنَا مَنْ هُوَ أَعْلَمُ مِنَّا فَضْلًا عَنِ الْإِقْلِيمِ الَّذِي نَحْنُ فِيهِ، ثُمَّ إِذَا جَرَى الْقَدَرُ عَلَيْنَا بِدَعْوَى الْعِلْمِ وَلَوْ فِي وَقْتِ غَيْظٍ.. فَالْوَاجِبُ عَلَيْنَا أَنْ نُبَادِرَ إِلَى التَّوْبَةِ وَالِاسْتِغْفَارِ عَلَى الْفَوْرِ خَوْفًا مِنْ نُزُولِ الْمَقْتِ عَلَيْنَا مِنَ اللهِ عَزَّ وَجَلَّ، وَهَذِهِ مُصِيبَةٌ لَا يُبْتَلَى بِهَا أَحَدٌ وَهُوَ عَاقِلٌ أَبَدًا، فَإِنَّهُ مَا مِنْ عِلْمٍ طَالَعَ الْعَبْدُ فِيهِ وَأَحَاطَ بِبَعْضِهِ عِلْمًا إِلَّا وَسَبَقَهُ إِلَيْهِ وَإِلَى وَضْعِهِ عُلَمَاءُ رُبَّمَا لَا يَصْلُحُ أَنْ يَكُونَ هُوَ مِنْ طَلَبَتِهِمْ.

وَقَدِ ادَّعَى شَخْصٌ مَرَّةً الْعِلْمَ وَقَالَ: وَاللهِ؛ لَا أَعْلَمُ أَنَّ أَحَدًا مِنْ أَبِي بَكْرٍ الصِّدِّيقِ إِلَى عَصْرِنَا هَذَا أَعْلَمُ مِنِّي فِي عِلْمٍ مِنَ الْعُلُومِ، فَقَامَ إِلَيْهِ شَابٌّ صَغِيرٌ لَا لِحْيَةَ لَهُ، فَقَالَ: هَلْ أَنْتَ أَعْلَمُ مِنَ الْإِمَامِ الشَّافِعِيِّ؟ هَلْ أَنْتَ أَعْلَمُ مِنْ سِيبَوَيْهِ؟ هَلْ أَنْتَ أَعْلَمُ مِنْ أَئِمَّةِ الْأُصُولِ؟ هَلْ أَنْتَ أَعْلَمُ مِنْ عُلَمَاءِ الْمَعَانِي وَالْبَيَانِ؟ هَلْ أَنْتَ أَعْلَمُ مِنْ أَئِمَّةِ التَّفْسِيرِ؟ هَلْ أَنْتَ هَلْ أَنْتَ، وَهَكَذَا فَمَا دَرَى الْمُدَّعِي مَا يَقُولُ، فَافْتَضَحَ فِي الْمَجْلِسِ.

I heard our Shaykh, the Shaykh al-Islām Zakariyyā ﷺ, say:

> It has reached us that Muhammad ibn Jarīr al-Ṭabarī wrote a *tafsīr* composed of one thousand massive volumes; the texts of knowledge that he had memorized were similar to what it would take one hundred camels to carry. Ibn Shahīn used to say, "I have copied more books than I can count. I once estimated the value of the ink that I had used to be two thousand *qinṭār*."[56] Someone else said, "If I were to write what I have memorized, no animal could carry it."
>
> In every age, the scholars bear knowledge unrivalled by the famous scholars among their students. Yet, I hear a person of a weak state, like mine, saying, "By Allah! I do not know of anyone in all of Egypt more knowledgeable than me. If I had known of someone, I would have walked to him and benefitted from him."

Such a person is insane. The smallest part of his punishment is that he is deprived of the blessing of the scholars of his age and will die ignorant. I also saw someone claim to be a Qutb, saying, "Allah (Exalted is He) showed me all the saints in the circle of sainthood; I did not see So-and-so among them", indicating someone who was among the pious of his time. Someone in the gathering said to him, "If you are truthful, tell me how many hairs are in your beard." He did not know what to say, and was humiliated in front of everyone. If Allah (Exalted is He) has forbidden the scholars from claiming knowledge,

---

(56) [The classical measurement of a *qinṭār*, by most classical estimates, is around four thousand dinars. It has also been said that it is four thousand dirhams. Either way, two thousand *qinṭārs* refers to a very large amount of money.]

وَسَمِعْتُ شَيْخَنَا شَيْخَ الْإِسْلَامِ زَكَرِيَّا رَحِمَهُ اللهُ يَقُولُ: بَلَغَنَا أَنَّ مُحَمَّدَ بْنَ جَرِيرٍ الطَّبَرِيَّ أَلَّفَ تَفْسِيرًا أَلْفَ مُجَلَّدَةٍ ضَخْمَةٍ، وَكَانَ مَحْفُوظُهُ مِنْ مُتُونِ الْعُلُومِ نَحْوَ حَمْلِ مِائَةِ بَعِيرٍ.

وَكَانَ ابْنُ شَاهِينَ يَقُولُ: كَتَبْتُ مِنَ الْمُؤَلَّفَاتِ مَا لَا أُحْصِي عَدَّهُ، وَحَسَبْتُ الْحِبْرَ فَبَلَغَ أَلْفَيْنِ مِنَ الْقَنَاطِيرِ.

وَكَانَ بَعْضُهُمْ يَقُولُ: لَوْ كَتَبْتُ مَا فِي صَدْرِي مَا حَمَلَهُ مَرْكَبٌ، وَلَمْ يَزَلْ فِي كُلِّ عَصْرٍ عُلَمَاءُ حَامِلُونَ الْعِلْمَ لَا يَجِيءُ الْعُلَمَاءُ الْمَشْهُورُونَ مِنْ طَلَبَتِهِمْ.

وَسَمِعْتُ شَخْصًا ضَعِيفَ الْحَالِ مِثْلِي يَقُولُ: وَاللهِ الْعَظِيمِ؛ لَا أَعْلَمُ الْآنَ فِي مِصْرَ كُلِّهَا أَعْلَمَ مِنِّي، وَلَوْ أَنَّنِي عَلِمْتُ لَمَشَيْتُ إِلَيْهِ وَاسْتَفَدْتُ مِنْهُ اهـ، وَمِثْلُ هَذَا مَجْنُونٌ وَأَقَلُّ جَزَائِهِ أَنَّهُ حُرِمَ بَرَكَةَ عُلَمَاءِ زَمَانِهِ وَمَاتَ بِجَهْلِهِ.

وَقَدْ رَأَيْتُ شَخْصًا يُدْعَى الْقُطْبِيَّةَ يَقُولُ: أَطْلَعَنِي اللهُ تَعَالَى عَلَى دَائِرَةِ الْأَوْلِيَاءِ كُلِّهِمْ فَلَمْ أَرَ فُلَانًا مِنْهُمْ، وَأَشَارَ إِلَى شَخْصٍ مِنْ صَالِحِي عَصْرِهِ، فَقَالَ لَهُ شَخْصٌ فِي الْمَجْلِسِ: إِنْ كُنْتَ صَادِقًا فَقُلْ لِي: كَمْ فِي لِحْيَتِكَ مِنْ شَعْرَةٍ؟ فَمَا دَرَى مَا يَقُولُ وَخَجِلَ بَيْنَ النَّاسِ. وَإِذَا كَانَ اللهُ تَعَالَى نَهَى الْعُلَمَاءَ عَنْ دَعْوَى الْعِلْمِ مَعَ عِلْمِهِمْ، فَكَيْفَ بِمَنْ يَجْهَلُ وَيَدَّعِي الْعِلْمَ مَعَ الْجَهْلِ.

despite the fact that they have it, how is it then with someone ignorant [who] yet claims knowledge despite it?

Our Shaykh, the Shaykh al-Islām Zakariyyā al-Anṣārī ﷺ, told us that once, five hundred scribes gathered in the circle of knowledge of al-Ḥasan al-Baṣrī ﷺ recording knowledge from him. Affected by some pride, he said to himself, "Those in this gathering will not ask me about any knowledge except that I will inform them of it." However, a weak, beardless child, leaning on a cane, stood up and asked him, "Our master, we have heard what you said. So, does a mosquito have a stomach or intestines?" Al-Ḥasan's colour changed; he became yellow and was carried out of that gathering unconscious. He then died after three days.

Shaykh Muḥyī al-Dīn ibn al-ʿArabī ﷺ told a story about himself. He was riding in a ship on the Atlantic Ocean when the wind became violent. So he said, "Be still, O sea, for upon you is an ocean of knowledge." Just then, a great sea serpent looked at him and said, "We have heard what you said. What do you say, then, about when a woman's husband is transmuted into something else? Does she await the *ʿiddah* of a divorcee or of a widow?" The *shaykh* did not know what to say, so the serpent said to him, "Take me as your *shaykhah*, and I will teach you the answer." He accepted, and she said, "If he is transmuted into an animal, her *ʿiddah* is a divorcee's. If he is transmuted into an inanimate object, her *ʿiddah* is a widow's." He related this story in his hagiographies of his *shuyūkh* among the Jinn, human beings, the Angels, and animals. It has reached us that, afterwards, no one ever heard him lay the slightest claim to knowledge.

So, investigate, O brother, the knowledge you have of *fiqh*, grammar, the religious fundamentals, and others: you will find that it does not equal a drop in the deep ocean, compared with

وَحَكَى لِي شَيْخُنَا شَيْخُ الْإِسْلَامِ زَكَرِيَّا رَحِمَهُ اللهُ قَالَ: اجْتَمَعَ يَوْمًا فِي مَجْلِسِ الْحَسَنِ الْبَصْرِيِّ رَضِيَ اللهُ عَنْهُ خَمْسُمِائَةِ مِحْبَرَةٍ تَكْتُبُ عَنْهُ الْعِلْمَ، فَحَصَلَ لَهُ بَعْضُ عُجْبٍ فِي نَفْسِهِ فَقَالَ: لَا تَسْأَلُونِي فِي هَذَا الْمَجْلِسِ عَنْ عِلْمٍ مِنَ الْعُلُومِ إِلَّا أَخْبَرْتُكُمْ بِهِ، فَقَامَ إِلَيْهِ صَبِيٌّ أَمْرَدُ ضَعِيفٌ يَتَوَكَّأُ عَلَى عَصًا، فَقَالَ: يَا سَيِّدِي؛ قَدْ سَمِعْنَا قَوْلَكَ، فَهَلْ لِلنَّامُوسَةِ كِرْشٌ أَوْ مُصْرَانٌ؟ فَتَغَيَّرَ لَوْنُ الْحَسَنِ وَاصْفَرَّ، ثُمَّ حُمِلَ مِنْ ذَلِكَ الْمَجْلِسِ مَغْشِيًّا عَلَيْهِ، فَمَاتَ بَعْدَ ثَلَاثَةِ أَيَّامٍ اهـ.

وَذَكَرَ الشَّيْخُ الْكَامِلُ مُحْيِي الدِّينِ بْنُ الْعَرَبِيِّ رَضِيَ اللهُ عَنْهُ عَنْ نَفْسِهِ أَنَّهُ كَانَ رَاكِبًا مَرَّةً فِي سَفِينَةٍ فِي الْبَحْرِ الْمُحِيطِ فَهَاجَتِ الرِّيحُ، فَقَالَ: اسْكُنْ يَا بَحْرُ؛ فَإِنَّ عَلَيْكَ بَحْرًا مِنَ الْعِلْمِ، فَطَلَعَتْ لَهُ هَائِشَةٌ مِنَ الْبَحْرِ وَقَالَتْ لَهُ: قَدْ سَمِعْنَا قَوْلَكَ، فَمَا تَقُولُ فِيمَا إِذَا مُسِخَ زَوْجُ الْمَرْأَةِ هَلْ تَعْتَدُّ عِدَّةَ الْأَحْيَاءِ أَمِ الْأَمْوَاتِ؟ فَمَا دَرَى الشَّيْخُ مَا يَقُولُ، فَقَالَتْ لَهُ الْهَائِشَةُ: تَجْعَلُنِي شَيْخَةً لَكَ وَأَنَا أُعَلِّمُكَ الْجَوَابَ؟ فَقَالَ: نَعَمْ، فَقَالَتْ: إِنْ مُسِخَ حَيَوَانًا اعْتَدَّتْ عِدَّةَ الْأَحْيَاءِ، وَإِنْ مُسِخَ جَمَادًا اعْتَدَّتْ عِدَّةَ الْأَمْوَاتِ اهـ. ذَكَرَ هَذِهِ الْحِكَايَةَ فِي تَرْجَمَةِ مَشَايِخِهِ مِنَ الْجِنِّ وَالْإِنْسِ وَالْمَلَائِكَةِ وَالْحَيَوَانَاتِ، وَبَلَغَنَا أَنَّهُ مِنْ ذَلِكَ الْوَقْتِ مَا سَمِعَ أَحَدٌ مِنْهُ رَائِحَةَ دَعْوَى الْعِلْمِ.

فَيَحْتَاجُ مَنْ يُرِيدُ الْعَمَلَ بِهَذَا الْعَهْدِ إِلَى شَيْخٍ يَأْخُذُ بِيَدِهِ وَيُدْخِلُهُ حَضَرَاتِ الْعُلُومِ وَالْخَزَائِنِ الْإِلَهِيَّةِ، حَتَّى يَرَى أَنَّ جَمِيعَ مَا عَلِمَهُ هَؤُلَاءِ لَا يَجِيءُ نُقْطَةً مِنَ الْبَحْرِ الْمُحِيطِ، وَقَدِ اسْتَخْرَجَ أَخِي الشَّيْخُ أَفْضَلُ الدِّينِ مِنْ سُورَةِ الْفَاتِحَةِ مِائَتَيْ أَلْفِ عِلْمٍ وَنَيِّفًا وَأَرْبَعِينَ أَلْفَ عِلْمٍ، وَذَكَرْنَا مِنْهَا فِي كِتَابِنَا الْمُسَمَّى بِـ «تَنْبِيهِ الْأَغْبِيَاءِ عَلَى قَطْرَةٍ مِنْ بَحْرِ عُلُومِ الْأَوْلِيَاءِ» ثَلَاثَةَ آلَافِ عِلْمٍ.. لَا يَتَعَقَّلُهَا الْإِنْسَانُ إِلَّا إِنْ رَأَى أَسْمَاءَهَا؛ إِذْ لَمْ تَخْطُرْ لَهُ قَطُّ عَلَى بَالٍ.

the knowledge of the people of Allah ﷺ.[57] Hence, whoever wishes to act upon this covenant needs a *shaykh* to take him by the hand and enter him into the presences of knowledge and divine treasures until he witnesses that what he has been taught is not even equal to said drop.[58]

From the benefits of travelling upon the hand of a *shaykh* is that the wayfarer arrives to a presence in which he sees his apparent and hidden attributes – in all their emptiness – as a trust which the Real has stored with him. Thus, he has no right to ever claim even one of them for himself, out of shyness before Allah (Exalted is He); people will see him as a scholar in their eyes while he considers himself ignorant. In that way, he is safe from such claims in word or state, in secret or openly. However, if someone does not travel in the way that we have mentioned, in most cases he will be veiled and declare misguided claims that are far from correct.[59]

So, O brother, travel the path of *adab* with Allah by the hand of a *shaykh*. Even if you are among the most knowledgeable, he will show you your ignorance when you travel the path. May Allah take charge of your guidance.

The story of Mūsā and Khiḍr ﷺ is enough of an example. That is because Khiḍr said to Mūsā ﷺ, "I am the most knowledgeable person on Earth, but, O Mūsā, your knowledge and mine, compared to the knowledge of Allah, is only like the water that this bird is pecking from this ocean."

---

(57) Ibn al-Subkī narrates in *al-Ṭabaqāt al-Wusṭā* that Abū al-Qāsim al-Junayd ﷺ used to say, "Allah has not sent down from Heaven any knowledge, to which He has made a way for people to obtain, except that He granted me a portion and a part of it."

(58) My brother, Shaykh Afḍal al-Dīn, extracted 241,000 sciences from Sūrah al-Fātiḥah. We mentioned in our book *Tanbīh al-Aghbiyā' ʿalā Qaṭrah min Baḥr ʿUlūm al-Awliyā'* around 3,000 of them, which would not occur to the mind of a human being unless he sees their name – for they would never even come to mind.

(59) In fact, one of them even said "I am Allah", and thus disbelieved. We ask Allah for His gentle mercy.

فَانْظُرْ يَا أَخِي؛ فِيمَا عَلِمْتَهُ مِنَ الْفِقْهِ وَالنَّحْوِ وَالْأُصُولِ وَغَيْرِهَا.. تَجِدُهُ لَا يَجِيءُ قَطْرَةً مِنَ الْبَحْرِ الْمُحِيطِ بِالنِّسْبَةِ لِعُلُومِ أَهْلِ اللهِ عَزَّوَجَلَّ.

وَقَدْ نَقَلَ ابْنُ السُّبْكِيِّ فِي «الطَّبَقَاتِ الْوُسْطَى» عَنْ أَبِي الْقَاسِمِ الْجُنَيْدِ رَضِيَ اللَّهُ عَنْهُ أَنَّهُ كَانَ يَقُولُ: مَا أَنْزَلَ اللهُ مِنَ السَّمَاءِ عِلْمًا وَجَعَلَ لِلْخَلْقِ إِلَيْهِ سَبِيلًا.. إِلَّا وَجَعَلَ لِي فِيهِ حَظًّا وَنَصِيبًا اهـ.

ثُمَّ مِنْ فَوَائِدِ السُّلُوكِ عَلَى يَدِ شَيْخٍ أَنَّ السَّالِكَ يَصِلُ إِلَى حَضْرَةٍ يَرَى جَمِيعَ صِفَاتِهِ الظَّاهِرَةِ وَالْبَاطِنَةِ عَارِيَةً عِنْدَهُ وَأَمَانَةً أَوْدَعَهَا الْحَقُّ عِنْدَهُ، فَلَا يَسُوغُ لَهُ أَنْ يَدَّعِيَهَا أَوْ شَيْئًا مِنْهَا لِنَفْسِهِ أَبَدًا حَيَاءً مِنَ اللهِ تَعَالَى، فَالنَّاسُ يَرَوْنَهُ عَالِمًا فِي عُيُونِهِمْ.. وَهُوَ يَرَى نَفْسَهُ جَاهِلًا، وَهُنَاكَ يَأْمَنُ مِنْ أَنْ يَدَّعِيَ لِنَفْسِهِ حَالًا أَوْ مَقَالًا سِرًّا أَوْ جَهْرًا. وَمَنْ لَمْ يَسْلُكْ كَمَا ذَكَرْنَا فَمِنْ لَازِمِهِ الْحِجَابُ غَالِبًا وَالدَّعَاوِي الْمُضِلَّةُ عَنْ سَوَاءِ السَّبِيلِ.. حَتَّى أَنَّ بَعْضَهُمْ قَالَ: أَنَا اللهُ، فَكَفَرَ. نَسْأَلُ اللهَ اللُّطْفَ.

فَاسْلُكْ يَا أَخِي؛ طَرِيقَ الْأَدَبِ مَعَ اللهِ عَلَى يَدِ شَيْخٍ وَلَوْ كُنْتَ مِنْ أَعْلَمِ النَّاسِ عِنْدَ نَفْسِكَ؛ فَإِنَّهُ لَا بُدَّ أَنْ يَظْهَرَ لَكَ جَهْلُكَ إِذَا سَلَكْتَ الطَّرِيقَ، وَاللهُ يَتَوَلَّى هُدَاكَ.

وَفِي قِصَّةِ مُوسَى وَالْخَضِرِ عَلَيْهِمَا الصَّلَاةُ وَالسَّلَامُ كِفَايَةٌ لِكُلِّ عَاقِلٍ، وَذَلِكَ أَنَّ الْخَضِرَ قَالَ لِمُوسَى عَلَيْهِ السَّلَامُ: أَنَا أَعْلَمُ أَهْلِ الْأَرْضِ، يَا مُوسَى؛ مَا عِلْمِي وَعِلْمُكَ فِي عِلْمِ اللهِ إِلَّا كَمَا نَقَرَ هَذَا الْعُصْفُورُ مِنْ هَذَا الْبَحْرِ، وَالْمُرَادُ بِعِلْمِ اللهِ مَعْلُومُهُ لِقَوْلِهِ تَعَالَى: ﴿وَمَآ أُوتِيتُم مِّنَ ٱلْعِلْمِ إِلَّا قَلِيلًا﴾ [الإسراء: ٨٥].

Here, the meaning of "Allah's knowledge" is the objects of His knowledge[60], due to His words: "And what you have been given of knowledge is only a little."[61] It is known to Khiḍr that the knowledge of Allah (Exalted is He) cannot be attributed with any decrease, while the drop of water on the beak of a bird will inevitably decrease. If the intended meaning had been the Divine (Attribute of) knowledge that exists with His Essence, it would not have been permitted to describe it as "a little" – that is, as decreasing by the amount that is on the beak of the bird. No one would say that.

However, it is possible that Khiḍr only wished to indicate the insignificance by way of comparison. If he had described it as the amount of water that a mosquito takes in its mouth, that would have been fitting as well, as it is smaller than that which the beak of a bird takes out.

I only interpreted the Hadith for you, O brother, because Khiḍr ﷺ is a knower by Allah (*ʿārif bi-Llāh*). So understand that, and beware of falling into error.

And Allah (Exalted is He) knows best.

(60) The objects of Allah's knowledge consist of the knowledge that He sprinkles in the hearts of His servants. It is different to His beginningless knowledge that is specific to Him; even if the knowledge of the Creation is included in the knowledge of Allah, it contains a subtle contingency from the standpoint of its being associated to Creation.
(61) *Al-Isrāʾ*, 85.

فَلَوْ كَانَ الْمُرَادُ بِهِ الْعِلْمَ الْقَائِمَ بِالذَّاتِ لَمْ يَصِحَّ وَصْفُهُ بِالْقِلَّةِ فَافْهَمْ، وَمَعْلُومُ اللهِ هُوَ الْعِلْمُ الَّذِي يَبُثُّهُ فِي قُلُوبِ عِبَادِهِ.. وَهُوَ غَيْرُ عِلْمِهِ الْأَزَلِيِّ الْخَاصِّ بِهِ، لِأَنَّ عِلْمَ الْخَلْقِ وَإِنْ كَانَ مِنْ جُمْلَةِ عِلْمِ اللهِ فَفِيهِ رَائِحَةُ الْحُدُوثِ مِنْ حَيْثُ إِضَافَتُهُ إِلَى الْخَلْقِ فَافْهَمْ. وَإِيَّاكَ وَالْغَلَطَ وَإِنَّمَا أَوَّلْنَا لَكَ يَا أَخِي الْحَدِيثَ لِأَنَّ الْخَضِرَ عَلَيْهِ السَّلَامُ عَالِمٌ بِاللهِ، وَمَعْلُومٌ عِنْدَهُ أَنَّ عِلْمَ اللهِ تَعَالَى لَا يُوصَفُ بِنَقْصٍ مَا، وَلَا بُدَّ لِمِنْقَارِ الْعُصْفُورِ مِنْ بَلَلٍ يَكُونُ عَلَيْهِ فَافْهَمْ، فَلَوْ جَعَلْنَا الْمُرَادَ بِعِلْمِ اللهِ الْقَائِمَ بِالذَّاتِ لَمَا صَحَّ وَصْفُهُ بِالنَّقْصِ عَلَى قَدْرِ مَا أَخَذَ الْعُصْفُورُ وَلَا قَائِلَ بِذَلِكَ، وَيَصِحُّ أَنْ يُرِيدَ الْخَضِرُ بِذَلِكَ الْإِشَارَةَ لِلْقِلَّةِ عَلَى وَجْهِ ضَرْبِ الْمَثَلِ، وَلَوْ أَنَّهُ عَبَّرَ بِمَا تَأْخُذُهُ النَّامُوسَةُ عَلَى فِيهَا مِنَ الْبَحْرِ لَسَاغَ لَهُ ذَلِكَ أَيْضًا؛ لِأَنَّهُ أَقَلُّ مِمَّا يَأْخُذُهُ مِنْقَارُ الْعُصْفُورِ فَاعْلَمْ ذَلِكَ.

وَقَدْ رَوَى الطَّبَرَانِيُّ مَرْفُوعًا: «سَيَظْهَرُ قَوْمٌ يَقْرَءُونَ الْقُرْآنَ، يَقُولُونَ: مَنْ أَقْرَأُ مِنَّا؟ مَنْ أَعْلَمُ مِنَّا؟ مَنْ أَفْقَهُ مِنَّا؟ أُولَئِكَ هُمْ وَقُودُ النَّارِ».

وَفِي رِوَايَةٍ لَهُ أَيْضًا مَرْفُوعًا: «مَنْ قَالَ إِنِّي عَالِمٌ فَهُوَ جَاهِلٌ». وَاللهُ تَعَالَى أَعْلَمُ.

The Prohibition of Disputing in Matters of Knowledge

A general covenant was taken from us by the Messenger of Allah ﷺ that we would not dispute regarding any of the sciences of the Sacred Law, except with the intention to give victory to the religion, but only on the condition that one has sincerity and presence with Allah (Exalted is He) in it – brought on by unveiling and witnessing, not with suppositions, showing off, heedlessness, or conjecture – and not to defeat the people of disputation in our school or any other school. Therefore, if someone wishes to act upon this covenant, he is in need of a *shaykh* who is an expert in the Sacred Law, who has investigated all the proofs of the schools of law – both those that are used and those that have been abandoned – and has travelled the path of the people in the levels of sincerity.

For the one who desires to act upon this covenant without a *shaykh*, he is, in most cases, aiming for the impossible. During my wayfaring, I – and all praise is due to Allah (Exalted is He) – have investigated the source from which stemmed all the schools. I contemplated all the schools of the *mujtahidūn* and their followers; through unveiling and certainty, I found them to all branch off from that source. Thus, by the praise of Allah, none of their contradictory statements were hidden from me. If I had travelled the path alone without a *shaykh*, I would have been veiled by the blind following of their statements without knowing their sources. *All praise is due to Allah, the Lord of all the worlds.*[62]

Hence, O brother, you should know that the follower of one Imam must not call the gathering of another Imam as disputants, as when one says, "The disputant has said such-and-such, while I say such-and-such." For having excellent *adab* in one's

---

(62) *Al-Fātiḥah*, 2.

أُخِذَ عَلَيْنَا الْعَهْدُ الْعَامُّ مِنْ رَسُولِ اللهِ ﷺ أَنْ لَا نُجَادِلَ فِي عِلْمٍ مِنَ الْعُلُومِ الشَّرْعِيَّةِ إِلَّا بِقَصْدِ نُصْرَةِ الدِّينِ بِشَرْطِ الْإِخْلَاصِ وَالْحُضُورِ مَعَ اللهِ تَعَالَى فِي ذَلِكَ عَلَى الْكَشْفِ وَالشُّهُودِ، لَا عَلَى الظَّنِّ وَالرِّيَاءِ وَالْغَفْلَةِ وَالتَّخْمِينِ وَمُغَالَبَةِ الْخُصُومِ مِنْ أَهْلِ مَذْهَبِنَا أَوْ غَيْرِهِمْ.

وَيَحْتَاجُ مَنْ يُرِيدُ الْعَمَلَ بِهَذَا الْعَهْدِ إِلَى شَيْخٍ مُتَضَلِّعٍ مِنْ عُلُومِ الشَّرِيعَةِ قَدِ اطَّلَعَ عَلَى جَمِيعِ أَدِلَّةِ الْمَذَاهِبِ الْمُسْتَعْمَلَةِ وَالْمُنْدَرِسَةِ، وَسَلَكَ طَرِيقَ الْقَوْمِ فِي دَرَجَاتِ الْإِخْلَاصِ.

وَأَمَّا مَنْ أَرَادَ الْعَمَلَ بِهَذَا الْعَهْدِ بِنَفْسِهِ مِنْ غَيْرِ شَيْخٍ فَهُوَ يَرُومُ الْمُحَالَ غَالِبًا، وَقَدِ اطَّلَعْتُ بِحَمْدِ اللهِ تَعَالَى عَلَى الْعَيْنِ الَّتِي يَتَفَرَّعُ مِنْهَا جَمِيعُ الْمَذَاهِبِ فِي حَالِ سُلُوكِي، وَتَأَمَّلْتُ جَمِيعَ مَذَاهِبِ الْمُجْتَهِدِينَ وَمُقَلِّدِيهِمْ وَهِيَ مُتَفَرِّعَةٌ عَنْهَا كَشْفًا وَيَقِينًا، فَلَمْ يَخْفَ عَلَيَّ بِحَمْدِ اللهِ تَعَالَى مِنْ مُنَازِعِ أَقْوَالِهِمْ إِلَّا النَّادِرُ، وَلَوْ أَنَّنِي كُنْتُ سَلَكْتُ وَحْدِي بِغَيْرِ شَيْخٍ لَكُنْتُ مَحْبُوسًا خَلْفَ حِجَابِ التَّقْلِيدِ لِلْأَقْوَالِ، لَا أَعْرِفُ مِنْ أَيْنَ جَاءَتْ.

فَـ (الْحَمْدُ لِلهِ رَبِّ الْعَالَمِينَ).

وَاعْلَمْ يَا أَخِي؛ أَنَّهُ لَا يَنْبَغِي لِمُقَلِّدِ الْإِمَامِ أَنْ يُسَمِّيَ جَمَاعَةَ الْإِمَامِ الْآخَرِ خُصُومًا كَقَوْلِهِ: إِنْ قَالَ الْخَصْمُ كَذَا.. قُلْتُ كَذَا، فَإِنَّ حُسْنَ الْأَدَبِ فِي اللَّفْظِ مِنْ أَخْلَاقِ الْعُلَمَاءِ الْعَامِلِينَ.

wording is from the conduct of the scholars who act upon their knowledge. Once, a scholar gave me a book to read, which was in refutation of Imam Abū Ḥanīfah ﷺ. That night, in a vision, I saw Imam Abū Ḥanīfah, with a light as bright as the sun's, rising around seventy forearms' lengths into the sky. I then saw that scholar who had attempted to refute him, as if a black gnat, in front of him. Furthermore, if our Imam al-Shāfiʿī ﷺ had said, "All people are like the children of Abū Ḥanīfah in *fiqh*", how could it be conceivable of the likes of us to attempt to refute him? That is beyond insanity.

Allah (Exalted is He) said, "He has legislated for you, as a religion, that with which He exhorted Nūḥ and those that which We have revealed to you, and that with which He exhorted Ibrāhīm, Mūsā, and ʿĪsā: to establish the religion and not to separate into groups regarding it."[63] Thus Allah (Exalted is He) has ordered that the religion be established without demolishing it by arrogating ourselves above its Imams.

However, this matter (behaving arrogantly) has become the norm among the followers of the schools. You see each person attacking the evidence of the schools other than in his own. It reaches a point where he hardly sticks to the Book and the Sunnah – that is one of the ugliest traits. The only response they deserve is to defend the Imams, either by saying that they had not come upon the evidence which he is using to refute them, or by the fact that the *mujtahid* has methods of deriving rulings, using the rules of the Arabic language, that are hidden to the likes of us.

It has reached us that when Imam al-Shāfiʿī entered Baghdad, he visited the grave of Imam Abū Ḥanīfah ﷺ. The dawn prayer came in, and he prayed without reciting the *qunūt*, though it is his ruling that it be recited. When asked about that,

---

(63) *Al-Shūrā*, 13.

وَقَدْ أَطْلَعَنِي إِنْسَانٌ مَرَّةً عَلَى كِتَابٍ فِي الرَّدِّ عَلَى الْإِمَامِ أَبِي حَنِيفَةَ رَضِيَ اللَّهُ عَنْهُ فَرَأَيْتُ تِلْكَ اللَّيْلَةَ فِي وَاقِعَةِ الْإِمَامِ أَبَا حَنِيفَةَ، وَقَدْ تَطَوَّرَ نَحْوَ سَبْعِينَ ذِرَاعًا فِي السَّمَاءِ وَلَهُ نُورٌ كَنُورِ الشَّمْسِ، وَأَجِدُ ذَلِكَ الْعَالِمَ الَّذِي رَدَّ عَلَيْهِ تُجَاهَهُ يُشْبِهُ النَّامُوسَةَ السَّوْدَاءَ انْتَهَى. وَإِذَا كَانَ إِمَامُنَا الشَّافِعِيُّ رَضِيَ اللَّهُ عَنْهُ يَقُولُ: النَّاسُ كُلُّهُمْ فِي الْفِقْهِ عِيَالٌ عَلَى أَبِي حَنِيفَةَ، فَكَيْفَ يَسُوغُ لِأَمْثَالِنَا أَنْ يَتَصَدَّرَ لِلرَّدِّ عَلَيْهِ؟ هَذَا فَوْقَ الْجُنُونِ بِطَبَقَاتٍ وَقَدْ قَالَ تَعَالَى:

﴿شَرَعَ لَكُم مِّنَ ٱلدِّينِ مَا وَصَّىٰ بِهِۦ نُوحًا وَٱلَّذِىٓ أَوْحَيْنَآ إِلَيْكَ وَمَا وَصَّيْنَا بِهِۦٓ إِبْرَٰهِيمَ وَمُوسَىٰ وَعِيسَىٰٓ ۖ أَنْ أَقِيمُوا۟ ٱلدِّينَ وَلَا تَتَفَرَّقُوا۟ فِيهِ ۚ﴾ [الشورى: ١٣].

فَأَمَرَ اللَّهُ تَعَالَى بِإِقَامَةِ الدِّينِ لَا بِإِضْجَاعِهِ بِالتَّكَبُّرِ عَلَى أَئِمَّتِهِ، وَهَذَا الْأَمْرُ قَدْ فَشَا فِي مُقَلِّدِي الْمَذَاهِبِ، فَتَرَى كُلَّ إِنْسَانٍ يَدْحَضُ حُجَّةَ مَذْهَبِ غَيْرِهِ، حَتَّى لَا يَكَادَ يَبْقَى لَهُ تَمَسُّكًا بِكِتَابٍ وَلَا سُنَّةٍ، وَذَلِكَ مِنْ أَقْبَحِ الْخِصَالِ، وَإِنَّمَا كَانَ اللَّائِقُ بِهِمُ الْجَوَابَ عَنِ الْأَئِمَّةِ إِمَّا بِعَدَمِ اطِّلَاعِهِمْ عَلَى ذَلِكَ الدَّلِيلِ الَّذِي ظَفِرَ بِهِ الرَّادُّ عَلَيْهِمْ، وَإِمَّا بِأَنَّ لِذَلِكَ الْمُجْتَهِدِ مَنْزَعًا فِي الِاسْتِنْبَاطِ مِنْ وُجُوهِ قَوَاعِدِ الْعَرَبِيَّةِ يَخْفَى عَلَى أَمْثَالِنَا.

وَقَدْ بَلَغَنَا أَنَّ الْإِمَامَ الشَّافِعِيَّ لَمَّا دَخَلَ بَغْدَادَ وَزَارَ قَبْرَ الْإِمَامِ أَبِي حَنِيفَةَ رَضِيَ اللَّهُ عَنْهُ، حَضَرَتْهُ صَلَاةُ الصُّبْحِ فَتَرَكَ الْقُنُوتَ مَعَ أَنَّهُ يَقُولُ بِهِ، فَقِيلَ لَهُ فِي ذَلِكَ، فَقَالَ: اسْتَحْيَيْتُ مِنَ الْإِمَامِ أَنْ أَقْنُتَ بِحَضْرَتِهِ وَهُوَ لَا يَقُولُ بِهِ. فَرَضِيَ اللَّهُ تَعَالَى عَنْ أَهْلِ الْأَدَبِ. هَذَا فِي بَابِ الْآدَابِ وَالسُّنَنِ، أَمَّا الْوَاجِبُ وَالْحَرَامُ فَإِذَا قَامَ عِنْدَ الْمُجْتَهِدِ دَلِيلٌ فِيهِ فَلَيْسَ لَهُ أَنْ يَتْرُكَهُ أَدَبًا مَعَ مَنْ يُخَالِفُهُ، فَافْهَمْ.

he said, "I felt too shy to recite the *qunūt* in front of the Imam whose ruling is that it is not recited (in the dawn prayer)."

Thus, may Allah (Exalted is He) be pleased with the people of *adab*. However, this is regarding acts that are considered *adab* and Sunnah. As for obligations and prohibitions, understand well: when the *mujtahid* rules on them with an evidence, he cannot leave it out of *adab* with those who disagree with him.

Shaykh Muḥyī al-Dīn related in *al-Futuḥāt al-Makkiyyah* that in Central Asia, there was a group of Shafiʿis and Hanafis that continued to dispute with each other for an entire year. In fact, some of them would refrain from fasting during Ramadan in order to strengthen their argument against the disputant. The Prophetic Hadith narrated by al-Ṭabarānī, where the Lawgiver ﷺ said, "*Indeed, the Sacred Law has been given on three hundred sixty paths*", is to close the door to disputation without knowledge, in order to strengthen the religion; for indeed, disputation demolishes it. Hence, it does not befit anyone to respond to anyone who disputes with him, unless he has investigated all those paths (methods), finding his disputant's statement to correspond to none of them.

I heard Sīdī ʿAlī al-Khawwāṣ ﷺ saying:

> The religion can only be established through agreement upon it, not by disputing over it. However, it is not possible for the scholars to come to an agreement unless they free themselves of the control of their egotistical desires. As long as they do not free themselves, it is not possible for them to consolidate their hearts with the hearts of others. So, know that the helpers of the religion, in reality, are those who have travelled the path and exited from the presence of souls into the presence of spirits, for the spirits have no desire for any egotistical objective. Thus, from that point of view, their assis-

وَقَدْ حَكَى الشَّيْخُ مُحْيِي الدِّينِ فِي «الْفُتُوحَاتِ الْمَكِّيَّةِ» أَنَّ مِنْ وَرَاءِ النَّهْرِ جَمَاعَةً مِنَ الشَّافِعِيَّةِ وَالْحَنَفِيَّةِ.. لَمْ يَزَلِ الْجِدَالُ بَيْنَهُمْ قَائِمًا طُولَ السَّنَةِ، حَتَّى أَنَّ بَعْضَهُمْ يُفْطِرُ فِي رَمَضَانَ لِيَتَقَوَّى عَلَى الْجِدَالِ مَعَ خَصْمِهِ.

وَقَدْ رَوَى الطَّبَرَانِيُّ مَرْفُوعًا: «إِنَّ الشَّرِيعَةَ جَاءَتْ عَلَى ثَلَاثِمِائَةٍ وَسِتِّينَ طَرِيقَةً».

انْتَهَى، فَلَا يَنْبَغِي لِأَحَدٍ أَنْ يَرُدَّ عَلَى مَنْ يُجَادِلُهُ إِلَّا إِنْ نَظَرَ فِي هَذِهِ الطُّرُقِ كُلِّهَا، وَلَمْ يَجِدْ كَلَامَ خَصْمِهِ يُوَافِقُ طَرِيقَةً وَاحِدَةً مِنْهَا، وَمَا ذَكَرَ الشَّارِعُ ذَلِكَ إِلَّا سَدًّا لِبَابِ الْجِدَالِ بِغَيْرِ عِلْمٍ تَقْوِيَةً لِلدِّينِ، فَإِنَّ النِّزَاعَ يُوهِنُهُ وَيُضَعِّفُهُ.

وَسَمِعْتُ سَيِّدِي عَلِيًّا الْخَوَّاصَ رَحِمَهُ اللهُ يَقُولُ: لَا يَقُومُ الدِّينُ إِلَّا بِالِاتِّفَاقِ عَلَيْهِ لَا بِالِاخْتِلَافِ فِيهِ، ثُمَّ لَا يَصِحُّ لِلْعُلَمَاءِ اتِّفَاقٌ إِلَّا إِنْ خَرَجُوا عَنْ رِقِّ الشَّهَوَاتِ النَّفْسَانِيَّةِ، وَمَا لَمْ يَخْرُجُوا فَلَا يَصِحُّ لَهُمُ ارْتِبَاطُ قُلُوبِهِمْ مَعَ بَعْضِهِمْ بَعْضًا أَبَدًا. فَعُلِمَ أَنَّ أَنْصَارَ الدِّينِ حَقِيقَةً هُمُ الَّذِينَ سَلَكُوا الطَّرِيقَ وَخَرَجُوا مِنْ حَضْرَةِ النُّفُوسِ إِلَى حَضْرَةِ الْأَرْوَاحِ، فَإِنَّ الْأَرْوَاحَ لَا شَهْوَةَ لَهَا إِلَى شَيْءٍ مِنَ الْأَغْرَاضِ النَّفْسَانِيَّةِ أَبَدًا، وَهُنَاكَ يَكُونُ نُصْرَتُهَا لِلدِّينِ خَالِصَةً مِنَ الشَّوَائِبِ، فَاعْلَمْ ذَلِكَ وَاعْمَلْ عَلَيْهِ، وَاللهُ يَتَوَلَّى هُدَاكَ.

tance of the religion is free of all defect. Know this, and act upon it. May Allah take charge of your guidance.

Al-Bayhaqī, al-Tirmidhī, and others narrated the following Prophetic Hadith[64]: "*No people have gone astray after having been guided except that they began to dispute with one another.*" Then he recited, "They only presented the example purely for argument's sake. They are a people who are given to disputation."[65]

Al-Bukhārī, Muslim, and others have narrated the Prophetic Hadith: "*Indeed, the most hated of people to Allah is al-aladd al-khaṣim.*" *Al-aladd* is a person who argues excessively; *al-khaṣim* is the one who demands proof from the one disputing with him and then invalidates his evidence – except if a heretical innovator shows us evidence that has no support from the Book nor the Sunnah, in which case we say that invalidating his proof counts as helping Allah, His Messenger ﷺ, and the Muslims.

And Allah is Most Forgiving, Most Merciful.

(64) Declared sound (*ḥasan*) by al-Tirmidhī.
(65) *Al-Zukhruf*, 58.

وَقَدْ رَوَى الْبَيْهَقِيُّ وَالتِّرْمِذِيُّ وَغَيْرُهُمَا مَرْفُوعًا وَحَسَّنَهُ التِّرْمِذِيُّ: «مَا ضَلَّ قَوْمٌ بَعْدَ هُدًى كَانُوا عَلَيْهِ إِلَّا أُوتُوا الْجَدَلَ. ثُمَّ قَرَأَ ﷺ: ﴿مَا ضَرَبُوهُ لَكَ إِلَّا جَدَلًا بَلْ هُمْ قَوْمٌ خَصِمُونَ﴾ [الزخرف: ٥٨].

وَرَوَى الشَّيْخَانِ وَغَيْرُهُمَا مَرْفُوعًا: «إِنَّ أَبْغَضَ الرِّجَالِ إِلَى اللهِ الْأَلَدُّ الْخَصِمُ».

وَالْأَلَدُّ: هُوَ شَدِيدُ الْمُخَاصَمَةِ. وَالْخَصِمُ: هُوَ الَّذِي يَحُجُّ مَنْ يُخَاصِمُهُ وَيُدْحِضُ حُجَّتَهُ، اللَّهُمَّ إِلَّا أَنْ يَقُومَ لَنَا صَاحِبُ بِدْعَةٍ لَا يَشْهَدُ لَهَا كِتَابٌ وَلَا سُنَّةٌ.. فَلَنَا إِدْحَاضُ حُجَّتِهِ نُصْرَةً لِلَّهِ وَلِرَسُولِهِ وَلِلْمُسْلِمِينَ:

(وَاللهُ غَفُورٌ رَحِيمٌ).

Made in the USA
Coppell, TX
04 February 2026

71037633R00100